44

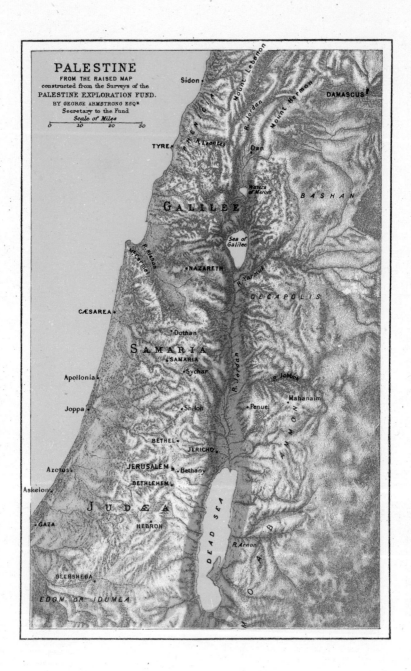

PALESTINE
FROM THE RAISED MAP
constructed from the Surveys of the
PALESTINE EXPLORATION FUND.
BY GEORGE ARMSTRONG ESQ.R
Secretary to the Fund
Scale of Miles
0   10   20   30

Sidon

DAMASCUS

Mount Lebanon

R. Jordan

Mount Hermon

TYRE

R. Leontes

Dan

Waters of Merom

BASHAN

GALILEE

Sea of Galilee

NAZARETH

R. Kishon

Mt. Carmel

R. Yarmuk

DECAPOLIS

CÆSAREA

Dothan

R. Jordan

SAMARIA

SAMARIA

Sychar

R. Jabbok

Apollonia

Mahanaim

Joppa

Shiloh

Penuel

AMMON

BETHEL

JERICHO

Azotus

JERUSALEM

Bethany

BETHLEHEM

Askelon

JUDÆA

GAZA

HEBRON

DEAD SEA

M O A B

R. Arnon

BEERSHEBA

EDOM OR IDUMEA

THE
RELIGIOUS BACKGROUND
OF THE BIBLE

by

J. N. SCHOFIELD

M.A. (Cantab.), B.D. (Lond.)
Head of Department of Hebrew,
University of Leeds

THOMAS NELSON AND SONS LTD
LONDON EDINBURGH PARIS MELBOURNE
TORONTO AND NEW YORK

First published 1944

PREFACE

THIS book is the outcome of a series of public lectures delivered at the invitation of the University of Leeds in the spring term of 1941. It attempts to connect, in the same way as a previous volume, *The Historical Background of the Bible*, the Old and New Testaments with each other and with the present day ; and to present a picture of the development of religion in the light of archæological research in Bible lands.

The writer believes that the difficulties of reconstruction with which the whole world will be faced can be overcome only if the experiences of men of the past in their relationship with God and their fellows are understood. Croce has written, " What constitutes history may be thus described : it is the act of comprehending and understanding induced by the requirements of practical life. . . . The practical requirements which underlie every historical judgment give to all history the character of ' contemporary history ' because, however remote in time events there recounted may seem to be, the history in reality refers to present needs and present situations wherein those events vibrate."

The book is not written with that air of " jaunty infallibility " which Saintsbury attributed to Matthew Arnold, but in the humble recognition that, to quote Donne,

> On a huge hill,
> Cragged, and steep, Truth stands, and he that will
> Reach her, about must, and about must go ;
> And what the hill's suddenness resists, win so.

In response to requests from readers of the *Historical Background* notes have been added as a help to students ; these notes also show, in part, the author's deep indebtedness to archæologists and writers whose labours have made this book possible. In particular he is glad to have this opportunity of expressing again how much he owes to Professor S. A. Cook, whose sympathetic insight and wide culture have always been available and have been generously given to him. His colleagues, Professors Bruce Dickins and E. O. James, and Professor H. H. Rowley of Bangor, have kindly read the work through and made many valuable suggestions. Miss Walton and Miss Wellburn have given generous help with the typescript. Without the constant help and encouragement of his wife the book would not have been written.

J. N. SCHOFIELD

Leeds 1944

CONTENTS

To my father

JAMES THOMAS SCHOFIELD

who taught me the importance
for personal religion as for academic
research of the biblical injunction

πάντα δὲ δοκιμάζετε, τὸ καλὸν κατέχετε

(1 Thessalonians v.21)

LIST OF PLATES AND MAPS

CHAPTER I

INTRODUCTION : SOURCES

THE primary source for any history of the development of religion in Palestine must always be the Bible itself, interpreted by one who knows from experience something of contact with the living God revealed through its pages. During the last fifty years, however, the comparative study of religions and the work of archæologists have provided two other sources which can be used to supplement and interpret the evidence from the Bible. But all the evidence, both from the Bible and from the new sources, should be used only with considerable care, and each source has its own peculiar limitations and difficulties.

§ THE BIBLE

So far as the Bible is concerned, difficulties arise at once because of the way in which the book has been put together. The literature is not arranged in the order in which it was written, and the course of development is not easily discernible. In Hebrew the Old Testament is called *Law, Prophets, and Writings*, and this threefold division shows that the literature has been grouped in reference to subject matter. The Law was set in a framework of the early history of the world and of Israel, and was collected into the five books of the Pentateuch known as the books of Moses. The Prophetic Writings were divided into two sections : the Former Prophets comprised the historical books—Joshua, Judges, Samuel, and Kings—the Jewish tradition being that they were written by prophets ; and the Later Prophets, which are the books we commonly call prophetic—Jeremiah, Ezekiel, Isaiah, and the book of the Twelve, *i.e.* the twelve smaller prophetic books of Hosea, Joel, Amos, Obadiah, Jonah, Micah, Nahum, Habakkuk, Zephaniah, Haggai, Zechariah, Malachi. All the remaining

1

books were classed together as Writings, a motley collection including the historical works, Chronicles, Ezra, Nehemiah, Ruth, Esther, the prophetic book of Daniel, as well as the Psalms and the Wisdom literature which we should expect to find there.

The order of the books within the groups was not constant even in Jewish tradition ; Massoretic scholars, from the seventh to the ninth centuries A.D., placed Isaiah before Jeremiah, probably because the book contained the writings of an eighth-century prophet, although earlier Jeremiah had stood first ; Ezra and Nehemiah were separated from Chronicles, of which they originally formed the continuation. In most printed Hebrew Bibles the order of the books in the third section, the Writings, has been influenced by the order in which they were used in the festivals of the Jewish Synagogue.

In Greek versions of the Old Testament the books were all rearranged in what seemed a more natural order : Ruth was placed after Judges because its background belongs to that period ; the other historical books were placed together, Chronicles following Kings, and Lamentations being put next to Jeremiah. It is of interest to remember that the problem of the order of individual books did not arise until the codex or book form replaced papyrus rolls. A papyrus roll normally contained only one book, and although often a number of rolls would be collected together in one box, no decision was then necessary as to the order in which the rolls should be preserved.

In the New Testament also the grouping of the literature appears to have been due partly to the exigencies of manuscripts, and the order within the groups is not constant. The four Gospels, grouped under the title *The Gospel*, formed the first group. This was followed by the Pauline Epistles, with or without Hebrews, the Acts, the Catholic Epistles, and the Apocalypse ; but the order of these groups differs in the different manuscripts, and the Catholic Epistles might precede the Pauline, and the Acts be given first, second, or third place. As with the Old Testament, the order of the books within the groups varies, reflecting different theories as to how the books should be arranged.

The Apocrypha, which the Christian Church took over with the Greek translation of the Old Testament, was also not arranged in any chronological order. In Greek manuscripts the books are interspersed among those books which had been accepted by the Jews. The Apocryphal additions to Jeremiah, Esther, and Daniel were treated as integral parts of those books; I Esdras and I and II Maccabees followed Chronicles as historical works; Judith and Tobit followed Esther; Ecclesiasticus was placed with the other Wisdom books, and the Prayer of Manasses was appended to the Psalms. The arrangement appears to be the result of collecting papyrus rolls together in boxes.

The partial use of the Apocrypha by the Reformed Church, and the printing of Bibles without these books, led to the belief that there is a gap of nearly four hundred years between the two parts of the Bible, but modern research has shown that such a gap does not exist. Within the Hebrew Bible there are writings that are now held to date from the second century B.C., and it seems probable that much of the older writings passed through the hands of revisers in that period, and was then adapted for current use. Some of the Apocrypha and the "Pseudepigraphal" writings—books written in the names of great men of the past, such as Moses, Isaiah, and Ezra—not only bridge the so-called gap, but actually overlap, and are contemporary with, New Testament writings. It must also be borne in mind that the text and contents of the Old Testament, even apart from the extra-canonical writings, were not fixed until the Christian era.

There is, however, a further difficulty in the use of the Bible as a source. When the books themselves have been arranged in chronological order, we have still to ask whether all the contents of a particular book belong to the period to which the book is assigned. A comparison of the books of Samuel and Kings with those of the Chronicler, or of Genesis with the book of Jubilees, shows that the idea that the text of the Bible was sacred and unalterable was unknown before the Christian era ; the writings of Josephus would also confirm this. Old poems, traditions, history, or even prophetic messages could be re-used by a later editor, and adapted to the new circumstances in which he was living. Again, before printing revolutionized the writing of books it was always easy for additions and glosses to be made in margins and incorporated into the text when the copy was re-written, thus becoming an integral part of the book.

For the past sixty years scholars have, in the main, accepted the view that variations within the Bible can best be explained by assuming that an editor has combined different documents.[1] This " documentary " hypothesis is beginning to be modified by a theory which recognizes to a fuller extent the importance of the scribes through whose hands the books passed ; their activity, it claims, has caused within the various books successive strata which give us clues as to the *milieux* of time, place, and thought from which they sprang. Whether we think of many documents combined by an editor at one time—the " documentary " theory—or stress more strongly the activity of many scribes, who at many times altered and supplemented an original work—the " supplementary " theory—it follows that the whole content of any particular book may not be of one and the same date, a fact of considerable importance when we attempt to trace, chronologically, lines of development. Some of the books thus incorporate genuine old traditions which were handed down orally, or perhaps were written in a form now lost. Other equally old traditions have been added later by writers who knew the folklore that existed in other levels of society, or had made new contacts with people whose background was different—perhaps a fresh invasion of nomads from the desert had swept their country, or they had gone as captives to Babylonia, or, so far as the New Testament is concerned, had visited another Christian Church. The result is often a knotty tangling of the skein of tradition extremely difficult to unravel. The different strata may offer evidence for the religion of the period to which they refer, or of the period in which they were first committed to writing, or of the period in which they were re-used by an editor for the comfort or teaching of his own generation ; but in every case no story or saying can be fully used to illuminate the course of the development of the religion, until we have explained why it was retained by the writer or re-used by the editor. Whatever theory of inspiration we may hold as true, there is always a human reason why each saying or story was saved from the vast mass of traditions and writings which lies behind the Old and New Testaments and is now lost ; often the discovery of that reason throws more light on the development of religion than does the saying or story itself.

In addition to old traditions, new material was continually added to the existent books, particularly after major historical crises, such as the three destructions of Jerusalem in 586 B.C. and A.D. 70 and 132, the return from the Babylonian exile, or the great Maccabæan revolt. These additions provide us with " finger-prints " that enable us to detect the presence of successive revisers, and to learn much about the particular circles to which they belonged.

It is very important to recognize the part played by different *milieux* of thought and place as well as of time. There is a danger—and the history of Old Testament criticism provides many examples—of treating all development in terms of date, but progress in religion did not, and seldom does, follow a clear straight line. We speak sometimes as though the Mosaic, Canaanite, Prophetic, Priestly, and Wisdom religion were successive stages, although in actual fact they probably represent in their present form different tendencies in contemporaneous types of religion. In one circle development might have reached a stage which another would take generations to achieve ; groups under the influence of Persian or Greek thought might develop beliefs in immortality which would take long to be accepted in conservative or secluded circles ; Christians at Antioch, Corinth, or Rome developed at a different rate and in a different way from those who remained in Jerusalem. If to-day an attempt was made to trace historical sequence through the writings of members of different contemporary Jewish or Christian communities, there would be amusing results which would probably reveal only the preconceptions of the investigator as to how the development ought to proceed.

When, however, the Bible is used with these facts in mind, it offers valuable cross-sections of the inner religious experience of groups and individuals in different ages and at different places, and enables us better to interpret much of the material from other sources.

§ COMPARATIVE STUDY OF RELIGIONS

During the last century the comparative study of religions has also added much to our knowledge of the history and meaning of the religion of the Bible. Dr. T. R. Glover [2] reminds us that this study began long ago when Greek writers such as Xenophanes noted the divergences in men's conceptions of the gods ; but real advance dates from the nineteenth century. By then the study of particular religions, and religion in general, provided a mass of material for comparative work, and men arose who were sufficiently emancipated from the belief that their religion alone was true and all others false to attempt to study the material objectively, and discover the peculiar contribution made by each religion. From the standpoint of biblical studies the most important contribution was made by Robertson Smith, who published in A.D. 1889 his epoch-making book on the religion of the Semites—the religion with which that of the Bible is most nearly kin. His claim that there is a close connection between the religion of the Old Testament and those of Edom, Moab, Ammon, the Aramæans, and the nomadic Semites is not now questioned, and his influence was so great that most attempts at writing a history of Old Testament religion begin with a recital of the survivals found there of features from the general religion of Semitic peoples.

This interest in survivals causes, however, one of the temptations that beset the study of comparative religion. It is increasingly fascinating to trace any well-known practice back to its source in some crude religious ceremony of primitive man ; but it is always necessary to remember that the discovery of the origin of a practice does not fully explain its meaning. A wealth of human experience, unknown to our far-off ancestors, enriches the rite for us. The use of linen vestments may be linked with Ezekiel's statement (xliv. 17f.) that God is fastidious and dislikes the sweaty smell of woollen garments on a priest, but this hardly explains their modern use in the services of the Church. Even in two closely related religions, common words or ritual may not have the same significance, and the similarity may be of little importance ; elements that have survived from an ancient past may have completely changed their meaning, and must be judged not by their early origin, but by their later development, for the key lies in the last stage, not the first.

On the other hand, it would be equally unwise to try to read back into the past a modern attitude to religious matters, and to explain the earliest stage by the latest development. There are post-biblical Jewish writings and practices which in Judaism have survived to our own day ; these have been called the " living traditions of a living people," and often they help us to understand biblical practices by providing an end of the thread which enables us to trace our steps into the maze of the past. The connection of a psalm or book with a particular Jewish festival may throw new light on the meaning of the biblical passage, but caution is necessary ; for example, the present Jewish rule that meat and milk must not be consumed at the same meal cannot be regarded as a true explanation of the ancient law that a kid shall not be seethed in its mother's milk ; that law must be connected, not with dietary rules, but, as in Exodus xxiii. 19, with fertility rites and the presentation of first-born.

When all this has been said, however, the comparative method has shown that the Bible cannot be studied in isolation.

Much of its religious symbolism can be understood only as we study other religions, and a common practice, like eating a communal meal before God, can be illustrated best from outside the Bible. In this book the main use made of the comparative study of religions will be to set the Bible against the background of the particular religions with which it came into contact, and which influenced its development. No attempt will be made to discuss general religious principles underlying that development.

§ ARCHÆOLOGY

In our attempt to trace the history of biblical religion the most interesting, and often the most tantalizing, assistance comes from the mute witness of archæological discoveries.[3] Under British rule during the years after A.D. 1919 considerable excavations in Palestine and the surrounding lands have provided so much material that it has hardly been possible to collate it and assess its significance. Many sites in the Holy Land itself have yielded strata in correct chronological sequence, revealing the material remains of the religious life with which they were contemporary. These strata provide the background of Palestinian religion in each succeeding age, carrying us back beyond the age of Abraham, and forward into the Roman period beyond the setting of the New Testament. The mode in which men buried their dead has given us clues to their ideas of the after-life ; plans of temple buildings and the remains of temple furniture show how men worshipped and thought of their gods ; figurines, amulets, and all the personal paraphernalia of religion reveal the daily practices of common people. If it be true that " history is a more intelligent witness than archæology because it arrives later on the scene and thinks "[4] it is equally true that the contemporaneous evidence provided by archæology, free from the propaganda of historians, can offer more reliable witness.

Unfortunately the data provided by archæology usually

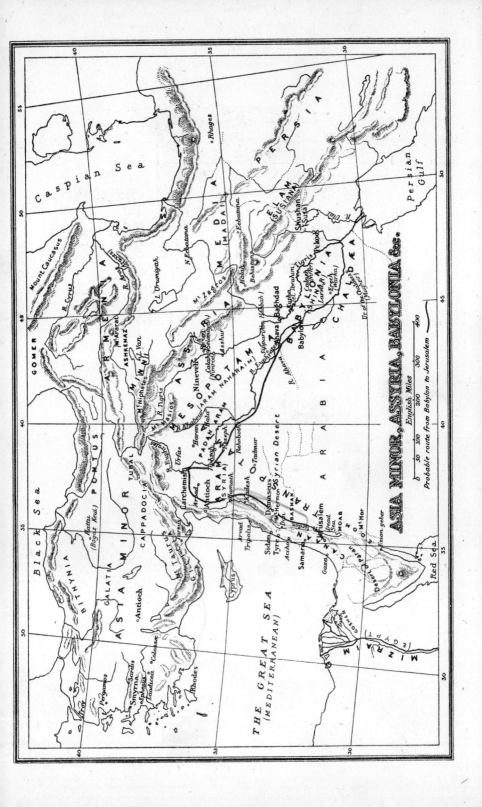

ASIA MINOR, ASSYRIA, BABYLONIA, &c.

English Miles
0 50 100 200 300 400

Probable route from Babylon to Jerusalem

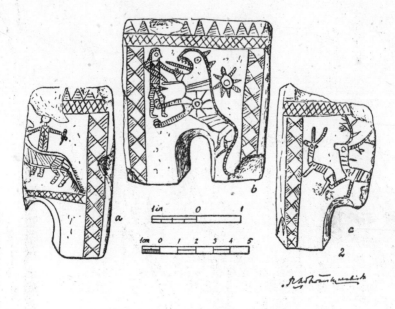

VOTIVE ALTARS FROM GEZER

(*From* " The Religion of Ancient Palestine in the Light of Archaeology," *by S. A. Cook,
British Academy, Oxford Press,* 1930)

need to be interpreted, and, as in the writing of history, the opportunity arises for the confusion produced by " thinking." Sometimes we are fortunate enough to discover writings which can still speak to us from those ancient times, and help us to interpret aright other material remains, but more often we are faced with the difficult task of trying to co-ordinate the evidence from archæology with that from the Bible, and with practices and beliefs known from elsewhere. Much of the difficulty of co-ordination is due to the fact that the " thinking historians " in the Bible have re-written and re-used their old records so often for spiritual and moral teaching, that there is a great gulf between the religion of ancient Palestine, revealed to us through archæology, and that assumed in the Bible as the religion of the same periods. For our purposes we shall find that it is often better to rely on archæological records than to attempt to determine from the Old Testament the oldest forms of the religion of Israel.[5]

This becomes obvious when we consider, for instance, the sensational discoveries made at Ras Shamra in Syria, and at Aswan in Egypt, which have made necessary considerable revision of previous theories of the development of biblical religion. These discoveries have shown us how much pre-exilic material has been lost, and how thorough has been the revision of what remained. We have learned that in Israel simple popular religion was not always early, nor the more elaborate priestly religion late; the latter often conserved extremely ancient beliefs and ceremonies, and simple religion was sometimes the outcome, not of primitive conditions, but of later reconstructive periods.

It is perhaps still necessary to provide a warning that archæological data must not be confused with a particular interpretation put upon them. Starkey—whose tragic death in Palestine was such a loss to archæology—used to insist that the task of the archæologist was to present the facts as faithfully as possible, and, so long as those facts were not distorted, to allow freedom of interpretation to any one who wished to use them. The attempt to use those facts for a study of the development of religion must involve some interpretation ; when, for example, we find the symbolic wings of the sun-god, or the Egyptian sign of life, on the seal of a man whose name proclaims him to be a Yahweh worshipper, we must ask what meaning those symbols had for the owner of the seal, and for what extent of syncretism they are evidence.[6]

Archæology has provided us with full accounts of ritual and mythology from Egypt, Babylonia, and Syria ; legends of their gods, and moral treatises, have given much material for comparison with the Old Testament ; but the whole jig-saw of what A. A. Bevan [7] called " the more disjointed and more miscellaneous fragments of archæology which are without the continuity which is of the essence of history " has not only to be fitted together, but must be inset in the mosaic of biblical pictures to reveal a development in line with accepted principles of progress, learned from the comparative study of religions.

BOOK I
THE RELIGIOUS GEOGRAPHY OF PALESTINE

CHAPTER 2

THE SETTING OF THE LAND

§ ITS CENTRALITY

As long ago as 1899 S. R. Driver wrote,[1] " The general result of the archæological and anthropological research of the past half century has been to take the Hebrews out of the isolated position which, as a nation, they seemed previously to hold, and to demonstrate their affinities with, and often their dependence upon, the civilizations by which they were surrounded." During the succeeding decades an ever-increasing mass of material has confirmed his judgement, and has made it as impossible to treat the religion, language, and literature of Palestine in isolation as it is to study her history apart from that of surrounding peoples.

A glance at the accompanying map of the Near East shows the central position of Palestine. Sir G. A. Smith[2] wrote of the country, "At most times the land has as much deserved the name ' Mediterranean ' as that sea on which her harbours open and of whose waves she was the first mistress." It is the land bridge between the two great continents of Africa and Asia, and, lying at the eastern end of the Mediterranean, is a place where East and West meet ; but though the Hebrew language pictured the land as facing east, it must be remembered that its gates were always open to the western sea of which it formed the eastern limit, and that consequently it was less oriental than Babylonia, and the Bible less Semitic than if it had been nurtured in the Euphrates valley. The influence

11

of Mesopotamian culture is shown by cuneiform inscriptions, and stories tell of Egyptian nobles who fled to Palestine for refuge or came to purchase cedar wood from the forests of Lebanon. All the trade between the civilizations in the river valleys of the Nile and Mesopotamia passed along the Fertile Crescent, of which Palestine forms the western end ; caravans from the north, through Damascus to the Gulf of Akabah, passed along her eastern border ; much of the traffic also from the Mediterranean and far distant Spain was unloaded on her western shores, and carried across the country to be re-shipped at the northern end of this Gulf, where Solomon built one of his navies.

In addition to this peaceful penetration by merchants, Palestine was continually overrun by invaders. Powerful Egyptian neighbours on the west, and successive empires on the east, in turn attempted to make it the outpost of their dominations—a buffer state to protect them against their rival or a stepping-stone to further conquest. From the mountains of Asia Minor, and the region around the Caspian Sea in the north, warlike hillmen entered the Fertile Crescent, and moved along it to Palestine, while from the south and south-east half-starved nomads raided its green and pleasant fields.

Israel Abrahams [3] said of Palestine, " No area of the earth's surface has so often re-echoed to the tramp of armed men as the short strip which stretches from Tyre to Gaza. Even the migrations of races were of the nature of campaigns ; the ancient world knew no peaceful penetration, but rushes red in tooth and claw. For more than four thousand years the story is continuous of armies and caravans moving by this road to battle or to trade."

§ EBB AND FLOW OF POPULATION

When we remember that Palestine is a country only about the size of Wales, although unlike Wales not a remote place of refuge but part of the actual high-road of the ancient world, it is obvious that the constant sojourning within its borders of so many peoples would have a great and complicating effect upon its whole life, and it is necessary to glance briefly at the more important of these invading peoples. In earliest times the contacts on the west were throughout with one and the same people, the Egyptians, and the story of their penetration of Palestine before the entry of the Israelites extends from the dawn of history.[4] Apparently the turquoise and copper of the Sinai peninsula first attracted their attention, and during the fourth millennium B.C. kings of the first dynasty to rule a united Egypt claim to have visited the mines and slaughtered the nomads there. But the visits of Egyptians to Syria in the north were equally early and extensive, and remains at Byblos in Syria reveal, just as do inscriptions on the rocks of Sinai, the presence of this early influence. Apart from the two hundred years when Egypt itself was overrun by the Hyksos invaders, Egyptian influence remained dominant in Palestine until the invasion of the Sea Peoples at the beginning of the twelfth century, but the extent of the influence varied with the strength of the ruling dynasty. In the middle of the second millennium B.C. under the eighteenth dynasty, which drove out the Hyksos in 1580 B.C., and again under the vigorous nineteenth dynasty founded by Ramses I in 1369 B.C., Egyptian monarchs led victorious armies through the heart of Palestine, leaving unmistakable traces on the country and its religion.

From the east came the influence not of one people but of many, and their story is more difficult to recount. It began at the same early date in the fourth millennium B.C., when Sumerians lived in southern Babylonia and their monarchs led armies across to the Mediterranean.[5] Many mounds containing remains of their cities have now been excavated, enabling us to understand why later Babylonians and Assyrians regarded them as the founders of civilization. Solid, elaborate temple buildings, carvings, pottery, and numerous clay tablets show the high stage of their culture. Examples of the pottery which is usually associated with them have been found on the sea coast of Palestine as well as in the Jordan valley. Sir

Leonard Woolley has, however, discovered evidence that suggests that this pottery was taken over and not originated by the Sumerians, and the fact that, though they themselves were bald and clean-shaven, their gods wore the Semitic beard and had hair on their heads, would tend to confirm his suggestion that their culture had been grafted on that of their conquered predecessors.

The Accadian kingdom in northern Mesopotamia later rivalled that of the Sumerians, and has left inscriptions showing how it exploited the silver mines of the Taurus mountains, and used building materials of stone and cedar wood from Syria. Many legends have gathered round the name of Sargon I, the greatest king of Agade. Perhaps the best-known legend is the one which is comparable to the story of the childhood of Moses. It relates how he was born of a temple woman, who set him floating on the Euphrates in a reed chest smeared with bitumen. After his rescue he was loved by the goddess Ishtar, who made him ruler of the kingdom. Recent study of the Accadian dialect shows how deeply this language influenced Hebrew, and it seems probable that this close linguistic contact was accompanied by equally strong religious influences.

Hammurabi, the most famous king of the first Babylonian dynasty, flourished toward the end of the second millennium B.C.[6] Like Moses, he has a reputation as both a law-giver and a religious reformer. The discovery at Susa of his legal code inscribed on a seven-foot stone has provided much material for comparison with the laws of the Old Testament.[7] In religion he took advantage of the decadence of the Sumerians to move the religious centre from Nippur to Babylon, and replaced Enlil by Marduk as the chief god of the country. He himself was a Semite, like the Amorites who at about the same time moved into Syria and Palestine, and the contacts between Babylonia and Syria in this period suggest that the Hammurabi dynasty belonged to the same general stock as the Amorites.

These first Babylonians were overthrown by Hittite invaders

from Asia Minor. Thousands of clay tablets comprising the records of their kingdom were discovered at its ancient capital of Boghaz-Keui in the bend of the Halys River about ninety miles east of Angora.[8] This early Hittite empire appears to have arisen from an Indo-European invasion of Asia Minor at the beginning of the second millennium B.C., and became equal in importance to Egypt. Sir Leonard Woolley's excavations at Atchana in north Syria show that there Hittite occupation followed a period in which the city acknowledged the overlordship of Hammurabi, and we know that the kingdom of Aleppo was conquered by them in the middle of the eighteenth century B.C.[9] Probably the Hittites were kin to the Hyksos, and little is known of them during the Hyksos domination, but after that had been broken in 1580 B.C. it was Hittites who for nearly two hundred years seriously challenged the Egyptian supremacy in Syria. Their empire finally fell before the Sea Peoples known to biblical tradition as Philistines, and from the twelfth century Carchemish[10] in Syria became the centre of a neo-Hittite confederation mentioned in Assyrian records and eventually conquered by Sargon II in 717 B.C. How far south they penetrated into Palestine is still a matter of keen controversy. From the Old Testament we learn that Abraham bought a cave near Hebron from Hittites (Gen. xxiii. 10), and that Esau married one of their daughters (Gen. xxvi. 34) ; David's faithful soldier Uriah is described as a Hittite (II Sam. xi. 3), and Ezekiel (xvi. 3) taunts Jerusalem with being inhabited by a mongrel people, born in Canaan from an Amorite father and a Hittite mother. Hittite domination over the western coasts of Asia Minor had repercussions in the period covered by the New Testament, for it was apparently through this domination that the veneration of the Hittite goddess spread thither and produced the worship of Artemis, or Diana of the Ephesians, against which Paul had to contend.

Another Asiatic invasion of Palestine which was of even greater importance for the development of religion in the country was that of the Hyksos,[11] who have already been mentioned. Much has still to be learned about this people, although many of their cities have been excavated. There are features that link them with the Hittites, and with the Kassite horsemen who became supreme in Babylonia after the Hittite invasion there. They had Aryan affinities, and their characteristic earthwork fortifications suggest an origin in the steppes of Asia or Europe, but many of the names of their leaders and their gods are Semitic. In the present stage of our knowledge it seems wiser to regard much of their culture as assimilated from Semitic peoples whom they conquered ; even pottery, which for long was regarded as typical of the Hyksos, has been found in the pre-Hyksos stratum at Lachish, and their scarab seals certainly come from Egypt. Their rule lasted for nearly two hundred years, and evidence of their influence comes from places as far apart as Cnossus in Crete and Baghdad in Mesopotamia. In Palestine their penetration was widespread, and remains have been found at Hazor north of the sea of Galilee, Askelon in the coastal plain, Lachish in the Judæan foothills, and Jericho.

The overthrow of the Hyksos by Egypt in 1580 B.C. made possible the rise of other smaller nations, who in the fourteenth century were jostling each other for control of the Syrian coast ; only two of these need be mentioned here, the Assyrians and the Mitanni. The former were an ancient people and their culture can be traced to the third millennium B.C. Excavations at Assur, their capital on the Tigris in northern Mesopotamia, show that they were influenced by, but distinct from, Sumerians and Accadians. In the reign of Hammurabi they were vassals of Babylonia, and letters found at Tell el-Amarna in Egypt show the same conditions in the fourteenth century ; by the middle of that century, however, Assyrian power had begun to grow, and we see the opening of the long struggle between Assyria and Babylonia for supremacy in Mesopotamia, a struggle that ended when the neo-Babylonians in 610 B.C. defeated the remnants of the Assyrians and took their place as conquerors of Palestine.

The Mitanni appear to have been of Aryan origin, and

spoke a Hurrian language, akin to that used by the modern inhabitants of the Caucasus. It is also probable that the people called in the Old Testament Horites should be called Hurrians and belonged to the same group. It is of interest to find among the gods worshipped by the Mitanni such names as Varuna, the Indo-Iranian ethical god (which according to some scholars lies behind the Old Testament name Araunah), Indra, and Mithra, but we can only speculate as to the influence of these gods on the growth of early ethical ideas in Palestine and among the Hebrews. We know that in the fifteenth century B.C. Egyptian monarchs found it necessary to make marriage alliances with the Mitanni, who were strong enough both to incite rebellion in Syria against their Egyptian overlords and to garrison many Syrian cities.

Consideration of the nomadic invaders can be left until we speak of the Israelites, who were themselves nomads, but here it may be noticed that it is the nomadic peoples who best illustrate the fact that Palestine was a country not only of immigration, but of emigration. Men entered it in order to pass through to Egypt or Babylonia ; they were driven from it in search of food when drought had caused famine there ; they fled from it through fear of the vengeance of a foreign overlord ; and they were sold into slavery by their own kings or carried away captive by a conqueror. But often they found life hard on their native hills, and set out to find wealth or ease in other lands. This emigration produced in time a large and widespread Diaspora, playing an important part in the development of the home country ; sending back there not only wealth to temples, Christian churches, and Jewish colonies, but impregnating the land with foreign ideas which altered the progress of religious life.

This ebb and flow of peoples caused syncretism in language, literature, and religion, but the fact that there were successive waves from the same general direction, and with the same general culture, often makes it impossible accurately to date a particular influence ; we know the direction from which an influence came but neither the period nor the channel through which it entered. For example, Babylonian influence on the laws and psalmody of Israel may have been mediated through Canaanite inhabitants of Palestine, or been the result of direct contact between Israel and Babylonia ; Persian influence on the religion of the land may have been due to old Iranian contacts with Palestine, to Cyrus's conquests, or to infiltration from the much later empire of Alexander the Great.

§ THE RELIGIOUS INFLUENCES FROM EGYPT, MESOPOTAMIA, AND SYRIA

We shall be better able to recognize some of the diverse threads in Palestinian religion if we look briefly at the religious influences that entered with these invading peoples. Erman [12] and Breasted,[13] in their accounts of the religion of Egypt, both emphasize the fact that it was the product of the land. The two outstanding natural phenomena were then, as now, the sun and the Nile. The sun shines from unclouded skies, from its heat there are no hills or valleys in which to take refuge, and the tall palm-tree gives but little shade ; the Nile, fed by the rains and melting snows of Central Africa, regularly brings its fertilizing flood-waters. These two phenomena under different names were worshipped as the great gods. The absence of impressive natural features in the landscape throws into greater relief birds and animals, Nile boats and human beings, and these became to the Egyptian the representatives of his gods. Dry sands, fringing his small area of cultivated soil, preserved for thousands of years papyrus reeds, human bodies, and buildings that elsewhere would have perished ; very early began to emerge beliefs that life did not end at the grave, and gradually there grew the elaborate cult of the dead which is the outstanding feature of Egyptian religion. At first the hereafter, like religion itself, was the affair of the king and his nobles, and, as to-day in Egypt, there was a great gulf between the rulers and the common people. But soon conscience began to develop, and men recognized that individual character was more important than material possessions. This recognition influenced the conception of judgement in the after-life, and to secure the future well-being of those whose character did not merit such treatment, elaborate magical rites were practised; but, to quote Erman, "among all the extravagant ideas concerning life and death, the feeling yet obtained that the righteousness of man would then be far more powerful than forms and ceremonies."

Movements towards monotheism can be traced in the religion of Egypt. At first each town or province had its own peculiar gods and forms of worship, but political unity led to religious syncretism. The god of the royal family or residence became the official state god worshipped everywhere, either separately or blended with local deities. This is illustrated in the history of Amon, the obscure god of Thebes. Two local families, worshippers of Amon, had successively dominated Egypt, and his worship spread throughout the kingdom; he was identified with the solar god Re, and as Amon-Re he became the state god under the rule of another strong Theban family who drove out the Hyksos invaders. The movement was carried a stage farther when Amenhotep IV,[14] a later king of the same family and father-in-law of Tutankhamen, attempted to break away from this syncretistic form of solar worship, and the myths and traditions of Amon-Re. He instituted a purer worship of the sun under the name Aten, represented by the sun's rays ending in human hands, and he changed his own name to Akhenaten. His attempt to introduce an intellectual and ethical monotheism, which could be universal through his empire, failed, but in many ways its influence remained, and our knowledge of it enables us better to credit the possibility of the early beginnings of the monotheism attributed by Jewish tradition to Moses. In Egypt the priestly reaction which followed the attempt led to renewed emphasis on the externals of religion—rites and ceremonies, and the building of great temples in which the gods were remote from the common people. As always, the remoteness of the great gods made men find intermediaries closer to themselves, and there was a tendency to worship lesser gods, such as the bandy-legged dwarf Bes, and his hippopotamus-shaped wife, who were thought of as protective ; people also venerated as divine incarnations living birds and animals—snakes, cats, rams, and above all, the apis bull of Memphis—which in earlier days had been regarded as representative of the gods. In more educated circles traces of Akhenaten's revolt and his monotheism lingered on ; religious poetry was emancipated from traditional forms ; and personal piety, the recognition of the meaning of moral sinfulness, and a new hope in life, sprang from the teaching of the fatherly care of Aten, the god whose hands reached out to men.

Mesopotamian religion reflects rather the history of the country, where frequent violent changes were caused by foreign invasions, and it is not so easy to trace development. The invader brought with him a new pantheon to be combined with the gods already there, and often his chief god was given the supreme place ; for in Mesopotamia also a tendency to monotheism can be seen in the fact that each of the conquering peoples had one god whom it worshipped as supreme, and who retained his position so long as his people were in power. Apart from deified princes, the gods seem to be mainly sky-gods, but it is not always easy to differentiate between them, for most bore both Sumerian and Babylonian names, and in any particular city the chief god tended to be given the functions of many others. It is interesting to notice that from earliest times they appear to have been arranged in groups of three ; there was one triad of Anu god of heaven, Enlil god of earth, and Ea lord of waters, and another of Sin the moon-god, Shamash the sun, and Ishtar the planet Venus, sometimes represented as a male but more often as the goddess of war and pleasure. But there is considerable confusion ; Enlil often usurped the place of Anu, and Ishtar, who was thought of as the daughter of Sin or of Anu, supplanted Anu in the worship at Erech and Lagash. When Hammurabi became supreme the old myths had to be altered to enable Marduk to depose Anu as chief of the gods ; Marduk was regarded as the son of Ea and took his father's power, and was also given the title Bel which had belonged to Enlil. It may be noted that though in Egypt the sun is more important than the moon, which is the representative of the sun-god at night, in Mesopotamia it is the moon which is more important, and at Ras Shamra the sun appears to be a goddess. Other gods worshipped in Mesopotamia which are important for Palestinian religion are Hadad or Adad, the god of atmosphere, who like the Syrian Rimmon became god of storms and thunder, Nergal the god of war, disease, and the underworld, and Nabu or Nebo god of wisdom. In Mesopotamia both goddess and priestess were more important than in Egypt, for each of the gods had his consort and family, and the anomaly of a lonely bachelor was almost unknown among the gods.

Every deity had its own symbolic animal,[16] probably regarded rather as the throne of the god than, as in Egypt, its living representative ; Ishtar is seen riding on lions ; Adad, or the lightning flash that represents him, appears on the back of a roaring bull ; Marduk drives a chariot drawn by a winged lion. If, therefore, we could discover whether the bull worship of the Old Testament was influenced more from Babylonia or from Egypt, we should know whether the bull was regarded as the throne or as the representative of Yahweh.

In many ways Hebrew religion was more closely connected with Babylonia than with Egypt. In Egypt, for example, an altar was simply a raised platform or table on which food was placed, and animal cults prevented sacrifices ; in Mesopotamia, as in Israel, the altar stood in front of the temple, and on it animals—goats and sheep generally—were slain or burnt. These sacrifices provided food for the gods, who were allotted definite portions, but they also acted as substitutes for men ; an offerer claimed that a lamb should be accepted in his place in expiation for sin, and in the signing of treaties we find such a sacrificed animal symbolizing one of the contracting parties. In both Mesopotamia and Israel worship consisted of public and private prayers, offerings, and sacrifices ; psalms of penitence and praise closely resembling those in the Hebrew

Psalter were sung, sacrifices were accompanied by libations, and public worship was carefully regulated by ordinances. Sin was regarded as causing the loss of the god's protection, and had to be expiated by magical and purification rites and by sacrifices. But the idea of sin here does not appear to be a moral conception ; it is a breach of ritual requirements, and often is thought of as due to inadvertence as in the laws of the Old Testament ; and the ritual in both was directed towards the expiation of sins of ignorance. The priestly religion of the Israelites has closer contact with Mesopotamia, while the morality of the prophets has more in common with the conscience which dawned so early in Egypt. The priesthood also played an important rôle ; usually the reigning monarch, who was regarded as the representative and deputy of the god, was the national high priest, and his son chief priest of the capital city ; his mother or daughter would usually be high priestess. Priests were divided into three classes : magicians, whose duty it was to win the favour of the gods and drive away demons ; soothsayers, who obtained oracles and foretold the future by dreams, observing the heavens and natural happenings, or studying the liver of sacrificial animals ; and finally singers, who were responsible for much of the worship.[16]

Close contact between Mesopotamia and the Old Testament is seen also in their ideas of the future life. In contrast to the elaborate ideas in Egypt, Mesopotamian religion thought of the dead as entering a dark world where existence, as in the Hebrew Sheol, was miserable and hopeless. This notion of the afterworld becomes more surprising when we remember the evidence from Sir Leonard Woolley's striking discoveries of large-scale human sacrifice connected with royal burials.[17] One cannot help wondering whether, both in Mesopotamia and in Israel, prophetic reformers in their revolt against an elaborate cult of the dead killed the belief in a real existence after death.

Numerous excavations in Syria are now revealing that the closest parallels with the Old Testament come, however, from that country, and that Syria was moreover the channel through which much of the external influence on Palestinian religion entered. Henri Berr [18] writes of Syria, "Lying at the crossroads of the ancient world, the highway of wandering peoples and victorious hosts, traversed by trade and the earliest movements of thought, Syria was the inevitable home of syncretism." It was the door for Egyptian as well as Mesopotamian and Hittite influence, and through it poured Hyksos, Philistine, Greek, and Roman conquerors. Sufficient excavations have not yet been made to render possible a connected history of its religious development. Each site makes its own peculiar contribution and suggests that the accounts given by classical writers—Lucian, Herodotus, and Philo of Byblos—are in the main accurate. Many a city bears a name revealing the nature of its patron deity ; Sidon was the city of Sid, who may be the god depicted at Arvad as a sea-god, half fish, half man, with scales, long plaited hair, and grasping a dolphin in each hand ; Heliopolis, or On, the modern Baalbec, was presided over by a youthful sun-god, whose conical hat, serpent, ostrich feathers, and horns witness to the syncretistic nature of his worship. His usual symbol was a young bull with sprouting horns.

The antiquity and prominence of the cult of fertility goddesses and of the mother-goddess are revealed from many sites, and agree with Lucian's account. Representations have been found of Kadish as a nude goddess riding on a lion, with Egyptian lotus flowers in one hand and serpents in the other. At Qatna the holiest shrine, a windowless room curtained off from the temple, contained a small golden statue of a goddess with a Sumerian name ; a mother-goddess was associated with the sun-god at Baalbec ; and the Lady of Byblos was at an early period assimilated to Hathor, the Egyptian cow-goddess of the heavens, whose characteristic head is described by Erman as " a broad kindly woman's face surrounded by thick plaits of hair and retaining nothing of the cow except the ears and two horns between which appears the disc of the sun." It is of interest also to remember that we find in Syria, as well as in Egypt and Mesopotamia, frequent representations of the mother-goddess suckling her babe or holding it in her arms—

a picture which was to reappear thousands of years later in Christianity.

Evidence from Egypt in the third millennium B.C. shows that many of the gods worshipped in Syria were those already seen in our survey of Mesopotamian religion : Shamash, Sin, and Hadad ; the sun, moon, and weather gods ; the Amorite god Amurru, or Amor ; the divine king Melk, and the Semitic god El.

The fullest account of Syrian religion comes from the excavations which have been proceeding since A.D. 1928 at Ras Shamra, the ancient Ugarit, on the coast. The earliest strata suggest that at first influence came from the Ægean ; in the fourth millennium Mesopotamian contacts were more numerous, and in the third those with Egypt. A Semitic invasion followed, and the oldest temple yet unearthed there is dedicated to Dagon, the food-god, who was worshipped also by Hammurabi. Later these Semitic invaders added to their pantheon Baal, a god of the Hadad type, and his images are the most numerous of all in the later strata. After this, Egyptian influence again became strong, and two sphinxes with the name of Amenhotep III carved on their breast were found at the entrance to Baal's temple ; at the same time there is much evidence for the entrance of Minoan culture from Crete. Under the Hyksos conquest, Hurrian and Mitanni elements entered the city, and in the fifteenth century we find from the Amarna letters that it allied itself with the Hittites against Egypt. Its overthrow came at the hands of the Sea Peoples who destroyed the Hittite empire.

A large library of cuneiform tablets in a new alphabetic script was discovered in the priests' house between the temples of Dagon and Baal. These have been deciphered, and although the translation of some of them is far from certain, they appear to leave no doubt as to the nature of religion at Ras Shamra during the first half of the second millennium B.C. The worship of El was carried to such a point that, although he was not the only god, it might almost be called monotheistic. He is a sun-god, represented sometimes by a winged disc, but

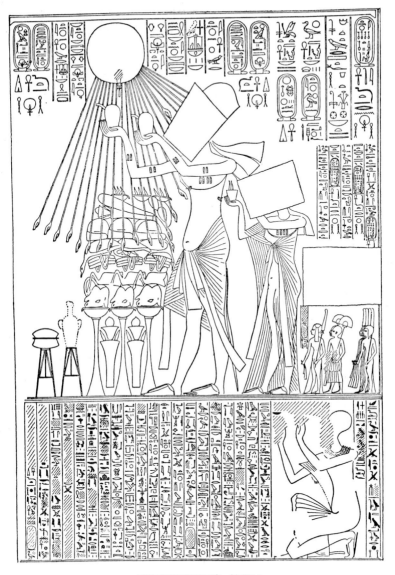

WORSHIPPING ATEN

(*Egypt Exploration Society*)

Bas-relief from Ras Shamra of a god—possibly Yahweh—before whom stands
the king, holding a sceptre and a libation vessel

(*Prof. C. Schaeffer*)

more often as a bull. Almost as important as himself is his consort Asherat of the Sea, who is called counsellor and creator of the gods. There is some doubt as to whether Baal is regarded as the son of Dagon or of El, but both El and Baal have sons who figure largely in the cult myths of the city. Some scholars claim to have found evidence too for the presence in the pantheon, as a minor figure, of a god whose name corresponds to that of Yahweh, the god known to us in the Old Testament as the national god of Israel.[19] Schæffer in his Schweich Lectures (for 1936) on the Ras Shamra tablets stresses the important place in the religion of magical rites which connect fertility cults with libations offered to the dead. Numerous pieces of clay piping, with holes to allow liquid to flow through, were used for pouring libations into the ground, and into large bottomless vases in tombs.

The findings here are of supreme importance for our purpose ; they give us first-hand evidence for the religion of Canaan, which previously we had known only from con- demnations in Israel's prophets and prohibitions in her laws ; they teach that much of the ritual and even many technical terms in the Mosaic law, which scholars had thought to have originated in the post-exilic period, were not only of high antiquity, but belonged to the religion of Palestine before the Israelites entered ; their presence in the priestly writings is not due to the originality of these later writers, but to the priestly tendency to conserve and adapt features in the old religion which could not be eradicated.

CHAPTER 3

THE CULT PATTERN OF THE NEAR EAST

ONE of the most important discoveries of recent years, in its effect on our ideas of biblical religion, is that the myth and ritual running through the whole of the Near East had certain common features, and that there are traces in the Bible that Palestine itself was influenced in its religious development by this cult pattern.[1] In this common pattern the cycle of religious feasts is based on the recurring seasons of the agricultural year. We can see it clearly in the religion revealed in the excavations at Ras Shamra, and it is possible that it was from Syria that it spread to Mesopotamia and Egypt, where also it is clearly discernible. The pattern is not everywhere identical; there are signs of adaptation and disintegration, but the main features are the same throughout.

There is everywhere a dramatic representation of the death and resurrection of a god. At Ras Shamra it is Aleyn who is slain by Mot in the heat of the summer, when the withering plants and the drying up of the ground proclaim his doom. Anath, his consort, searches for his body, and finds it with the help of Shapsh, the sun, who here is a goddess. Numerous animal sacrifices are offered, and, again with the help of the sun-goddess, Aleyn is restored to life and placed on Mot's throne to rule with Baal, so that the return of rains and fertility is assured. A passage describing Anath's conflict with Mot shows clearly the vegetation nature of the myth:

Anath seized Mot, the divine son, with a sickle she cuts him, with a winnow she winnows him, with fire she scorches him, with a mill she crushes him, she scatters his flesh in the fields to be eaten by the birds that his destiny may be fulfilled.

In Egypt the Nile god Osiris is the hero and Set the villain.[2] There are many versions of the myth, but in all Osiris is murdered by his brother Set ; Isis his faithful wife seeks her husband's body, and after her search has been successful Osiris is raised to life. Scenes on the walls at Denderah and in the Isis temple at Philæ depict some of the annual ritual linked with this resurrection ; wheat or barley is sown in a mummy-shaped vessel, and under the heat of the Egyptian sun quickly springs up as a symbol of the living Osiris.

In Mesopotamia it is Marduk who dies and rises again. He has here replaced the Sumerian hero Tammuz, the god who, drowned in the floods at the summer solstice, was lamented and sought by his lover Ishtar. A Babylonian seal depicts Marduk imprisoned in the underworld, and a kneeling figure corresponding to his consort Zarpanit bewailing him or praying for his return. Of particular interest is the fact that here the creation myths, known to many of the Old Testament writers, were used as incantations to help to restore Marduk to life. It is clear too that his son Nabu or Nebo has a share in his rescue, just as in Egypt Horus helps to restore his father Osiris ; at Ras Shamra the story appears to differ in that both Aleyn and his father Baal seem to go down together into the underworld, but it is the son and not the father who dies and rises again.

These myths are all variant forms of the well-known Tammuz-Adonis story, which cannot be dissociated from the fact of the annual dying of vegetation, and its renewal through autumn rains or summer floods. That the myth was known in Palestine is proved by references in the eighth-century book of Isaiah (i.) and the sixth-century Ezekiel (viii.), both of which speak of the presence of the cult in Jerusalem ; and it seems probable that the myth cannot be separated from the Old Testament poems relating the death and resurrection of the Servant of the Lord (cf. Isa. lii. 13–liii.), and that it prepared the ground for the acceptance of the records of the death and resurrection of Jesus in the New Testament.

It is also of interest that the ritual was often enacted at the death of the reigning monarch, who was regarded as the embodiment of the god. Mesopotamian seals show that there

was a time when, at the annual festival, a human substitute
for the god-king was sacrificed. It is well-known that in
many parts of the world the fertility of the land was thought
to be dependent on the virile strength of the king, and men
feared that a failing king meant failing crops. Such ideas are
important when we seek to understand the religious significance of the revolts which the Old Testament relates as taking
place at the end of the reign of David (1 Kings i.).

These ideas bring us to another common feature of our
cult pattern—the enthronement of the king as god. Though
so far we have no relevant material from Ras Shamra, there is
ample evidence in Egypt and Mesopotamia of deification rites
performed at the coronation of a new king who thereby becomes made, or acknowledged as, the son and representative
of the god. In Babylonia there appears to have been an annual
ceremony of the coronation of the king and his enthronement
at the New Year festival ; his crown and sceptre were laid
before the statue of the god, and both before and after he took
the hand of the god and received them back, he was struck
on the cheek by the priest as a sign of humiliation. Perhaps
from the sight of such an act of abasement there came to post-
exilic Jews the idea of a day of national humiliation expressed
in the annual Day of Atonement, linked with the New Year
feast. Such enthronement ceremonies are witnessed to from
the end of the third millennium B.C., and an inscription found
at Persepolis shows that the ceremony persisted until 484 B.C.,
when Xerxes altered the Persian policy of religious toleration
and ceased to show deference to Marduk. Mowinckel in his
studies in the Psalms claims to have found considerable evidence
for such annual coronation ceremonies in Palestine. Possibly
Psalm ii. may retain an example of the form liturgy would
take at such a ceremony : " I have set my king upon my
holy hill of Zion. The Lord said unto me, thou art my son,
this day have I begotten thee," a verse echoed in the story
of the baptism of Jesus.

Another prominent element in the cult is sacred marriage,[3]
which formed the climax of the fertility rites. Evidence for

this goes back at least as far as the fourth millennium B.C., and has been gathered from many widely separated districts. It is natural that in details the ceremony varied, but we usually find that one of the two chief actors was the king dressed as a god. In Egypt there are myths telling of the marriage of earth and sky, of the wings of the dead Osiris overshadowing his wife ; and the picture of Isis nursing her child is one upon which Egyptian fancy loved to dwell. Wall paintings depict the sacred rite enacted between the king and queen as deities; and the heir to the throne was regarded as son of the god.

From Ras Shamra the tablets tell only of sacred marriages among the gods, though in one tablet there appears to be evidence that priests played the part of the god. From Mesopotamia we get continual evidence that the rite was central in the New Year festivities, usually held at the beginning of the autumn. The king as god was here also the chief actor, his partner being sometimes the high-priestess, sometimes a maiden. The more we learn of this part of the cult-pattern the more clearly we realize that many of its features are reflected in the Bible ; incidental sayings, stories of David and of Shiloh, as well as the protests of prophets and lawgivers, become easier to understand in the light of it.

A further element, which often precedes that of the enthronement of the king and the sacred marriage, is the ritual combat of the gods with evil powers who would destroy creation. In Mesopotamia the account of the conflict between Marduk and Tiamat, the goddess of the watery abyss, is too well known to need repeating. This myth has entered Old Testament writings particularly in the account of creation, where Chaos is represented in Hebrew by a word that corresponds to Tiamat ; in Ezekiel, where Yahweh is spoken of as having a net (xxxii. 3), like that with which Marduk entrapped Tiamat ; and in the Psalms. In Egypt it is the son of the slain god who carries the fight to a victorious issue, and assists in the restoration of his father. At Ras Shamra there appear to be several accounts of the conflict. There is a fight between Baal and a god of the sea, which may correspond to the Old

Testament idea of God's conquest of the sea and the fixing of its bounds ; Baal also fights Lotan, the seven-headed serpent, whose name reminds us of the Old Testament Leviathan. Representations of this monster have been unearthed at other places. There are, moreover, fights between Mot, the god of death and winter, and Aleyn with his consort Anath. In all of them the forces of rain, life, and fruitfulness are victorious over death and destruction. Summer heat and storms cease, and the way is prepared for the coming of the crops.

The last element to be mentioned is the new creation, which is made possible by victory over destructive forces. At Ras Shamra, as in Babylonia, the building of a new temple, in the one place for Baal and in the other for Marduk, appears to be part of a ceremonial of making this brave new world. In Babylonia there was a ceremony of fixing the Destinies, which took three days at the end of the New Year festival. The Tablets of Destiny were part of the trophies of victory in the divine conflict, and by them Marduk, in consultation with Nabu, the god of wisdom, fixed for the ensuing year the destiny of the world ; at Ras Shamra the magical objects which were used are called Teraphim—a word well-known to Old Testament students. This rite secured the proper functioning of all created things—sun, moon, stars, men, and animals, heaven and earth. It seems probable that the creation tablets were part of the ceremony, and it is well to recognize that the story in Genesis of the six-day creation is not simply a myth relating how the world was made, but springs from this functional use of myth, in which the annual recital of the creation account secured the proper functioning of created things for the coming year. The connection of Nabu, the god of wisdom, with the new creation, may be reflected in the later Jewish conception of Wisdom, who was personified as helper at creation (Prov. viii.).

The basis of the whole cult-pattern would appear to be mimetic magic, performing an act in order that a corresponding act may be repeated on a larger scale by cosmic forces, as a sailor whistles for a wind. The instinct behind the cult must be deeply implanted within us, since examples of it are found all over the world and down to our own day ; this makes all the more striking the bold assertion of the writer in Genesis, who declares that because God's bow has been set in the sky such rites are unnecessary : " While the earth remaineth, seed-time and harvest, and cold and heat, and summer and winter, and day and night shall not cease " (Gen. viii. 22).

CHAPTER 4

THE PHYSICAL FEATURES OF PALESTINE

IN the foregoing pages we have attempted to put Palestine and
its religion in its setting in the Near East, and to show how it
was influenced by surrounding nations and the common cult-
pattern which ran through their religious life. To complete
the religious geography of Palestine, it is necessary to look
at the country itself, and see how its physical features affected
the development of religion.

§ ITS INDIVIDUALITY

That the central position of the land continually subjected
it to influences from many directions is beyond doubt, but
it is equally important to recognize that throughout its long
history Palestine has retained an individuality of its own. The
power often attributed to the Hebrew people of reshaping and
adapting what they have received from outside is in reality a
characteristic inherent in the country itself. Pottery forms,
as well as myths, traditions, and religious institutions, have
from the most remote period been taken over, altered, and
re-used in the land. Professor S. A. Cook in his Schweich
Lectures for 1925 [1] summarizes thus his conclusions :

The land of Israel—Palestine itself—is in completest touch, archæo-
logically, with the larger area of which it is an organic part, but it has
an individuality of its own. There is in fact a certain protest or reaction
against other religions, even those which best enable us to understand
Israel. In close contact with Egypt, but un-Egyptian, lying at the tail
end of states which were bound up with Mesopotamia and Anatolia, and
throughout exposed to the incursions of desert tribes, the small land must
hammer out its own career or be swallowed up. The evidence seems
to show that the exclusiveness and creativeness, the self-consciousness one
might say, which characterize the religion of Israel, date from an early,
if not a pre-Israelite, period.

This individuality may be, in part, due to the fact that for much of its history the land formed the boundary, rather than an integral part, of neighbouring kingdoms. Outside influence appears to have penetrated furthest when Palestine was incorporated in a larger empire. Early Mesopotamian and Egyptian rulers, as we have seen, invaded the land, but did not pass beyond its borders. The Hyksos for two hundred years made it part of their far-flung empire, and left indelible marks on the archæology of the country. Afterwards for a thousand years it was the boundary of Egyptian or Assyrian rulers, and an eighth-century prophet shows how Israel leaned for support first on one and then on the other, " fluttering to and fro like a silly dove " (Hos. vii. 11). Babylonians and Persians successively penetrated Palestine, and with varying degrees of strength held sway over Egypt, but their domination was maintained only by continued invasion, and Palestine remained the limit of effective military control. For a short time it was part of the empire of Alexander the Great, but after his death the division of his possessions among his generals left the country as a bone of contention between the Ptolemaic power in Egypt, and the Seleucids in Syria. Even the Romans did not extend their power eastwards beyond Trans-Jordan, and on more than one occasion they were driven out of Palestine by the Parthians. This characteristic of the political history of the land made her inhabitants ever ready to revolt and react against the cultural and religious, as well as the military, control of her neighbours.

The individuality was also, in part, due to the physical nature of the land.[2] The writer of the book of Deuteronomy, who knew Palestine as well as he knew Egypt, brings out some of the outstanding features of the land when he is contrasting the two countries :

For the land whither thou goest in to possess it, is not as the land of Egypt, where thou sowedst thy seed, and wateredst it with thy foot as a garden of herbs ; but the land is a land of hills and valleys and drinketh water from the rain of heaven, a land which the Lord thy God careth for (xi. 10f.).

In contrast with the flat Nile valley it is the natural features of Palestine which are impressive. In Egypt, as we have seen, attention is attracted to human beings and man-made things —men trotting along mud roads on donkeys or walking beside buffaloes or laden camels ; women with long black robes, the lower part of their faces veiled, picturesque with water jars on their heads, or babies sitting astride on one shoulder ; villages with mud houses and tall minarets standing out on the sky-line; primitive water-wheels turned by patient oxen; the slow, stately movement of flat-bottomed boats driven along the Nile and its canals by sails on long curved masts that catch the wind above the banks. In Palestine, it is hills and valleys that compel attention—the rugged broken line of hills that bound the fertile plain of Esdraelon, or form the eastern edge of the broad coastal plain ; narrow barren ravines or steep mountain sides that fall to fertile green valleys ; the changing colours on the hills of Moab beyond Jordan ; the snow-covered peak of Hermon, rising above the cedars and fir trees of Lebanon. It is possible that from the beginning the tribal God of Israel may have been a God who dwelt among mountains, and was, as to Amos, a universal God comparable to the old sky-gods of other nations. But increasingly from the sixth century B.C. he was worshipped, as was natural in such a land, as a personal God who controlled Nature—the one " who laid the founda-tions of the earth " (Isa. li. 13), " weighed the mountains in scales and the hills in a balance " (Isa. xl. 12), and to whom " the hills shout for joy."

The Deuteronomic contrast between Egypt and Palestine emphasises another feature of the country which had an im-portant influence on the development of religion. To that writer the fertility of Egypt was man-made (Deut. xi. 10). The rainfall there is almost negligible, and cultivation is possible only where the waters of the Nile flood can be conserved and used for irrigation. To-day, as then, the land is watered by the foot of man, and visitors to the country can still see the peasants watering their fields by opening or closing, with bare feet, the mud barriers that block the water channels. In Egypt men

could rely on the regular rising of the Nile, and forget their
dependence on the rains which, falling in equatorial Africa,
cause the flood ; but in Palestine it was impossible to forget
that all prosperity was due to the fact that " the rain cometh
down and the snow from heaven, and returneth not thither
but watereth the earth, and maketh it to bring forth and bud,
and giveth seed to the sower and bread to the eater " (Isa. lv.
10).   Although in contrast to Egypt it can be called a " good
land, a land of brooks of water, of fountains and depths,
springing forth in valleys and hills " (Deut. viii. 7) yet Palestine
lacks any perennial streams, apart from the Jordan, and that
is useless for irrigation. This river too, like the Nile, has an
annual flood and " overfloweth all its banks all the time of
harvest " (Josh. iii. 15) ; every year it too carries down tons
of fertile soil washed from the hills by torrential rains, but the
Nile mud is spread over the wide fertile delta and made to
produce two crops a year, while the Jordan mud is heaped up
around the barren Dead Sea in weird-shaped unproductive
mounds. The river—whose name means " the Descender "—
dropping at forty feet a mile as it leaves the Sea of Galilee,
flows swiftly along a channel cut deeply into the old river bed
at the bottom of the valley. Even the flood waters fill only
this old river bed, and cannot be used on the land that towers
two thousand feet above the valley. Wherever in Palestine
there was a good perennial spring a town was built, and
excavations have shown the care that even the earliest inhabitants took to conserve the spring waters ; but many of the
towns were dependent entirely on water caught in large rock-
hewn cisterns.

This lack of water gives point to many of the religious
ideas of the Bible and the language in which they are expressed.
Deborah and Samuel worshipped a God who manifested himself in the thunderstorm that defeated their enemies ; Elijah
proved his God to be the true rain-giver ; Deuteronomy
taught men the lesson of humble dependence on the God who
rewards obedience by " the rain of your land in its season,
the former rain and the latter rain, that thou mayest gather in

thy corn and thy wine and thy oil " (Deut. xi. 14) ; Jeremiah, describing the sins of his people in forsaking God, proclaimed, " My people have committed two evils ; they have forsaken me, the fountain of living waters, and have hewn themselves out cisterns, that can hold no water " (Jer. ii. 13) ; Jesus too spoke of the living waters he gave (John iv. 10), of the rivers of living water that flowed from those who believed on him (John vii. 38), and in contradiction to the Deuteronomic writer he claimed that the love of God is shown by the fact that " He maketh his sun to shine on the evil and on the good, and sendeth rain on the just and on the unjust " (Matt. v. 45).

Dependence on an uncontrollable rainfall made the peoples of Palestine always peculiarly susceptible to religious cults that claimed to produce fertility, the increase of crops, cattle, and children. Excavations are continually providing fresh evidence of the widespread worship of the mother-goddess, the guardian of fertility ; and we are beginning to realize how deeply Palestine was influenced by the religions we have described, that reflected the passing of the seasons, worshipping a god who every year died when the summer sun parched the ground, and rose again when autumn rains brought new life to vegetation. That the importance of the seasons in religion persisted can be seen in the festivals of the modern Jews, and of the Christians, who worship One whose birthday is commemorated in mid-winter, and whose resurrection from the dead at springtime.

§ Its Natural Divisions

There are two other features of the country which had an important bearing on its religion. We have already seen how frequently it was entered by neighbouring peoples. The reasons for this spring from the nature of the land, for in the first place, apart from the Mediterranean it had no natural dividing lines between it and the outside world, and in the second, there were divisions within the country which caused a constant lack of unity.

To Old Testament idealists the northern limit of their land
stretched to the " entering in of Hamath "—the southern end
of the valley between the Lebanons which gave access to
Hamath—but in fact the actual boundary did not reach much
beyond the northern end of Lake Huleh, where Dan was
situated, and where the present artificial line between Palestine
and Syria runs. The most important break in the contours
at the north is caused by the broad plain of Esdraelon, and
pre-Israelite inhabitants built their line of forts along the hills
south of the plain, from Bethshan in the Jordan valley, through
Megiddo and Taanach, to Dor on the Mediterranean ; but to
Israelites invading from the east it was no barrier, and they
spread both north and south of it.

In the south one passes almost imperceptibly from the
cultivated land to the desert, and the extent of both fluctuates
with the rainfall. Beersheba is usually regarded as the outpost
of cultivation, but ruins of large cities far to the south of it
prove that, at least in Roman times, with careful cultivation
and the conservation of water the so-called desert could support a numerous and prosperous population. Moreover the
desert has never been impassable. The Bible tells of the
journeys of patriarchs, history relates the movement of large
bodies of troops, and to-day as one crosses it by car, or on the
railway built by British troops, Bedouin can be seen trekking
freely across it with nothing to prevent them entering Egypt
on the one side or Palestine on the other. The Amorites built
most of their strong fortresses—" walled up to heaven "—
north of Beersheba, and even to-day the population of Beersheba is far more akin in appearance to the Bedouin and fella-
hin of Egypt than to the Palestinian Arab. There has always
been a constant stream of desert wanderers entering the cultivated land, and these infiltrations were an important factor
in the religious life of southern Palestine.

On the west there are no cliffs to shut the land off from
the waters of the Mediterranean. The shallow water in the
bay at Acre is useless for large modern ships, but provided
excellent anchorage for earlier smaller boats. Cyprus and the

islands and coasts of the Ægean were within easy reach, and
Second-Isaiah, the great prophet of the sixth century in Palestine, often addressed his stirring messages to their inhabitants.

On the east the Jordan valley has never proved an effective
barrier. Hebrew tradition pictures the tribes as settling both
sides of it ; Israelite kingdoms stretched across into Trans-
Jordan ; and both Roman and Turkish administrations ignored
it when drawing the limits of their provincial governments.
South of the Sea of Galilee the wadis leading to it from east
and west formed highways for trade and tribal invasions, and
northern Palestine was in closer contact with Trans-Jordan than
with southern Palestine. In the south the real barrier was not
the Jordan valley, but the rocky desolate wilderness which
stretches from the edge of the valley to the central hill country
of Judæa, almost to the gates of Jerusalem, Bethlehem, and
Hebron.

The second reason for the frequency with which the land
suffered invasion, was that by nature it was a house divided
against itself, and continual dissension and internal warfare
brought successive invaders, often invited by one party to
assist it against another. The Amarna letters [3] show how petty
kings of small city states fought one another, slandered each
other to the Egyptian overlord, and found it utterly impossible
even to combine against the common invader.

It is usual to find the reason for this disunity in the presence
of great natural divisions running from north to south, which
are obvious from a glance at a relief map, or to anyone flying
over the country. Crossing from west to east the four main
sections are the coastal plain, the central hill-country, the deep
Jordan valley, and the fertile land of Trans-Jordan shading off
into the Arabian desert. But it is important for our purpose
to notice that these natural divisions form real barriers only
in the south. The wilderness on the east, which we have
mentioned, shuts Judæa off from Trans-Jordan, and on the
west the valleys leading up from the coastal plain do not run
straight into the hills, but form long parallel lines, rising from
south to north, and making a boundary difficult to cross.

§ Contrast between North and South Palestine

All this had the effect of isolating the little mountainous kingdom of Judæa, and separating it, not only geographically but politically, from its neighbour in the north. The history of Palestine shows that never was it possible to unite the land in a self-contained kingdom that endured for any length of time. The military domination of the north by the southern kingdom under David ended after eighty years with the death of his son Solomon, and afterwards, except for short periods when one part controlled the other, Palestine was divided into two kingdoms—the northern and the southern—which were essentially different from each other.

In the north Galilee lay along the main line of communication in the ancient world. The roads westward to the coast, as well as those between Egypt and Mesopotamia, passed through it, so that it was open to influences from both sides. Its affinities were with the great river civilizations of the Nile and Euphrates, and with the fertile lands of Trans-Jordan. From every direction it was easy of access. Valleys from the coastal plain and from the Jordan ran straight up into its broken hills in the centre, and the deep valley between the two Lebanon ranges brought traffic from Syria and the north. It contained rich agricultural lands and was famous for its figs, vines, and olives ; so fertile was it that there was a Jewish saying that it was easier to raise a legion of olives in Galilee than a single child in Judæa.

Judæa, on the other hand, was hemmed in on east and west by natural barriers, strong enough to prevent easy access to its bare mountain heights. What Henri Berr says of Palestine is particularly true of Judæa :

A certain exclusiveness and love of independence were fostered as in Greece by the nature of the country which, between coastal plain and the desert, was cut up by mountain ranges, and allowed small groups in separate districts to live in a relative isolation, secluded from the main lines of communication.

Thus it became conservative and exclusive, and foreign influences did not easily penetrate its rocky fastnesses. Because it lay open only at its southern end, its chief affinities were not with the lavish and varied civilizations of the Nile and Euphrates, nor with the agriculturalists of the north, but with the lean, ascetic nomad of the desert.

Racially, too, these two peoples of north and south appear to have been different. Both belonged to a common Semitic stock, but many of the invaders who swept across the country from the north and north-west, as well as from Egypt, missed Judæa secluded on its high plateau. The Israelite tribes who settled in the north appear themselves to have belonged to a different wave of immigration, coming from northern Trans-Jordan, while those of the south entered from Edom and the Sinai desert. Compulsory evacuation also played its part in altering the character of the racial stock ; the Old Testament contains evidence of the transportation of inhabitants from the north and the replacing of them by settlers from Babylonia, Cuthah, Avva, Hamath, and Sepharvaim in 721 B.C. (2 Kings xvii. 24), and later by others in the time of Esarhaddon (Ezra iv. 2). Perhaps because of this the land in later times was called Galilee—the Ring—of the Gentiles, and even in the second century B.C. the foreign element so predominated that Judas Maccabæus sent troops to rescue small groups of Jews who were being persecuted there. In contrast, the Judæans regarded themselves as of purer stock, although the genealogies of the Old Testament show that they too were a mixed race. When Israelites first entered Judæa they intermarried with the Canaanite inhabitants, and later we have considerable evidence from prophets and historians that neighbouring tribes entered in the sixth century, after the Babylonian conquest, and mingled their blood with that of the Jews left behind in the country.

Contemporary accounts suggest that in the New Testament period also the Judaism of Galilee and of Judæa remained essentially different. Although in the Old Testament in its present form the religion of Judæa has in the main become dominant, yet we shall find that throughout the time covered

SLAYING THE SEVEN-HEADED SERPENT

SACRED MARRIAGE

RITUAL SLAYING OF KING-GOD

THE GOD IN THE MOUNTAIN

(From " The Origins of Early Semitic Ritual," *by S. H. Hooke, British Academy, Oxford Press,* 1938)

The cow-goddess Hathor, from
the Temple of Deir el-Bahri
(*Cairo Museum*)

Bronze statuette of Isis nursing
the infant Horus
(*British Museum*)

both by the Old and by the New Testament the north brought its contribution and played an important part in the formation of Judaism and Christianity ; but the study of the geography of the country helps us to understand why Judæa produced the stern prophets of morality and uncompromising conscience, why the pleasant hills of Samaria listened to Hosea's message of a loving Father, and why the fairest flower of religion grew amid the natural beauty of Galilee.

BOOK II

THE MINGLING OF CULTURES

CHAPTER 5

PALESTINE BEFORE THE TWELFTH CENTURY B.C.

§ CAVE DWELLERS OF THE STONE AGE [1]

DISCOVERIES in pre-historic caves in Palestine have shown that human beings existed there long before 4004 B.C., the date given for the creation of the world by Archbishop Ussher, and printed in the margin of the Authorized English version of the Bible. At three sites in northern Palestine—near the Sea of Galilee, near Nazareth, and in the Wadi el-Mugharah at the foot of Carmel, as well as in a cave near Bethlehem in the south—skeletons have been found which carry back human history many millenniums. The way in which these earliest inhabitants of the country buried their dead gives us evidence for the first rudimentary beginnings of religion in Palestine.

Under the floor at the mouth of one cave was found a group of eight skeletons, one of them that of a child about two years of age ; all had been flexed with the knees towards the chin in a contracted position, and with them were buried treasured personal possessions. The place of burial, where the living continued to dwell, suggests that at that time the dead were neither feared nor regarded as in any way unclean, but still remained part of the family circle. The contracted position shows that care was taken in the interment, and may point to a belief that death and burial were the preparation for a new birth from the womb of Mother Earth. The view that to these people death was not the last line of all is strengthened

42

by the fact that the bodies were buried with bone necklaces and garters, and the child was given a cap made of the toe bones of goats or gazelles. Perhaps they would be needed in the after-world, perhaps they were thought of as having a magical power to benefit the wearer, an idea certainly associated with pierced shells found in other burials. Near many of these early burials were found cup-holes scooped out of the rock ; their purpose cannot be determined with certainty, but similar cup-holes have been found in other places in Palestine so close to burials as to suggest that the two are connected.[2] Possibly they were to hold food for the dead, or more likely to receive libations, like the clay pipes and bottomless jars at Ras Shamra.

From other caves also comes increasing evidence that these people had developed some form of religious cult : there are drawings on walls and on bones, and figures which were possibly cult objects have also been found. One—a young bull carved in bone and dated in the fifth or sixth millennium B.C.—has been described as the finest pre-historic art object yet found in Asia. At Jericho [3] were found animal figurines, dated about 4000 B.C., which suggest some rudimentary pastoral cult possibly linked with the worship of the moon-god, and hence also, still in the Stone Age, came a most interesting pottery group, consisting of a man, woman, and child, which may represent one of the earliest forms of a divine triad. The most plentiful evidence, however, comes from Gezer, where in very ancient times the caves were used for dwellings and sanctuaries and later, when houses began to be built on the surface, became cemeteries and storehouses. Such prolonged occupation, continuing without abrupt breaks even when new-comers put the caves to new uses, makes it difficult to be precise in dating some of the objects found.

One cave here, which was buried beneath thirty-six feet of debris and whose contents must be dated in the fourth millennium B.C., had the familiar cup-holes at its entrance, and inside around the walls a band of rock which had been smoothed and covered with drawings, some of which suggest the presence of magical ideas. A picture of a human foot may perhaps be linked with a similar clay model found in the same cave, and with a tablet on which was the impression of a bruised foot of a child, made perhaps to heal or to harm him, or as a thank-offering ; there are sketches of animals, and scenes depicting hunting and pastoral activities, as well as the drawings of cup-holes arranged in spirals. From Mesopotamia of about the same date come scenes from agricultural and pastoral life depicted on friezes around the inside of temple buildings, and Ezekiel shows that such practices persisted in the temple at Jerusalem as late as the sixth century B.C.—" So I went in and saw and behold every form of creeping things, and abominable beasts and all the idols of the house of Israel, portrayed upon the walls round about. And there stood before them seventy men of the elders of the house of Israel, with every man his censer in his hand ; and a thick cloud of incense went up " (viii. 10f.).

There are other points of particular interest in the caves at Gezer. One cave is perhaps the oldest sanctuary yet found in Palestine ; on the rock surface above are many cup-holes, one of which has been connected by a channel with the cave below—a feature found also at Megiddo, where the channel pierced three feet of rock. In one end of the cave itself were the bones of pigs, which may have been sacrificed, as at other places, by being thrown into the cave ; and it is interesting to notice that figurines of pigs and pigs' teeth used as amulets were also found at Bethshan, Gezer, and at Jericho as late as the Jewish period. This presence in Palestine of pig-cults is of significance when we remember the Jewish abhorrence of this animal, and it may have a bearing on the date at which the prohibition against eating swine flesh was first introduced.

There is further a complex of two caves linked together by a narrow crooked passage, perhaps suggesting one of the earliest examples of a place where an oracle was given. The entrance to the smaller cave was blocked, and it was possible for a man to be hidden in it and give messages to those who had entered the larger cave and were ignorant of his presence. The dark windowless room in the later Jewish temple, known to us as the " Holy of Holies," is called in Hebrew by a word which connects it with this small cave at the back of the sanctuary.

That all the inhabitants of Palestine in the Stone Age were not of the same race, is shown by their different funeral customs. A pre-Semitic people at Gezer evidently cremated their dead— a practice rare in Palestine, although we know it was prevalent much later in the seventh century B.C. in a Phœnician colony at Athlit near Mount Carmel.[4] The successors of these early inhabitants at Gezer used the cave in which cremation had taken place for burials in the embryonic position. From else- where in Palestine there is evidence for megalithic burials in the form of dolmens, and in two places the dead were interred in trenches lined and covered with small slabs of stone, and with stone cairns built around them.

One form of culture which deserves special mention is that called Ghassulian,[5] first found at the tells at Ghassul in the Jordan valley, but since discovered at many other sites. It is definitely a flint-culture, and has been linked with the pre- Semitic inhabitants at Gezer, although the dead were not cremated ; it probably dates from before the fourth millennium B.C. A well-preserved wall painting of a large sun with eight rays driving away monsters in animal forms, and with a female figure beside it, has been thought to suggest some worship of the sun as a female deity, and there is evidence too of animal worship, including particularly the bull. Their fine painted pottery is of a type widespread through northern Mesopotamia and Syria, and has been shown by Sir Leonard Woolley to be pre-Sumerian. Possibly it was disseminated by the Sumerians, for we know that in the Stone Age Palestine lagged far behind the cultures of the Nile and the Euphrates. The presence of this culture is of considerable interest, because the people who brought this pottery into Palestine may also have brought with them the Sumerian creation myths ; and these myths may thus have been handed down for many centuries in Palestine and been taken over by the Israelites after they entered the country.

§ AMORITES OF THE EARLY BRONZE AGE

The date at which Semites first entered Palestine, bringing with them the culture of the Early Bronze Age, has recently become the subject of controversy. At Bethel the earliest Canaanite settlement is dated at about 2200 B.C., when the Semites were thought to have entered the land, but Dr. Wright[6] in his study of Palestinian pottery contends that the Bronze Age began at least a millennium earlier, in about 3300 B.C. This controversy is an example of the difficulty we shall often find of being precise as to the dating of successive cultures. But whatever the date of their entry may have been, we know that a Semitic people called Amorites, kin to Semitic dynasties which ruled in Mesopotamia, overran Palestine, giving their name to the hill country of Lebanon. Research has shown that their culture was higher than had been thought; they were skilled in building construction and in pottery making, and perhaps were even able to express themselves in writing.

These people seem to have been the first in Palestine to build sanctuaries as places specially set aside for community worship. The most outstanding feature of these shrines was the Mazzebah, or large upright stone,[7] on or near which are cup-holes like those we have already described. Such holy places have been discovered at many sites, including Megiddo, Taanach, Tell es-Safi, and Bab ed-Dra, but the finest example in Palestine is at Gezer, where there is a line of fine pillars still standing. One of these is obviously intended as a phallic symbol, another has patches worn smooth by the kisses of worshippers or by rubbing with sacrificial fat and blood. Three pillars have cup-holes carved on a smooth side; if these were used for libations the liquid would have to be dashed against the side of a pillar, as blood was thrown against the altar in Jewish ritual. There is a hollow block of stone in the centre of the line which may have been a basin for washing purposes or to hold blood; it may, however, have been intended to hold a wooden post. Such a cult object was later connected with Asherat, the consort of the Amorite god Amurru, and the book of Deuteronomy (xvi. 21f.) classes together the Mazzebah and the Asherah as objects forbidden near an altar. At this holy place, as at others, there were burials.

The site of the holy place at Gezer appears to have been determined by the presence of the oracle caves, but usually sanctuaries of this period were open-air shrines built outside the city walls, often on a neighbouring high place. Abraham is said to have built his altar outside Bethel between Bethel and Ai (Gen. xii. 8). At Jerusalem the holy place, which later became the site of the temple, was on the high ground north of the city wall, and at Bab ed-Dra it lay on the hill above the fresh-water wadis leading down to the Dead Sea. Such shrines were probably pilgrim centres for the particular districts visited at certain festivals ; and the fact that these sanctuaries are also burial places suggests that the times of the festivals may have been determined by the cult of the dead. From the Bible we learn that at later times festivals were held at such holy places for a coronation, and to rally the people against an enemy. It is of interest too to recall that at the present time the Samaritans at Nablus dig their altar and hold their Passover festival on the neighbouring hill of Gerizim, where the whole of the people encamp for the sacred week.

In Mesopotamia, by the end of the Early Bronze Age, complex pantheons were worshipped with elaborate ritual ; in Egypt pyramids had been constructed, and the lavish cult of the dead and of the solar god had grown up ; and in both there was the developed mythology of the cult-pattern of which we have spoken, but there is no trace that these developments had yet reached Palestine. In her simple shrines were found no figurines of the mother-goddess, but only the bones and images of sheep and goats, which formed the background of a shepherd's life.

There is at least one sanctuary from this period which shows progress toward the type of buildings we shall find in the Late Bronze Age ; this is the covered shrine at Ai. It is evident from its contents that it was built under Egyptian influence, and the fact that this influence had penetrated thus far into the central hills by the fourth millennium B.C. is remarkable. The building was constructed against the wall of the citadel. No figures were found to tell us to whom it was dedicated, but in one room were two stands for burning incense, and there was also an inner holy place with an altar. The position of the altar suggests that as in Egypt it was intended for food offerings to the god, rather than for animal sacrifices.

Although from this sanctuary at Ai we cannot tell whether the food was only an offering to divine beings or was part of a meal shared by the worshippers, yet we have evidence at other sites of communal religious meals in this period. The Early Bronze Age people used special pots for ordinary cooking purposes, but at Megiddo in some of the cup-holes, used as we have seen in the cult of the dead, are traces that animal flesh had been cooked there by throwing in hot stones—animal bones were found and stones fused by heat to the inside of cup-holes. These meals may have been part of a communal feast in which the whole group, dead and living, shared. It was customary among a nomadic people to regard the god also as part of the community and as partaking of the feast. That Jeremiah, at the end of the seventh century B.C., talks of eating the bread of the dead (xvi. 7), and Deuteronomy finds it necessary to prohibit setting aside food for the dead from sacred tithes (xxvi. 14), may indicate the persistence of such practices for many centuries.

As yet it is clear that these people drew no definite line to distinguish the dead from the living ; they were careful over the disposal of the dead, and usually buried them beneath the floors of their dwellings. Toward the end of the period we find shafts sunk into the ground leading to a tomb at the bottom—a form of burial which becomes more fully developed in the next period.

§ Hyksos Influence in the Middle Bronze Age

If we follow the dating in Dr. Wright's book on the pottery of Palestine, we shall consider the Middle Bronze Age as beginning about 2200 B.C., when there were changes in Palestinian culture previously attributed to the arrival of Amorites. However this may be, changes which have been described as " a tremendous and rapid religious metamorphosis in the country" took place after the arrival of the Hyksos about 1800 B.C. The new elements which appear at this time must not, however, be thought of as peculiar to the Hyksos, for their culture shows a mingling of features from civilizations in Crete, Asia Minor, Syria, and Mesopotamia. We have already seen that this people came apparently from the same general Indo-European stock as the Hittites and Mitanni, and its culture has many features in common with theirs, as for example the worship of the great mother-goddess ; but the Hyksos readily absorbed the culture of conquered populations, and consequently their invasion strengthened many elements which formed part of the heritage of Semitic peoples in Syria and Mesopotamia, and which had already influenced Palestine. Hyksos names like Jacobel and Anatel proclaim adherence to Syrian deities.

The aim of the Hyksos appears to have been the building of a wide empire, and there is no evidence that they had any fanatical allegiance to particular religious beliefs. Because of this, and because they easily absorbed other cultures with which they made contact, they had a broadening, syncretistic effect on religion ; religious ideas and customs peculiar to different parts of the Empire began freely to circulate within it. Palestine was the centre of their kingdom and felt most strongly the throb of its pulse. From the more advanced civilizations of Mesopotamia came new life to quicken the stunted religious growth of the poorer pastoral folk and, as we should expect, these militant Hyksos also spread through Palestine and Egypt the cult of war-like Semitic deities.

Among the revolutionary ideas which appear in Palestine at this time three are of particular importance. Now, for the first time, the dead were separated from the living, and shaft tombs were constructed in special burial grounds outside the city walls. We can only conjecture that this change meant that the dead were in some way feared, or regarded as unclean. This idea permeated the priestly ritual of the Old Testament, in which contact with a dead body brought ceremonial defilement, although in some other phrases in the book we hear reminiscences of the earlier practice when men were gathered to their fathers in the family vault within the precincts of the home (2 Kings xxii. 20).[8]

Even more significant is the fact that although there are these shaft tombs outside the city walls for ordinary burials, we find numerous burials of infants in jars, not only inside the cities but inside houses, under walls, floors, and thresholds. Similar burials of infants are found much earlier in Mesopotamia, but, so far as we can judge, not in Palestine. The position of some of these burials suggests that they were foundation sacrifices, and the account of the rebuilding of Jericho in the book of Kings shows that the custom persisted until the ninth century, for Hiel " laid the foundation thereof in Abiram his first born, and set up the gates thereof in his youngest son Segub " (1 Kings xvi. 34). It is, however, of interest to see how early substitutes were found for human sacrifice. Already in the Bronze Age lamps and bowls were buried instead, and we have examples of jars containing rough bronze and silver human figures.

It is unlikely, however, that all these jar burials were the result of sacrifice. Many of the young children, especially those found under the floors of private houses, must have died a natural death, for the rate of infant mortality was probably high ; but, if so, it must be recognized that in some way they were differentiated from the adults buried outside the cities. There are examples in other cultures of premature births being disposed of under the floors of dwellings in order to retain the new life within the house, and some of these jar burials may have had a similar motive. In this connection it is suggestive that the bodies in the jars were thrust head downward toward the mouth of the jar, and the pointed bottom of the jar then closed up, both the form of the jar and the position of the body being reminiscent of an embryo in a womb.

Some of the bodies are unquestionably those of infants who had been sacrificed. Considerable numbers were found over the whole area of the holy place at Gezer, all of them being about eight days old; two showed signs of burning, and in one of the caves on a limestone altar was the skeleton of a child. Similar burials were found near a rock altar at Taanach and at Megiddo, while at Ras Shamra the child burials were made in a place separate from that used for ordinary interment. Archæology reveals that once the practice had begun it was not confined to any one period, though it becomes less frequent later, in the Hellenistic age. From the books of Jeremiah and Ezekiel we learn that the custom continued at Jerusalem until the sixth century B.C. Jeremiah tells us that the children were made to pass through the fire in a place specially rebuilt in his time in the valley of Hinnom, south of the city, and he finds it necessary to repudiate strongly the claim that such sacrifice was required by God (vii. 31f.); Ezekiel does not repudiate the claim, but says it was a commandment of God to punish and make desolate the people (xx. 26). Although some of the Old Testament laws demand that an animal substitute shall be offered in place of the human first-born, there are passages which class human with animal firstlings as equally the property of God—" Thou shalt not delay to offer the first of thy ripe fruits, and of thy liquors; the firstborn of thy sons shalt thou give unto me. Likewise shalt thou do with thine oxen and thy sheep; seven days shall it be with his dam; on the eighth day shalt thou give it to me " (Exod. xxii. 29f.). It has therefore been suggested that these bodies were those of firstborn children; perhaps they were sacrificed at some more primitive form of the passover, before children were redeemed from the Destroyer by the blood splashed on the doorposts. It should be noticed that the

Hebrew word translated " Passover " in the English versions of the Bible is " Pesach," which means " to limp or dance with a limping gait," and there are vivid descriptions of such sexual dances accompanying child sacrifice among the Carthaginians, who were kin to the Phœnicians ; it is the word used to describe the actions of the Baal priests on Carmel (1 Kings xviii.).

It cannot be without significance that these child jar burials came in with the third element brought by the Hyksos— fertility cults and the worship of the mother-goddess. In these cults the goddess is represented in human form. Especially abundant in Palestine are nude female figures in which maternal features are emphasized, but closely associated with these female figurines are animal symbols, in particular the snake and the dove. Evidence from Babylonia suggests a connection of snakes with winding streams and the fertilizing element ; similar use of the image is frequent in Crete in this period ; and many figurines found in Palestine, particularly one at Tell Beit Mirsim, make clear this connection between the snake, the goddess, and the fertility cults. There is much evidence that the serpent-cult was well known in Palestine ; a temple at Bethshan was dedicated to it, and bronze serpents have been found at Gezer and at Gath. From the Old Testament the connection with fertility is obvious in the story of the serpent instructing Eve (Gen. iii.). Another feature of serpent worship is brought out in the story of the bronze serpent made by Moses for healing the people—a serpent which we are told was destroyed in the seventh century by Hezekiah because it had become an object of worship in the temple (2 Kings xviii. 4). The dove too is commonly associated with the mother-goddess, and at Tell el-Ajjul, for instance, we find Hyksos pottery decorated with a dove and the star of the goddess. It will be remembered that, after the birth of Jesus, Mary offered two doves in accordance with the requirements of the Levitical law (Luke ii. 22ff. ; Lev. xii.). Is it possible that when Jesus associated these two creatures, telling his followers to be wise as serpents and harmless as doves (Matt. x. 16), he was calling attention to figures still found together even in Herod's temple ?

Only one temple has yet been discovered in Palestine which can definitely be assigned to this period ; this was at Shechem. It comes rather at the end of the Hyksos rule, and provides a link between the more elaborate structures of the Late Bronze Age and the open-air shrines which had preceded this period. In the centre of this temple lay a large unroofed courtyard in which stood an altar and possibly an image, but rooms were built round the court, suggesting that the institutional elements in religion had developed sufficiently to need permanent habitation. Within the open courtyard would be room for stone pillars and for the sacred tree, which was associated in Palestine with the Hyksos invasion. This sacred symbol was at first probably a living tree, but it has also been found conventionalized as a tree trunk, or a wooden post with the branches lopped off. At Tell en-Nasbeh was unearthed a pottery figure of such a tree with a dove and a lamp in its fork. Prophets from the eighth and sixth centuries, as well as the laws of Deuteronomy, condemn the high places, where fertility worship still took place by altars under green trees.

Under the Hyksos Palestine ceased to be a secluded land with a simple primitive religion. It was laid open to outside influences, became aware of developments that had taken place in the general culture of the Near East, and ceased to lag so far behind neighbouring civilizations. This is particularly noticeable in the growth of various forms of institutions, which resulted from being part of a great empire. It has been suggested by Professor Alt [9] that there are many laws in the Old Testament which presuppose secular organization and the gradual formation of case precedents, in contrast to others springing from a theocratic society, in which laws were given as oracles or directions through priests ; and it seems possible that the former secular type, which was part of the common culture of the Near East, entered Palestine under Hyksos domination, and thence was transmitted later to the conquering

Israelites. A similar development can be seen also in the growth of religious institutions, which is the distinctive feature of the next period.

§ EGYPTIAN DOMINATION IN THE LATE BRONZE AGE

The Hyksos were, as we have seen, driven out of Egypt and Palestine at the beginning of the sixteenth century when Egyptian power became dominant. The leaven of the Hyksos, however, continued to work, and in many ways it was the religion introduced by them which was elaborated in the building of great temples containing treasuries, storehouses, and living-rooms for the professional religious classes, which rapidly increased in the Late Bronze Age. The period affords abundant material for the archæologist, and during recent years fine examples of these complex temple buildings have been excavated. They were found in what were probably the civic centres of particular districts, just as in Mesopotamia the great temples were built in the central cities of particular provinces. Possibly under the Hyksos rule, but certainly under the loose Egyptian domination, these provincial cities in Palestine became centres of small city-states, which had each its own ruler and, we may conjecture, its peculiar ceremonies of the king-cult. A common feature of many of these temples is that they were rebuilt several times during the period, for no apparent reason ; at Bethshan there is evidence of four superimposed temples, and even the little temple in the old Hyksos fosse at Lachish was twice rebuilt. There is no sign of burning or destruction by invaders to account for this, but it seems from the evidence at Lachish that there was growing prosperity, and fresh interest displayed at different periods by successive Egyptian monarchs, who elaborated the temples in Palestine, as they did those in Egypt, for their own glory.

The temples at Bethshan [10] are worthy of description, because they reveal evidence for a highly syncretistic cult.

In the first temple the furniture shows influence from many sources—there are a Cretan incense altar, Cypriote vases and golden pins, and cylinder seals from North Syria ; the inscriptions are in Egyptian, and the conical headdress of the god is Babylonian. Also, as we should expect in such a building, the religion apparently catered for different cults. There is evidence that at the temple were practised the early pig-cult and the cults connected with the Amorite pillars and cup-holes, as well as that of the Hyksos period. It is possible that the temple was built on the site of a still older shrine, like the temple at Shechem which stood over an ancient cave sanctuary, and that the old cult was not abandoned when the new temple was built. This fact may also account for the presence of so many altars, some of stone and others of brick, possibly for different types of offerings.

Throughout all four strata at Bethshan the complex consisted of twin temples, one to the mother-goddess symbolized by a serpent, the other to a god Mekal, " the Great God, Lord of Bethshan," who is worshipped only here. His image was found engraved on a limestone stele, representing him as bearded, holding the Egyptian sceptre and sign of life, wearing the conical horned helmet with streamers, and receiving an offering of lotus flowers. At the entrance to the sanctuary stood a fine basalt panel three feet high, depicting on its upper half Nergal the god of disease and the underworld, in the form of a lion, trying to fight his way in past a dog, while on the lower half the dog is victorious and the lion is making off with its tail between its legs and the teeth of the dog sunk well into its haunches. Possibly the dog also symbolizes a divine being, and we are reminded of the many dog figurines in the south of Palestine, and the presence there of the tribe of Caleb—the Hebrew word for a dog. There is evidence also that a watch-dog was kept tied at the door of the temple. Within the sanctuary there are a large courtyard and many rooms, with offering tables, stone benches, altars, a stone pillar, and a libation bowl. Among the objects found in the temple a sacrificial dagger and the horns and shoulder of a three-

year-old bull give an idea of the sacrifices ; the close connection between the worship of the two temples is shown by the
finding of frequent representations of the mother-goddess—
one a lovely incised gold pendant. There have also been
found clay models of the round cakes which we know from
the book of Jeremiah were baked by the women for the
Queen of Heaven (Jer. xliv. 15ff.), and one of them was
stamped with an Egyptian word meaning " daily." In the
companion temple some articles are of interest : there is a
pottery serpent with female breasts; and a two-handled jar open
at both ends has serpents twined round it and entering it
through openings at the side. Such a jar might be used in
fertility rites, just like the pipes and jars at Ras Shamra. Another
object was a pottery shrine of two storeys with human figures
at the upper windows, and decorated on the outside with a
serpent and lion. This portable shrine may be similar in
purpose to the Ark carried by the Israelites as the throne or
dwelling of their God.

Foundation deposits under the steps of the altar prove the
next temple to have been built by Amenhotep III (1411–1375
B.C.). Its plan was similar to that of contemporary buildings
in Egypt, and it contained a small narrow shrine behind the
main altar. In this temple the goddess is wearing a conical
hat with streamers and two horns, showing her to be Astarte
Karnaim—the Astarte of the two horns—who gave her name
to a city in southern Palestine. Objects in this temple too
show evidence of syncretism, and include a bronze figure of
Teshub, the Hittite thunder-god. Finally Seti I (1313–1292
B.C.) and his successor Ramses II (1292–1225 B.C.) restored the
temples, and in the latter restoration they are dedicated
respectively to Anath, of whom Ramses himself was an ardent
devotee, and whose worship is witnessed to by such place-
names as Anathoth and Beth-anath, and to Resheph, the
Syrian god of war and thunder, whose bronze images are found
also at Ras Shamra, Megiddo, Gezer, and Lachish.

The temple at Lachish [11] is of interest because it appears to
have been used, not for the chief cult of the city, but for some

BEDOUIN ARAB
(*Photo by the Author*)

THE PYRAMIDS
(*Photo by the Author*)

CUP-MARKED SURFACE OF OLD ROCK-ALTAR,
JERUSALEM
(*From* " The Religion of Ancient Palestine in the Light of Archaeology,"
by S. A. Cook, British Academy. Oxford Press, 1930)

Model of the Fosse Temple, structure III, showing niches in the east wall

General view of the Temple showing benches, altar, shrine, and
the three niches

*(From " Lachish II, The Fosse Temple," by O. Tufnell, C. H. Inge, and
L. Harding, Trustees of the late Sir Henry Wellcome, Oxford Press, 1940)*

subsidiary religion, for it was built outside the walls in the disused fosse of the Hyksos fortification. The first construction is contemporary with the first temple at Bethshan, and so dates from the reign of Thutmose III ; it contained a sanctuary and two small rooms. Each successive temple grew in size. The second, again contemporary with the second at Bethshan, had foundation objects of Amenhotep III, and in it the sanctuary had been enlarged and two vestries added. The third building, possibly of the time of Ramses II, was again enlarged by the addition of an extra room. In all the buildings the shrine was against the south wall, and consisted of a base to support a cult object, and an altar ; while nearby was a hearth in the floor and a store of lamps and pottery receptacles for meat and drink offerings. The first temple had no hearth but three altars, and in the third the altar was missing—possibly it had been a portable one and was removed before the building was destroyed by fire ; around the walls of the second and third temples were benches for offerings, and there were enormous quantities of pottery apparently deliberately broken, especially chalices or goblets decorated in red like those found in the temple of the goddess at Bethshan. The roofs were supported by wooden pillars set on stone bases, as in the buildings found at Gezer and Gaza, which have been attributed to the Philistines, and remind us of the one described in the story of Samson's exploit (Jud. xvi. 23ff.). It is of interest that neither here nor elsewhere in Palestine is there evidence of the altars being used for burnt offerings ; but at Bethshan there is a pit with charred bones and baked clay, suggesting that as in the modern Samaritan ritual on Mount Gerizim, offerings were burnt in the pit. At Lachish the bulk of the animal bones found were right forelegs of sheep or goats—the portion which in the Old Testament is reserved for the priests in the communal sacrificial feasts. Gold plaques of the mother-goddess occur, and the figurine of Resheph. In the debris of the last structure were the remains of an ewer on which was an inscription whose interpretation has caused considerable difference of opinion ; it may possibly be a reference to a triad of deities comparable to some at Ras

Shamra—Shor, the bull-El of Ras Shamra, Mot his son, and Elath, a feminine form of El.

These excavations all make it clear that there was no monotheism in Palestine at this period. Individual temples were dedicated to local deities, as the temple at Bethshan was to Mekal, who is unknown elsewhere in the country. As new deities were introduced, whose worship was more widely spread, there was a tendency to fuse the local gods and goddesses with them—as, for example, in the last temple at Bethshan, Mekal has given place to Resheph, and his consort becomes Anath, who was as much at home in Syria and Egypt as in Palestine. The Old Testament writers give us a hint that this fusion had been carried a stage further, for there all the local gods and goddesses are classed together as Baalim and Ashtaroth—representations of the great Baal and his consort.

A further source of information as to the religion of this period is provided by letters found in Egypt at Tell el-Amarna, the site of the new capital founded by the monotheistic reforming king Akhenaten. These letters contain diplomatic correspondence between the Pharaoh in Egypt and princes in Palestine and Syria. They reveal a state of anarchy in these countries, local city-states each with its own king protesting loyalty to Egypt. One king, Abd-Khiba of Jerusalem, has a name which suggests that he was a worshipper of the Hittite goddess Khiba, and in his letters he uses a phrase similar to that used in the Bible to describe Melchizedek, an earlier priest-king of the same city. Writing to Pharaoh he says, "Behold neither my father nor my mother has set me in this place, but the mighty hand of the king has led me into my father's place." Possibly some such phrase was used in the king-cult at Jerusalem, and influenced the description of Melchizedek in the New Testament as "without father or mother, having neither beginning of days nor end of life" (Heb. vii. 3).

This use of phrases which can be paralleled in the Bible is an interesting feature of the letters, and suggests that in their address to the Egyptian king the princes used expressions taken from a common liturgy of the king-cult: he is spoken of

as " my god before whom I prostrate myself seven times,"
and the writer speaks of himself as the footstool of the king.
Numerous examples could be quoted to illustrate this use of
phrases which treat Pharaoh as a divine king ; he is the breath
without which his subjects cannot live. " To my lord I seek
the way : from my lord I cease not." " The Pharaoh has set his
name in the land of Jerusalem for ever, therefore it cannot be
deserted." " He has set his name at the rising of the sun and
at the setting of the sun " (cf. Mal. i. 11). " If we go up into
the heavens or if we descend into the earth, yet is our head in
thy hands " (cf. Ps. cxxxix. 8).[12]

Many of the phrases used passed later into the worship of
the Israelites, particularly into the language of the Psalter,
giving rise to the theory that much of the language used in
the worship of the Jewish temple was drawn from very early
pre-Israelite cults. In this connection it may be remembered
that the writer of Psalm civ. used the hymn in which was
summarized the ethical teaching of Akhenaten's monotheism.
Some of the Amarna letters contain phrases reminiscent of the
hymn, suggesting that it was already known in Palestine in
this period.

Egypt did not contribute only ethical teaching in this age.
An outstanding feature of the excavations has been numerous
figurines of Egyptian gods and goddesses used as amulets and
for magical purposes ; there are horus eyes—still used by Arabs
in Palestine on the bonnets of their cars—and figures of the
bandy-legged dwarf Bes, as well as those of Isis with her child.

This, then, was the religious culture of the country which
the Israelites entered.

CHAPTER 6

THE SEMITIC NOMADS

IT is obvious that archæology cannot give us much assistance in painting a picture of the religion of wandering nomads, and although there is considerable evidence for a general survey of such religion,[1] it would not be wise to give a detailed account of the religion of the Israelites when they entered Palestine, because we cannot be sure what stage of development they had reached. We know, for example, that a feature of nomadic religion was animism, in which natural objects such as streams, springs, rocks, or trees are regarded as inhabited by spirits, or later by gods; but we do not know how far such beliefs were really active in the religious life of the Israelites who entered the land. In the more ancient civilizations of Egypt and Mesopotamia such beliefs had receded into the background before the end of the fourth millennium B.C. Moreover, such animistic beliefs are shown by archæology to have been characteristic of the early religion of Palestine, so that survivals of them in the Old Testament may be Canaanite rather than nomadic. The same applies to other features which are regarded as important elements in nomadic religion, such as animatism, the belief that every object has a life of its own as distinct from being inhabited by a spirit; totemism, in which members of a group regard themselves as related in kinship to some animal or plant; and ancestor worship, in which a relationship with the dead is maintained by some form of cult or ritual. It is this that makes Kautzsch [2] say that when dealing with the pre-Mosaic religion of Israel caution is necessary, because we are dealing with hypotheses, not with facts. It thus seems wiser to confine our attention to features which are peculiar to nomadic religion, and which influence the development of later biblical religion.

§ SOLIDARITY OF THE GROUP

Everywhere in ancient times society consisted of small communities bound together by kinship whether regarded from the father's or from the mother's side.[3] Normally this social unit eventually developed into a nation or kingdom by the joining together of a number of tribes or communities ; but it is important to notice that among the nomads this development did not take place. The formation of large communities was prevented by the natural conditions of desert life, for although a tribe or social unit had to be large enough to defend itself, its herds, and its pastures, it could not grow beyond the limit its pastures could support, so that often it became necessary for sections of a tribe to separate, like Abraham from Lot. Various words are used to denote the different-sized groups within which the members were regarded as kindred, very much as we might talk of tribes, clans, families, or households, the smallest unit being spoken of as a " father's household." But whatever the size of the group, the basic idea was that of physical relationship expressed in the phrase Adam used to welcome his wife, " Bone of my bones, flesh of my flesh " (Gen. ii. 23). It was a community of the same flesh, and perhaps more important still, through whose veins ran the same blood. Robertson Smith emphasises the fact that the degree of kinship was unimportant ; the group consisted of " persons whose lives were so bound together in what may be called a physical unity, that they could be treated as parts of one common life. The members of one kindred looked on themselves as one living whole, a single animated mass of blood, flesh, and bones of which no member could be touched without all the members suffering." So close was the relationship that a nomad would describe the killing of a member of his group by saying, " Our blood has been spilt." The relationship of blood passed from parent to child, and the unity was so complete that the whole people was thought of as descended from one ancestor, whose name they bore. This idea of carnal unity produced a community which was closer and more exclusive than any of which we form part to-day. Others who in fact were not of the same blood could join the group, either temporarily by sharing a common meal, or permanently by undergoing some blood covenant rite, but it was not possible for any individual to form a close relationship with anyone outside the blood bond, for the blood tie was always the primary obligation.

This leads to the fact that "the practical test of kinship is that the whole kin is answerable for the life of each of its members," and each member is bound to avenge the death of any other member ; thus there is laid upon him the duty of blood revenge. The life of the group was thought of as residing in the blood—an idea which passed into later Jewish ritual, where we are told that "the blood is the life" (Deut. xii. 23). If that life blood was shed, accidentally or of intent, every member was bound to avenge it by shedding the blood of the group to which the slayer belonged. Blood revenge constituted the nomads' only form of protection, and the duty was a sacred one which overrode all other duties ; in blood revenge there could never be any question of divided loyalty. Robertson Smith tells a story to show how it even preceded a divine command. A man who was forbidden by an oracle to make war on the slayers of his father, broke the sacred lot, and with foul oaths dashed it in the face of the god with the words, " If it had been thy father that was killed thou wouldst not have refused me vengeance."

In more civilized times the vengeance was curbed by laws which placed the duty of blood revenge on the next-of-kin, allowed places of refuge to the accidental slayer, introduced the principle of an eye for an eye, and when the idea of the blood tie had partially broken down, limited it to the person of the slayer himself ; originally the vengeance appears to have been unlimited, any number of the slayer's group could be killed, and the song of Lamech shows a strong tribe delighting in exploiting the desert law : " I have slain a man for wounding me and a young man for my hurt. If Cain be avenged sevenfold, truly Lamech shall be seventy times seven " (Gen. iv. 23). The vengeance was also at first exacted without respect of rank or age, and had a levelling effect on nomadic society, for all members of a group equally shared the common blood, and were liable to be slain by an avenger of blood.

The aspect of tribal solidarity seen in blood revenge, in which any member of the group, irrespective of age or relationship, might suffer the penalty, has been so much emphasised that it tends to be treated as the only principle on which tribal life was organized, and to obscure other interesting features which have considerable importance for the development of religion. The story of Achan tells how, after he had stolen battle spoils which had been devoted to God, the whole family of which he was the head, with women, children, cattle, and all their possessions, were destroyed (Jos. vii.). This and other such stories in the Old Testament remind us of the words of the second commandment : " Visiting the sins of the fathers on the children to the third and fourth generation." Here it is not a question of people through whose veins ran the same blood, but of a social unit whose head had sinned ; the man had brought suffering only on that part of the family of which he was head. There is an importance attached to the father of the family or head of the group which is not shared by ordinary members, and his actions involve them. Achan was not simply part of a corporate personality composed of all those of the same blood—as he would have been considered if it had been a question of blood revenge—but the life of his family was focused in him as its representative, and when he sinned he committed them as though they too had sinned. This importance of a representative head is seen in the fact that the descendants continued to be called by his name, as though they were still inextricably bound up in the bundle of life with him (1 Sam. xxv. 29), and he was still their embodiment. So God can say to Abraham, " I will make thee as the stars of the heavens for multitude " ; and the prophets can call the people " Abraham my friend," or " Jacob my servant." This idea persisted into much later times, so that we hear of a whole household joining the new Christian faith, and Paul differentiates between the groups who have been committed by the act of their representative head, " As in Adam all died, so in Christ shall all be made alive " (1 Cor. xv. 22).

§ THE RELATIONSHIP OF THE TRIBE TO ITS GOD

To nomadic people the same close tie that bound together the various members of a group, united the group to its god. He too was thought of as part of the family circle, and treated as integral to the community, just as any other member. There is considerable evidence to suggest that the relationship was not thought of metaphorically but physically. This physical flesh and blood relationship was the only permanent one known to the nomad, and it was natural for him to think and speak of his god in terms of it. Even as late as the seventh century, Jeremiah says that a worshipper before stone pillars and wooden posts says to the stock, " My father," and to the stone, " Thou hast begotten me " (Jer. ii. 27). In the book of Numbers the defeat of Moab is spoken of in the words, " Woe to thee, Moab, thou art undone, O people of Chemosh ; He hath given his sons as fugitives and his daughters as captives " (Num. xxi. 29), and it is interesting to see how this ballad was modified in the sixth century to, " Woe unto thee, O Moab, the people of Chemosh perisheth ; thy sons are taken captive and thy daughters made exiles " (Jer. xlviii. 46).

A confirmation of this idea, that the tie between the people and its god was physical, can be seen in the use of personal names composed of two words, one expressing the human relationship of father, brother, uncle, and in Mesopotamia mother and sister also, and the other the general name for god, El, or the personal name of the tribal god. It is common to find in one period of Israelite history names compounded of " ab," father, or " ah," brother, and the name of God in the form " Yah," i.e. Abijah and Ahijah. It is not clear whether these names mean, " My father or my brother is Yahweh," or as other analogies might suggest, " father or brother of Yah-weh." The former would at first sight appear to be more likely, but the variety of meanings which the genitive con-struction has in Semitic languages might make it possible to treat the latter as meaning, " One who acts as father for Yah-weh," just as Daniel might mean, " One who acts as judge for Yahweh." The exact meaning is not so important as the basic fact that the names contain some belief in a family relationship between the worshipper and his god, and because of this were discontinued in post-exilic Judaism. An interesting survival of the belief occurs in Second-Isaiah and Job, where God is depicted as the next-of-kin—usually translated Redeemer—whose duty was to avenge blood and buy back an enslaved kinsman.

The circle into which a man was born consisted of divine as well as of human members, and the man had equally im-portant duties to perform towards both these kinds of relatives ; his religion was thus part of his social environment, not some-thing he chose to do if he wished, but as natural and normal a part of his social life as his relationship to other members of his group. Because the most rudimentary form of this physical relationship has been seen in totemism, where the bond was renewed by animal sacrifices in which the god and the wor-shipper both partook, in various ways, of the blood, it has been suggested that totemism explains this type of religion. That it may have so developed among some peoples is possible, but it is unlikely that the development was universal, for we have seen that the communal meal between god and people, and the pouring out of libations of blood, may have arisen from ancestor worship. It seems clear that to the nomad the dead as well as the god formed one group with the living, and the nomad would offer sacrifice whenever he encamped near the tomb of one of his dead.

The theophorous names suggest that the god was thought of as the head of the group, the husband or the father in a patriarchal society, and the brother or uncle in one that was organized on a matriarchal basis. There is evidence that the giving of the name sometimes involved not only the idea of a parent-god, but the actual attribution of physical fatherhood, and there are many examples of kings who claim to be of divine descent—Syrian kings, for example, called themselves Benhadad, son of Hadad ; but normally the parent-god was regarded as father of the whole people rather than of individual members of the group. That this idea of God as " Our Father " rather than " My Father " persisted, is seen in the New Testament story that Jews tried to stone Jesus for calling God his own father (John v. 18) ; such a use of the phrase, "My Father," would imply a claim to be in the privileged relationship to God enjoyed by a leader or king. The individual member had each his own share in the family religion, but being part of a corporate unit he obtained his contact with God through the head of the family, who acted as priest and was regarded as representative of his people in religion as in everything else.

The idea of god as parent had, as Robertson Smith points out, an important bearing on the development of religion. Though magic played a large part in nomadic religion, the basic idea was not to placate or coerce an angry god who was feared because he was unknown or mysterious ; the parent-god of the nomad was known, and was essentially friendly. Sometimes—perhaps for no discernible reason—his wrath would flare up against his people, but that was only for a moment, and would pass when the cause passed, or the offence was expiated ; the ties of kinship which knit him to his own people were permanent and far stronger than his anger, so that in later times in the Old Testament, though men had sinned they could still claim the forgiveness and protection of their God " for his loving-kindness' sake." It was unthinkable that he would ever desert or destroy his own people.

The idea of a parent-god passed naturally into that of a tribal god, whose fortunes were bound up with those of the tribe. Just as among settled peoples there were city gods and national gods, so among nomads there were tribal gods. Chemosh was the god of Moab, Moloch of Ammon, and Kos of Edom, just as Yahweh became God of Israel. How far this tribal god was thought of as having a fixed abode is dubious. At one period Israel pictured her God as at home on Sinai from whence he came to answer his people's need. At least it seems true that he was not thought of as bound to any one holy place. As tribal god he protected his people, fought for them against their enemies, and was probably the supreme judge whose decisions were made, in cases that could not otherwise be settled, through trial by ordeal, and perhaps by oracle. He was also guardian of the morals of his people in all matters, whether of justice, honesty, or sex, but he was not in a full sense of the word a god of justice or even a moral god, for his relationship to other tribes, like that of his people, was governed not by justice or honesty, but by the principle of blood revenge. He supported his people in their quarrels with the outsider, though they cheated, stole, and were altogether in the wrong. His moral character was perceived only when it was realized that the tribal ethics must be applied beyond the bounds of kinship, and that right and wrong were more important than blood ; though it must always be recognized, when we say that the nomadic god was not moral, that the beginning of morals is found in the application of a rigid code within an exclusive circle, whether of tribe or of family ; honour among thieves is not honour, but it has the germ of honour within it.

We have used throughout the singular "god," as though the tribe or family were monotheistic and offered exclusive worship to one deity, but this is hardly accurate.[4] Though there is a word for a singular god, and personal names for tribal gods, yet throughout the Semitic world the singular or the plural can be used for god, and the plural can be construed with a singular or plural verb. The usage may express the vague "they" used often in colloquial speech to relate something which is true of, or common to all, members of a particular class, but it seems probable that the nomad thought of his god as he did of men. An individual man could be only one who had been driven out from his people, and must perish unless accepted in some other group. So deity also was thought of as social, and as with men there was a representative head who embodied the life of the group, so deity had its representative head who could be worshipped as the embodiment of deity ; but always there was around him the richer social background of other divine beings. Neither polytheism nor monotheism is adequate to express this idea ; it is rather " social godhead " embodied in one supreme being, and it is easy to understand how from such a conception it was possible on the one hand to fuse other gods and their functions in the one godhead, or on the other to associate with the supreme god other beings, even consorts and children, corresponding to human relationship in the corporate unit.

§ Festivals

The writer of the first chapter of Genesis tells us that lights were put in the heavens for signs and seasons and days and years ; the regular appearance of the moon has always had its influence on the fixing of festivals, and still to-day the movable feasts of Jews, Christians, and Moslems are fixed by the moon. Especially to nomadic people who during the heat of the summer months must travel by night, the moon is the most important of natural phenomena ; to these wandering dwellers in tents the light of the moon brought security, and answered the prayer which to them was more real than in peace-time to us, " Lighten our darkness, we beseech thee, O Lord." That the period of the full moon was also the natural occasion for social festivities is obvious to anyone who travels or lives in the Near East ; the heat of the day drives the Arab into his tent, and the few remaining hours of daylight are necessary for work, but in the warm, clear moonlight he can hope for time to feast with his companions and his god.

Each month the appearance of the new moon gave a natural reason for rejoicing. At Ras Shamra, as in Arabia, the word for the crescent moon is from the same root as the word for praise we know so well—Hallelujah, Praise ye Yahweh ; the nomad greeted the new moon with joyous shouts which became the synonym for praise. Images of the moon as a crescent or a disc were worn on the necks of camels, and from Ras Shamra and Isaiah we learn that they were used as ornaments by the women. At Ras Shamra, too, the crescent appears as a divinity to which sacrifices were made, and as we have seen in Babylonia the moon-god was of considerable importance.

Phœnician inscriptions and the Hebrew ritual in the book of Numbers show that the new moon was an occasion for feasts and sacrifices. At Saul's court it was a festival of two or three days, during which all courtiers were expected to be present, so that David had to beg leave of absence to attend at his father's house at Bethlehem an annual sacrifice, also held at the new moon (1 Sam. xx. 24ff.). Because the early Hebrew codes ignored all lunar feasts except possibly Passover and Sabbath,[5] it seems likely that originally they had no connection with Yahweh, and that they continued to retain their character as celebrations in honour of the lunar god.

Many Old Testament references connect the new-moon feasts with Sabbaths, as days on which trading ceased, assemblies were held in the temple, and joyous gatherings took place ; they were, too, the days on which " Men of God " were consulted, for when the woman of Shunem set out to tell Elisha of the death of her son, her husband said, " Wherefore wilt thou go to him to-day ? It is neither new moon nor Sabbath " (2 Kings iv. 23).

There is considerable difference of opinion as to the origin of the Sabbath,[6] but it seems probable that originally it was the name given to the feast of the full moon. The cognate word in Babylonian means the day when the moon ceased to grow, and it appears possible that the earliest reference of the Hebrew word—which also means to cease—was the same, and had nothing to do with resting from labour. In Babylon it was one of the days on which meat and bread could not be cooked, and it may be that the original prohibition was against kindling a fire. It is of interest to notice that a similar connection between moon, fire, and Sabbath is preserved in the folk tale of the man condemned to be set in the moon because he gathered firewood on the Sabbath day. When later the day was detached from the moon-cult, and became a regular seventh day festival, other prohibitions were added to that of kindling fire—prohibitions which had been attached to other days marking other phases of the moon ; and it thus became a day of general cessation from work, the reason given being that God rested from creation on that day.

The most important full-moon festival to the nomads appears to have been that held at the full moon nearest to the spring equinox, a feast that coincided in time with the agricultural feast of unleavened bread, and later was combined with it to form the Passover. In Arabia all small cattle bear their young at about the same time in the spring, and it seems likely that at this full-moon festival some firstborn lambs and kids were sacrificed. In some modern Arab tribes the sacrifice of the firstborn of the flocks is still a great occasion, but it is the firstborn of the whole flock, not of every animal, that is slain, so that, as among the Samaritans to-day, there would be one animal for each family. This may represent the original practice.[7] Some of the provisions of the later Passover ritual in the Old Testament (Exod. xii.) have the appearance of being survivals from this nomadic feast : the animal had to be eaten with loins girt, staff in hand, and in haste, as though in preparation for a journey. The prohibitions in the Hebrew ritual may also have been directed against features in this primitive feast : it must not be eaten raw, nor with the blood, no bones must be broken, and no-one may leave his tent till the morning. St. Nilus[8] tells of an Arab feast at which the group killed a camel, and, falling on the quivering carcase, devoured the whole animal raw—flesh, blood, and bones. Possibly the lamb was eaten in the same way. If originally it was an offering made in the presence of the moon-god in all its full glory, we can understand the reason for the later prohibition against leaving the tent, and the survival of the requirement that all must be eaten so that none remained till morning. How soon the blood became used for ritual sprinkling is not clear. The Old Testament mention of doorposts and lintels which had to be marked by the blood presupposes a settled community, but there is evidence of sprinkling of blood on the curtains of tents on other occasions, and we also know of such sprinkling on the flock from which the sacrifice had been taken. It seems certain that in origin it was a magical rite to secure the fertility of the flock, and only later was it linked with the ancient sacrifice of human firstborn. Some examples have been found in ancient and modern Greece of the eating of bitter herbs to prevent the entry of demons and disease. If this custom was an original feature of the feast, we should have a further confirmation of its magical character.

The other nomadic festival that should be noticed is that connected with sheep-shearing. It is mentioned three times in the Old Testament, and the impression is given that it partook of the same joyous social character as other communal feasts ; friends were invited and a sacrifice offered. In the book of Deuteronomy (xviii. 4) the first of the fleece is part of the first-fruits that belong to God, and the offering of this would naturally be a feature of the sheep-shearing festival. No indication is given as to the date of the feast, but it would presumably come after the lambing season, and before the hot weather, which even in Palestine begins early in May. Probably both Passover and sheep-shearing were originally part of the same week of festivities.

§ HOLY PLACES

In our survey of the old religion of Palestine we saw that its earliest form may have consisted in pouring out libations to the dead, who were thought of as alive, and that later there were great open-air sanctuaries which appear to have been rallying places for a people in the pastoral stage of development. These two features probably were the factors that determined the location of holy places to nomadic people, although archæology does not give us so much information about them, and much of our reconstruction must be conjectural. That the nomad sacrificed whenever, on his customary treks, he encamped near the tomb of an ancestor, suggests that in some sense a tomb was to him a holy place, whether because of his desire to care for the tomb or as part of a regular cult of ancestor worship. M. Dhorme [9] maintains from the Old Testament evidence that there were always three features of a holy place—a tomb, a stone pillar, and a sacred tree ; the third feature may seem to be dubious unless there was also water present, but it is probable that in any holy place fixed by the location of a tomb, the stone pillar or cairn of stones was a constant feature. The original significance of the stone is uncertain ; possibly it was simply to mark the place, and later was thought of as the abode of the spirit, when the dead were not thought of as dwelling in an underground cave. It provided a convenient means of establishing communion with the spirit by receiving the blood or the fat.

As well as holy places marked by a tomb there were others whose site had been chosen by the god. Some natural phenomenon had occurred that made known the fact that the place was the seat of a spirit or a god ; a dream, or the sight of a burning bush, was sufficient to link the place to a god who was revealing himself. Such a place might also be provided with a pillar or stones as a mark of identification or as a Beth-el—a house for the god to dwell in. Later the reputation of this sanctuary naturally grew as men frequented it to obtain revelations or guidance—sleeping there if the first revelation had been through a dream. Some of these places possessed natural features which led men to expect the presence of the supernatural : a mountain on which a thunderstorm had broken, a block of stone, a curious shaped rock, or a gnarled isolated tree. Possibly, as at Bab ed-Dra, worshippers buried their dead there and set up more pillars, and so there were special times and occasions when festivals were held at the shrine.

A third type of holy place grew up around a spring or well, which offered the possibility of a more protracted stay for the nomad and his flocks. An oasis with trees and pasture around living water was to him the ideal holy place ; its bounds, as

Pottery model from Beth-shan representing the
hippopotamus wife of Bes, and showing
Egyptian religious influence

*(Alan Rowe, Pennsylvania University Palestine Expedition
and Amalgamated Press Ltd.)*

Teshub, the Hittite god of war and storm, with battle-axe and forked lightning
(From " Reich und Kultur der Chetiter," by Meyer: courtesy of Amalgamated Press Ltd.)

KADESH WITH MIN AND RESHEPH
(Louvre)

IMPRESSIONS OF CYLINDER SEALS

From the Necropolis at Ras Shamra : examples of exquisite design
and workmanship on a minute scale, with lively figures engaged in
scenes of battle or religious ritual

(Prof. C. Schaeffer)

Robertson Smith remarks, were easily defined, and the whole tribe could gather there for some days for such an annual festival as that of the spring full moon. The water and the trees were also regarded as a means by which the will of the god became known ; in the Bible we hear of trees that were oracles and springs that gave judgements. Springs were always of particular importance, and it is easy to understand how readily supernatural associations were attached to the bubbling waters which were often addressed as living beings. Such holy places were often visited by nomads on pilgrimage or in fulfilment of a vow.

Often this larger holy place had a permanent custodian or priest who supervised it, knew the manner of the god, and had charge of the paraphernalia of the sacred oracle ; but his presence was not essential for the offering of sacrifices. Usually the priesthood was hereditary, and was held by the family who owned the rights over any cultivated ground or over a well that had been dug.

All these three types of holy places probably contained a place of slaughter or an altar, though we have no precise information as to the form it took. St. Nilus talks of a specially prepared heap of stones ; in other places a flat outcrop of rock has been used ; and elsewhere, as on Mount Gerizim, a trench was dug in the ground and the sides built up with stones to prevent them collapsing on the fire. There is also no certainty as to the type of sacrifice celebrated in these sanctuaries. The customary one was a communal meal, shared between the god and his worshippers ; but it is likely that there were others in which none of the carcase was eaten. The goat of Azazel was sent off into the wilderness bearing the sins of the people, and animals were slain to expiate sin. Others might be cut in pieces as the sign of a covenant—the early Hebrew always spoke of " cutting a covenant," and there is a vivid picture in Genesis xv. of God making such a covenant with Abraham. Men performing such a sacrifice passed between the pieces, and invoked the curse of a like fate on the one who broke the pact.[10]

CHAPTER 7

THE HEBREWS IN PALESTINE

§ THE PATRIARCHAL STORIES AND THE RELIGION OF THE " TWELVE " TRIBES

IF, as seems probable, all the Israelite tribes did not go down into Egypt and share the experiences of the Exodus, we should expect to find, in the Old Testament, accounts suggesting different perspectives of the past. It is therefore not surprising that Jewish tradition recognizes that there were two occasions when Hebrews entered Palestine : the first time as a wandering nomadic family led by Abram, and the second as a united nation forcing an entry under the victorious leadership of Joshua. The dominant tradition speaks as though the two entries were separated by a period in which all the tribes that had sprung from Abram lived in Egypt, so that all the holy places in Palestine, when the tribes re-entered, were Canaanite, and to be condemned. But there are traces of other traditions in the Old Testament which knew of no complete break, and speak as though the Hebrews continued to live in the land without going down into Egypt. Such traditions find con-firmation in the records of Egyptian kings who invaded Palestine, and appear to have found people or places whose names resemble those of the tribes—Jacob, Joseph, Simeon, and Asher. Whichever form of these traditions may appear more likely, it is difficult to fit the patriarchal and tribal stories into the picture of the religion of ancient Palestine given us by archæology, and it is equally difficult to assess the place of the stories in the development of religion.

The writers of the stories have given them a nomadic setting. Abraham with his household wandered from Haran Palestine, and through it to Egypt. For no apparent reason to he built altars on the high ground outside Shechem, Bethel,

Hebron, and at Beersheba; he paid tithes to the priest-king
of Jerusalem, and visited Gerar on the road to Egypt. Isaac,
his son, was more settled at Beersheba, but he too visited Gerar,
and like Abraham was buried at Hebron. The Philistines, whom
he is said to have met at Gerar, did not arrive there until about
1200 B.C., and from excavations at the site it would appear
possible that in the time of Isaac Gerar was a Hyksos centre.[1]
Jacob went farther afield; on his journey from Beersheba to
Haran to find a wife, he met God at Bethel, and later, on his
return to Palestine, he lived and worshipped there. He worshipped at places in Trans-Jordan—Gilead, Mahanayim, Suk-
koth, and Penuel—and he also visited the holy places of his
fathers, Shechem, Bethel, Hebron, and Beersheba, as well as
Bethlehem.

As time went on, other stories were told about these
shrines, providing them with the customary features of a
simple nomadic sanctuary—tombs, pillars, sacred trees and altars.
At Shechem Joseph was buried, and there was an oracle tree
called the oak of Moreh under which Joshua set up a great
stone, as a witness between Yahweh and his people. At
Bethel Jacob set up a stone pillar, anointing it with oil and
pouring on it a drink offering, and there Deborah, Rebecca's
nurse, was buried under the Oak of Weeping. At Hebron
there were the sacred oak of Mamre, the tombs of the patriarchs,
and in the vicinity the sacred pillar erected at Rachel's tomb.
At Beersheba worship centred round a sacred tree, the wells of
Abraham, and an altar. M. Dhorme suggests that the prominence of these places in the traditions shows that they lay
on the route taken by the patriarchs from Haran to Palestine,
but it seems more likely that they marked stages on the pilgrim
routes leading originally to one of the three great religious
centres, at Dan, Bethel, or Beersheba, and later to Hebron or
Jerusalem. Examples from other national literatures show
how cycles of stories were collected containing the tales
pilgrims were told as they journeyed to pilgrim centres,
each tale reflecting a particular tradition of the shrine at which
the travellers were spending the night. Most of these places

mentioned in the patriarchal and tribal stories retained their character as holy cities ; many of them would continue to be used by pilgrims for centuries, and it is thus difficult to date the developments in the traditions related at them.

As to the origin of the stories, we cannot be sure whether originally they belonged to the Israelite people and were deliberately attached to the sanctuaries or whether they were originally preserved at the sanctuaries and later fused into Israelite history. Perhaps different stories had different origins. The use made of the Abraham traditions by the natives of Palestine in the time of Ezekiel suggests that he was a figure attached to the land, his stories belonging to the shrines—" Abraham," they said, " was one, and he inherited the land, we are many, the land is given to us for an inheritance " (xxxiii. 24)—and the fact that at Ras Shamra myths relate the doings of peoples in Palestine known by the name of Abraham's father, Terah, confirms this suggestion ; on the other hand, the Israelites were named after Jacob, and he would appear to be a national hero.

But the problem of the stories becomes acute when we attempt to fit them into the Palestine of their time as revealed by archæology. Abraham is not likely, according to the biblical traditions, to have entered the land until the Middle Bronze Age, when, as excavations have shown, the places where he is related to have set up altars were already provided with sanctuaries of a developed character. We could understand the patriarchs visiting these shrines and worshipping there because they were ancient holy places, but we can no longer think of them as founding the sanctuaries at such a late time. Moreover as the patriarchs chose to worship at these places, it is difficult to separate entirely their worship from the character of the religious observances which excavations show to have been practised there ; when, for example, Jacob slept at Bethel, he would enter an elaborate Canaanite shrine to obtain a dream oracle as an omen for the journey on which he had set out.

It is interesting to notice that none of the patriarchs has

a name that suggests Yahweh worship [2]; Abraham contains
the word for father and a word meaning high or exalted; Jacob
and Joseph, if we may judge from the Egyptian records, were
shortened from Jacob-el and Joseph-el, and like Israel were
words that assert something about the activities of El. That
the writers thought of these early figures as worshippers of
El, is shown by the place names given in the records to explain
the appearance of a divine being, Beth-el, House of God,
El Roi, the seeing God, El Olam, the everlasting God; but
there is confusion in the stories, for Jacob says, "Surely Yahweh
is in this place," though he calls the place, House of El
(Gen. xxviii. 16), and similarly Hagar calls the name of Yahweh,
who appears to her, "The Seeing El" (Gen. xvi. 13). Some of
the names used in the stories have been thought to show a
survival of totemism—Leah means antelope, Rachel is a ewe,
Simeon a hybrid hyena, Caleb a dog. Other names definitely
show the worship of other gods: Gad is the name for the god
of fortune; Asher may be a similar name, or be connected
with the national god of Assyria, Assur; Zebulun reminds
us of the Baal-Zebul, or lord of the high place, worshipped
by the Phœnicians and at Ras Shamra, and the "Blessing of
Moses" (Deut. xxxiii. 19) suggests that Zebulun and Issachar
were custodians of a shrine to which Phœnicians brought the
treasure of the sea as offerings.

In their present form the stories have been retold for a
purpose: they assert rights of ownership of a cave at Machpelah, the reason why Jerusalem should receive tithes or the
origin of the holiness of a sanctuary. As in the New Testament,
they are used to teach the meaning of faith or God's attitude
to the sacrifice of the firstborn. In the same way equally
old stories of Daniel, Job, and Enoch, or the story of the
prophet Jonah, were retold in a new way to serve new didactic
ends, and it is the discovery of these new ends which gives the
stories their place and value in the development of biblical
religion.

§ THE MOSAIC TRADITION

The figure of Moses may also have been used in the same way. In the present form of Jewish tradition the elements which differentiate Judaism from other religions were given through Moses. He is regarded as the founder of the mono-theistic worship of the national God. Through him the covenant was made which united the people to their God, and he was the medium through whom was given the civil, ritual, and moral laws which later governed the life of the people, and later still were regarded as the supreme revelation of God and his will. Most scholars agree that considerable accretions have gathered to the person of Moses, and that the whole account of the Sinai law-giving has been inserted later into the story of the wilderness wanderings between Egypt and Palestine, but there is no unanimity as to the extent of the Mosaic kernel, although the fact of such a kernel is not questioned. The dis-covery of the stone containing Hammurabi's laws, and later the finding of similar codes used by Sumerians and Hittites, have shown that many of the civil laws belonged to the com-mon heritage of the Near East, and were active in Palestine before the entry of the Mosaic group ; many of the ritual laws have their roots in practices at the ancient Canaanite sanctuaries ; and as for the moral laws contained in the deca-logue, there is no conclusive evidence that any of the great prophets knew of a group of ten commandments which had been accepted by all the nation from this remote antiquity.

But traditions have usually a basis in historic facts, and there is nothing inherently improbable in the main outlines of the story ; even the claim that this man, "learned in all the wisdom of the Egyptians" (Acts vii. 22), was the founder of a moral monotheism is easily intelligible when we remember the monotheism of Akhenhaten ; and a body of legal decisions would certainly grow up from the judgements of such a leader as Moses. The biblical statement that the laws were written by the finger of Yahweh (Exod. xxxi. 18) finds an interesting parallel in a tablet found at Taanach, which speaks of guidance given by " the finger of Astarte."

There have been many efforts to rationalize the details of the Mosaic stories—notably the one made by Gressman—but they need not detain us. In the biblical tradition Moses fled to the desert, and became adopted by a Kenite or Midianite tribe, into which he married, and whose religion he accepted. This may also have been the religion of his mother, for her name, Jochebed (Exod. vi. 20), suggests Yahweh worship. Later, other members of his tribe accepted his leadership, and when they were driven from the cultivated land of Egypt to the nomadic life of the desert, were willing to worship the new God as their deliverer and accept him as the God whom their fathers had worshipped under other names. The father-in-law of Moses conducted a sacrifice (Exod. xviii.), the new members were incorporated into the people of Yahweh, and a covenant was made between the people and God ; but neither the contents of the covenant nor the character of the God is known. Jeremiah says the covenant consisted of the simple statement, " I will be your God and ye shall be my people " (vii.), and included the promise to obey the will of God as it should be revealed ; he emphatically repudiates the claim that was being made at the end of the seventh century, that the covenant included sacrificial laws. As to the people's idea of the character of Yahweh, other old elements in the traditions give the impression of a mountain God who controlled the thunderstorms and the weather like Hadad, Teshub, Rimmon or Baal.

We can think, then, of a section of the Israelites coming up out of Egypt and eventually entering Palestine, bringing with them the vivid memory of Moses and the covenant with Yahweh ; but one of the major problems of biblical religion is where this section settled and how soon its influence was felt in the development of the national religion. For the Mosaic tradition itself the first evidence, outside the Hexateuch, appears in the writings of the Deuteronomic authors in Palestine during the exilic period of the sixth century, and it is during this period that it may have become dominant. The period was one of *rapprochement* between the north and south of Palestine and of upheaval, when the upper layer was taken away and the traditions of the less literary were brought to the surface— we hear, for instance, that nomadic Rechabites, whose ancestors bore a Yahweh name and who had dwelt in the country for centuries, were forced to take refuge near Jerusalem, and brought their traditions and customs into the capital (Jer. xxxv.). The tradition that some of the people were brought up from Egypt appears in eighth- and seventh-century prophetic books, and in a phrase often used in the worship of the golden bulls at Bethel and Dan, " These be thy Gods, O Israel, which brought thee up out of the land of Egypt " ; it is of interest, too, that one of the earliest traditions in the book of Judges locates the Kenites in the plain of Esdraelon (Jud. v.), and another connects Yahweh worship and the family of Moses with the idolatrous worship which the Danites carried north from the hills of Ephraim (xviii. 30).

The early development of Yahweh worship is equally obscure.[3] There is sufficient evidence to show that the name was neither peculiar nor original to Israelite tribes in the south of Palestine in the time of Moses ; the name was probably known at Ras Shamra, and we have perhaps a representation of Yahweh from the same place. The Yahweh element occurs in the name of the Ephraimite Joshua, who led the conquering tribes, and in the Mosaic family ; it is infrequent until the time of David, when its use rapidly increases, and we find it especially in names of the Davidic royal family. Buchanan Gray[4] has shown that though no usurper to the throne of the northern kingdom had such a name, if his line continued to rule, his sons were so named. The inscription of Mesha, king of Moab in the ninth century B.C., discovered in Trans-Jordan, relates his destruction of a Yahweh temple on Mount Nebo, the height from which the Bible asserts that Moses viewed the promised land ; the stone provides an interesting confirmation of the connection of the Mount with Yahweh worship, and a contact with the Mosaic tradition. If we may accept the evidence of Hebrew names, we might perhaps say that Yahweh was worshipped by the family of Moses' mother ; that he was accepted by Moses, and by the group which came out of Egypt and which became his covenanted people ; that Yahweh worship obtained a hold on the nation at the time of the Davidic monarchy—perhaps because David himself adopted it ; and that in the northern kingdom it was the custom for the king, by the name he chose for his son, to show his adherence to the cult, perhaps because it was the religion of the royal sanctuary at Bethel. It is interesting that there still survive in the Old Testament traces of the traditions of the group of people from whom the Mosaic Israelites took Yahweh worship. These traditions do not know of a covenant with Yahweh at a time when Yahweh worship was adopted, but trace the worship to Enosh at the beginning of the world (Gen. iv. 26).

§ INFLUENCE OF THE CANAANITE CULTURE

There are a number of traditions in the Bible of the entry of the Israelites into Palestine. One of them, in the book of Joshua, represents the tribes as entering in a united force under Joshua, and conquering rapidly and completely the whole of the country. Another shows the tribes acting in isolation, or in groups of perhaps two tribes (Jud. i.), settling in particular areas, intermarrying with the native population, and adopting the customs and religion of those among whom they settled. A third tradition hints at a successful penetration from the south of Palestine, perhaps following the victory at Hormah over the king of Arad (Numbers xxi.). We have no external evidence to enable us to decide whether any of these traditions relate to the Mosaic Israelites, and archæology does not help us. It does, however, give us an ever-increasing mass of material to prove that in the religious culture of Palestine there were no changes to mark the entry of the tribes.[5] There are considerable signs that, at the end of the thirteenth century, the land was invaded by two groups of people, the one of a lower culture than the Canaanites, and the other bringing influences of Mycenæan and Cypriote civilization. The latter appear to have been the sea-people known to biblical tradition as Philistines, and the former those whom we call Israelites.

The Israelite invasion was marked, especially in the south and centre of the country, by wanton destruction of cities, and by pottery forms and building construction greatly inferior to those already found there—as we should expect from a nomadic people. But the religion of the land persisted unchanged. At many cities the old temples were re-used by the invaders, and where new temples were built the old worship centring round pillars, cup-holes, and stone altars remained. At Gezer and Megiddo temples built during this period included monoliths of unequal height, in addition to the columns that may have supported a roof; and at Bethshan, which remained under Egyptian influence until the twelfth century, there is nothing to mark the entry of a distinctive Israelite religion. Everywhere there was respect shown for the ancient sanctuaries, and the evidence, both from digging and from the Bible, shows that these places long continued to be treated as holy.

It follows, of course, that the Israelites also accepted the deities worshipped at these holy places. This becomes the more likely when we consider that the contemporaneous Philistine invaders readily accepted the gods of the lands they conquered. Dagon, the corn-god of Syria, became their food-god, although, as they were a maritime people, he was connected with fish rather than with grain, and was possibly confused with the fish-god of Sidon (Jud. xvi. ; 1 Sam. v.). A glass figure, half fish and half human, found at Lachish,[6] may be a representation of this god ; the Syrian god Baal-Zebul, whom we learn from the Bible was worshipped on Mount Carmel, was spoken of as god of Ekron, one of the five Philistine centres (2 Kings i.).

This willingness to accept the deities of the land springs

from a recognition that the deities have certain rights and powers in the new sphere which the invaders have entered. The very word used by the Israelites to describe these Canaanite gods expresses this recognition; they are called Baal, the general word for one who possesses rights—a husband is the baal of a woman, and Joseph the dreamer is a baal of dreams ; so the local gods possessed rights in their own district or sphere. These Baalim and their consorts ensured success to the agriculturalist, and it was necessary to make to them the usual offerings of first-fruits, and of corn and wine and oil. It should be noticed that this general word is the same as the name given in Syria to the great god Baal, who is often in the Old Testament confused with these local gods. It is easy to understand how the tendency, already noticed in Canaanite religion, to fuse local deities with newly introduced ones whose worship was more widespread would affect the relationship between Yahweh and the local Baalim. There were many points of contact between them ; the thunder- and weather-god would soon be thought of as the giver of rain and fertility, and the warrior god would become associated with the war goddesses of Canaan. Gradually, too, the god of the invading people became thought of as the god of the country, so that David could speak of being driven out of Palestine as being driven out from the presence of Yahweh (1 Sam. xxvi. 19).

Our biblical source for this period of transition is the book of Judges, and it gives us interesting sidelights on the syncretism that resulted from the invasion. One of the Israelite judges, Shamgar, son of Anath (Judges iii. 31), traced his parentage to Anath the goddess of fertility, whom seven hundred years later we find a Jewish community in Egypt still worshipping alongside Yahweh. Gideon's father worshipped Baal, and had a young bull called the bull of Shor (Judges vi. 25), a name we know from Ras Shamra as expressing the bull nature of El. Gideon himself made a golden ephod for divination, which became an object of worship (viii. 27), and a young man called Micah had a house of gods in which were golden images, teraphim, and an ephod. When these images were stolen he

cried, " They have taken away my gods " (Judges xvii.). The
story of Jephthah's daughter (Judges xi.) contains features
which belong to the fertility cult-pattern, and the same is true
of the story of the maidens who, dancing in the vineyards at
Shiloh at the end of the wine harvest, were seized by youths
from the tribe of Benjamin (Judges xxi.). Other elements
which became incorporated in the Israelite religion will be
seen as we follow the development of religion in the Bible.
Gradually, as moral conscience emerged, these elements were
thrown out, and we can recognize them from legal prohibitions
and prophetic condemnations ; and where they were too strong
to be eradicated, we can see them adapted and accepted in the
post-exilic priestly legislation.

But fortunately for the growth of religion everything
nomadic did not perish. The God of a roving people could
never be completely bound to any one place, and so we find
Yahweh at Sinai, Kadesh, in the temple on Mount Nebo, and
entering Palestine with Israel. He seems to have been accepted
by all Israelites as a war God—perhaps this is why the fugitives
under Moses made a covenant with this God, whose help they
greatly needed. In his name the tribes were rallied to battle
by Deborah, and later by Saul, and one of the sources quoted
by later historians is a book of poems, called the *Book of the
Wars of Yahweh* (Num. xxi. 14). Conquering invaders were
not likely to exchange this ally for another god while there
was still fighting to be done. It was peace that brought the
recurring danger of worshipping fertility deities, but always
it was to Yahweh they cried when oppressed by Canaanite,
Moabite, or Philistine, and he delivered them out of all their
distresses. This alternating apostasy from, and return to, a
war God appears to offer only a low type of religion, and there
is a great gulf between this tribal God of battles to whom men
called in time of need, and the universal God of love who,
in the teaching of Second-Isaiah and of Jesus, is depicted as
sending his worshippers out to give their lives in service ; but
in these crude beginnings lies the vision which was to enable
prophets to find God revealing himself in historic acts, and so

to interpret all history as the activity of God. The psalmist recognizes the gulf and reveals the cause of much of the world's misfortune when, picturing the God to whom men cry in their trouble, he bursts out with the refrain, " Oh that men would praise the Lord "—not only with their lips but in their lives— " for his goodness, and for his wonderful works to the children of men ! " (Psa. cvii.).

BOOK III
THE NATIONAL CULT AND THE INDIVIDUAL CONSCIENCE

CHAPTER 8

THE EARLY MONARCHY

THE gradual discovery and deciphering of the Ras Shamra tablets have proved conclusively that many elements that appear in the Pentateuch, and have been regarded as post-exilic, existed in Syrian religion in the fifteenth century B.C. Thus not only the condemnations that appear in the so-called " Priestly Code " may be regarded as evidence for religion in early monarchical times, but also much of the ritual in Numbers and Leviticus, which reveals the practices of that age.

§ RELIGION AT SHILOH

From the books of Samuel (1 Sam. i.) we learn that the religious centre in Palestine for the Israelites, after they had established themselves, was Shiloh. This was a pilgrim shrine at which were held annual New Year festivities in the autumn, and we have already seen from the book of Judges a picture of some of these festivities. The Danish archæological expedition at Shiloh [1] has found evidence that the city was ancient, but that there was considerable building activity at the time when the Israelites entered. Not long afterwards it was destroyed by fire, and remained practically deserted for centuries. In Jeremiah vii. 14 we read that more than four hundred years after its destruction it was still referred to as the place where Yahweh had been worshipped at the first, and the ruins of which testified to his punishment of his people's sins.

Neither from archæology nor from the Bible have we any evidence of a worship at Shiloh different from the Canaanite religion we have described; moreover, it seems that in many ways Canaanite ritual had deteriorated. Eli the priest, seeing a woman muttering her prayer, expects to find that she is drunk; the fertility rites have become an occasion for immorality between the priests and women worshippers; and the priests are no longer willing to share the communal meal with the worshippers, but demand special treatment. A three-pronged fork found at Lachish vividly illustrates the story of Eli's wicked sons (1 Sam. ii. 14) [2]—the long prongs and short handle would enable the priest's servant to obtain the lion's share of the animal seething in the pot. It is of interest that neither Eli nor his sons, Hophni and Phineas, bore a name compounded with the Yahweh element; the sons' names are Egyptian.

There are two traditions of the house of God at Shiloh, one calling it a tent, and the other giving the impression of a solid temple (cf. 1 Sam. ii. and 2 Sam. vii.), but both traditions agree that the central cult object was a portable shrine called the Ark. This ark, according to Exodus and Deuteronomy (x.) had been made by Moses to hold the two tablets of the ten commandments, and from the book of Numbers (x. 35f.) we learn that in the wilderness, " When the ark set forward, Moses said, ' Rise up, O Lord, and let thine enemies be scattered; and let them that hate thee flee before thee.' And when it rested, he said, ' Return, O Lord, to the ten thousand thousands of Israel.' " The words show that it was regarded as the dwelling place of Yahweh the God of battle, and this is further proved by the stories which relate that at Shiloh (1 Sam. iv.), and in the reign of David (2 Sam. xi. 11), the ark was carried into battle by the Israelite armies.

No wooden shrines of this kind have been found, [3] but many temples have yielded pottery shrines, small model buildings usually decorated with lions, snakes, or cherubim, perhaps originally containing an image of the god or goddess —most of these shrines are found in temples dedicated to goddesses—and treated as a special guarantee of the presence of the deity. Their use persisted, and we find them prominent not only in the worship at the Jewish temple, but in later Jewish synagogues, to hold the scroll of the law, and in parts of the Christian Church to house the emblems of the presence of Jesus.

§ Saul

When the temple and its priests at Shiloh had been destroyed and the ark captured by the Philistines, the way was open for the emergence of a new kind of religious leader. Samuel and Saul were both in different ways prophets. Samuel was a seer with the gift of second sight, earning money by revealing the whereabouts of lost asses, but he was also an itinerant "man of God" who officiated at communal feasts on local high places (1 Sam. ix.). Saul, however, was not a professional holy man, but a local farmer, and if we may judge from the remains of his capital at Gibeah, possessed common sense and good judgement.[4] A proverb twice repeated (1 Sam. x. 11, xix. 24)—"Is Saul among the prophets?"—shows that he was the last person whom one would expect to catch the prophetic contagion, but we find him with a band of prophets, using music as a help to obtaining oracles, stripping off his clothes, and lying naked all day and night prophesying. Saul's form of prophecy seems to have been exclusively of this ecstatic type, a type we find also among the Canaanites and in many other religions. Samuel was more than an ecstatic prophet, although there is evidence that he was capable of ecstasy. We see him hewing King Agag in pieces before the Lord (1. Sam. xv. 33), and we find him as head of a community of such prophets at Ramah (1 Sam. xix. 24).

Meanwhile the new religious centre, where Samuel anointed Saul as king and where he rallied the people against their enemies, was Mizpah,[5] the modern Tell en-Nasbeh. It was an ancient holy place with a sacred cave and a sacrificial rock marked with cup-holes. Badé's excavations there have shown

GOD OF THUNDER AND WAR
FROM RAS SHAMRA

(Prof. C. Schaeffer)

Gold pendants from the necklaces of a royal lady at Ras Shamra. The centre pendant of each necklace was a golden plate. On one of these, second from the right, is shown Astarte, Goddess of Love and Fertility, with her holy creatures, the lion, the ram, and the snake *(Prof. C. Schaeffer)*

Limestone incense altar of Assyrian origin from Gerar
(Sir C. Flinders Petrie)

Limestone table of offerings with three lions in relief ;
from Tell Beit Mirsim *(Prof. W. F. Albright)*

that it did not become a monotheistic city when the Israelites
under Samuel and Saul occupied it ; against the Israelite wall,
and lasting until the fall of this wall in the eighth century, were
built twin temples like those we have seen at Bethshan, one
possibly dedicated to Yahweh, and the other certainly the
shrine of his consort. In this second temple were found fragments of a goddess figurine, a conical stone pillar, and a pottery
dove and lamp nesting in the fork of a three-branched tree.
Though Saul himself appears to have been an enthusiastic
Yahweh worshipper and named his eldest son Jonathan—
Yahweh gave—that he was not a monotheist is shown by the
names he gave other children : a daughter Michal is called
after the god of Bethshan, and a son by the name of Baal.
Possibly the names are compliments to powerful religious
centres in his kingdom, and show that there was no attempt
at creating a national religion with Yahweh at its head. His
own devotion to Yahweh probably sprang from his need of the
help of the war-god, and the Bible records that he built his
first altar to Yahweh on the battlefield after victory (1 Sam.
xiv. 45).

§ DAVID AND THE " CULT-PATTERN "

A greater leader arose to succeed Saul, David, who has
become one of the heroes of Jewish religious history. As late
as the time of the Chronicler, we find him rivalling Moses as
the founder of temple worship and the Levitical order of
priesthood. The traditions that gather around his name are
difficult to unravel, and a comparison of the history in the
books of Samuel and Kings with that in the Chronicles shows
the direction in which the traditions grew. Far more than
Saul, he appears to have been a king like the kings of surrounding folk, and the centre of a king-cult ; on two occasions he
speaks of his rival Saul as the " anointed of Yahweh," and
regarded him as so inviolable that he killed the youth who had
slain Saul (2 Sam. i. 14f.). His capital at first was the holy
place of long-standing at Hebron, but after his capture of

Jerusalem he attempted to give religious prestige to the new capital by placing there the ark, which according to the Bible had dwelt at Shiloh, been captured by the Philistines, and for years had lain forgotten. The manner in which it was brought into Jerusalem is instructive in view of our knowledge of the earlier religion of Palestine (2 Sam. vi.). There is little trace of the presence of the Levites who loom so largely in the later account in Chronicles ; David himself acts as priest-king, dancing in front of the ark in such a shameless way as to disgust his wife, the daughter of Saul, who was not accustomed to seeing a king behave thus ; when the procession is over he distributes to the people the flat raisin cakes which at Bethshan are associated with the worship of Anath, the consort of the god. This act becomes all the more significant for the meaning of the ark when we remember the connection of these portable shrines with the worship of a goddess, the persistence of the association of Yahweh and Anath, the depicting of Anath with a shield and spear in one hand and a club in the other, and the presence at David's court of Abiathar, a priest from Anathoth. It is also of interest that the lion on which Kadesh the war-goddess stands, and which appears as a decoration on the pottery shrines, is the animal associated with David's tribe—the lion of Judah—and that both the six-pointed star of David, and the five-pointed star of his son Solomon, are found at the base of a plaque, found at Tell es-Safi, depicting a nude mother-goddess holding a serpent in each hand. The Davidic star was found also cut on the wall of a temple of a goddess at Megiddo, in the same form in which it has become so familiar in Judaism.[6]

It seems probable that like Saul, David was not a monotheist, nor did he strive towards religious unity in his kingdom. Two of his sons—Absalom and Solomon—are named after the god worshipped probably in Jerusalem, the god Shalem[7] whom we find at Ras Shamra, as god of the summer solstice, or possibly of the full moon. His own name, we learn from the Moabite stone, was connected with some cult object kept in the Gadite temple at Ataroth. At the end of his reign his connection with the king-cult again becomes clear ; the story of his last bride (1 Kings i.), the revolt of Adonijah, and even the earlier revolt of Absalom, who signalized his rebellion by spreading a marriage tabernacle on the roof of the palace in the sight of all Israel and thus laid claim to royal rights (2 Sam. xvi. 22), all may reflect the widespread belief that a failing king meant failing crops. But his importance to the development of religion is not solely along this line. Whether or not he wrote any of the Psalms in the form in which they have come down to us, it is clear that he was a man with considerable poetic gifts, who spontaneously expressed his sorrow in laments of great beauty. The tradition is strong that connects his name with at least two of the collections of hymns which have been incorporated in the book of Psalms, and his importance here cannot be overestimated. Such a man would make articulate for common people religious emotions which they themselves could not express, and so enable them to rise to higher levels of religious experience.

§ THE TEMPLE

No excavations have yet been possible on the site where the Jewish temple stood, and it is doubtful whether, even if such were allowed, they would reveal much, for the destruction of the successive buildings has been very thorough, and probably the foundations of Herod's magnificent edifice were laid on the rock surface. The books of Samuel (2 Sam. xxiv.) and Chronicles (1 Chron. xxi.) relate that the site was a threshing floor on which the angel of Yahweh appeared to David, when God stayed the great pestilence, and there the seer Gad commanded David to erect an altar. The story is comparable to those which give the origin of other places of worship in Palestine, and as in the account of Abraham and the cave of Machpelah, care is taken to state that David actually purchased the land. The site of the threshing floor on high ground above the old city was almost certainly an ancient Jebusite "high place" before it was taken over by David, or rather by Solomon, for we have no evidence that David continued to use it for sacrifice. Until Solomon built the temple, there were other religious shrines for Jerusalem. Solomon himself was anointed king at Gihon (1 Kings i. 33), in the Kidron valley near the spring. He offered his coronation sacrifices at Gibeon (iii. 4), probably Nebi Samwil, the great high place overlooking Jerusalem. There was a holy place on the Mount of Olives, where we are told David was wont to worship (2 Sam. xv. 32), and before the temple was completed the ark was kept in the old city, not on the high place.

The central feature of the temple site was the great rock altar, now covered by the beautiful Arab building known as the "Dome of the Rock." Near its southern side a channel has been cut through the rock to a cave beneath, and at the northern end three steps give access to the surface. Against the use of such an altar the law in Exodus xx. 25f. must have been directed : " Neither shalt thou go up by steps under thine altar, that thy nakedness be not uncovered thereon."

The rectangular shape of the temple described in the book of Kings shows the general plan to be similar to that of temples found elsewhere, but no others have been found with the many rooms in a three-storied building at the side, nor with the porch in front fifteen feet long. Two free standing bronze pillars—Jachin and Boaz (1 Kings vii. 21)—twenty-seven feet high, were set at the door, similar to the stone ones used at Shechem, and their decoration of pomegranates shows the persistence of fertility symbolism. Many of the other decorations in the building—palm trees, open flowers, and cherubim —can be illustrated from the carved ivories found at Samaria. The inner shrine was a windowless room, thirty feet cubed, shut off by carved doors of olive wood, and within were two large cherubim with outstretched wings, under which the ark was placed. These winged cherubim had lion bodies [8] and human heads, and are reminiscent of the sphinx of Egypt and the gigantic stone figures which guarded the way to Mesopotamian temples and palaces. That in Israel also they were looked on as guardians is shown by the description in Genesis of the cherub with the whirling flame barring the entrance to the garden of Eden (iii. 24). From the Psalms we learn that they were wind symbols on which Yahweh was thought to ride, and which acted as his messengers : " He rode upon the cherub and did fly, yea he flew upon the wings of the wind " (xviii. 10). It is possible that there was a connection between the cherubim and sun worship, for one of the cherubim found at Megiddo was wearing the disc of the sun as part of its headdress.

The orientation of the temple reveals the presence of the solar cult.[9] It was five degrees off the true north and south line, facing directly to the Mount of Olives, so that, it is estimated, at the New Year festival at the autumn equinox the rising sun shone through the eastern gates straight into the inner holy shrine. This cult remained until the destruction of the temple in 586 B.C., for Ezekiel tells us that in his time in the inner court, " at the door of the temple, between the porch and the altar, were about twenty-five men with their backs toward the temple and their faces toward the east ; and they worshipped the sun toward the east " (viii. 16). It may have been the practice of this cult that brought into the Psalter the hymn to the sun, Psalm civ., and the first half of Psalm xix., with its picture of the sun as a bridegroom, rejoicing as a strong man to run his daily course. The worship of the sun did not take place only in Jerusalem ; the name of the town Bethshemesh—the house of the sun—shows the same cult, and model chariot wheels found at Megiddo, and a complete pottery model of a chariot and its rider at Gezer in the Solomonic stratum, suggest the chariot of the sun-god.

Compared with Solomon's palace buildings, the temple was only a small royal shrine, ninety feet long by thirty feet wide, and it is probable that, like the temple at Bethel, throughout the early monarchy it remained a royal chapel rather than a national religious centre. It is clear that Solomon did not aim at centralizing religion at Jerusalem, for he built other temples. At Megiddo, where he erected his great stables, he also built temples, one of which was for the worship of a goddess, and from this temple come examples of portable shrines, and of an incense altar with the same proportions as that required by the priestly laws in the Old Testament ; this altar, moreover, had horns at each of the top corners, like those on the altar at Jerusalem, to which Joab clung for refuge when about to be slain at the command of Solomon (1 Kings ii. 28).

Of Solomon's personal religion we know little, though we learn from the Bible that his enthusiasm for Yahweh was not so great as it should have been, and that he was led away by the influence of his foreign wives. The other name given to him in the Old Testament is Jedidiah (2 Sam. xii. 25), which contains both the Yahweh element and the Dod or " loves " element seen in the name of his father David, as though here the two were definitely combined, but the name of the son who succeeded him—Rehoboam—is without the Yahweh element. Solomon enjoyed prosperity and apparently did no fighting, and consequently would not need to appeal to the god of battles. His place in the development of Jewish religion is that he built with lavish wealth this shrine, which gradually grew in importance until finally the Jerusalem temple became the only legitimate place of national worship.

§ DISRUPTION OF THE KINGDOM

At the accession of Rehoboam the northern part of Palestine, including ten of the twelve tribes, revolted against the oppressive taxation which had become necessary to keep up the magnificence of the Davidic court, and the story of the disruption throws considerable light on the contemporary religion. Jeroboam, the northern leader, signalized his independence by three religious changes, designed to wean his subjects from the temple at Jerusalem : he set up calf images at Bethel and Dan, introduced a non-Levitical priesthood, and altered by one month the date of the annual feast of Tabernacles (1 Kings xii. 25ff.). It seems a fair assumption that at such a moment he

would not risk offending his new subjects by needless innovations, and we may assume that the calf images replaced others,
destroyed perhaps by David when he had conquered the north.

In view of this it is interesting that the two accounts in the
Old Testament of the making of bull or calf images are not
independent of each other. It is generally admitted that
Exodus xxxii., which relates how Aaron made the golden calf
in the wilderness, in its present literary form is later than the
reform of Jeroboam ; and it is probable that the Exodus story
reflects some of the actual history of calf worship in the north.
In that story the Levites were rewarded for their zeal in the
destruction of the golden calf, they were praised for fighting
against their brethren and deserting their family, and the ark
was made to replace the calf as a symbol of the divine presence.
Now, from Judges xviii. we learn that the founder of the
priesthood at Dan in the extreme north was a Levite and grandson of Moses, and we know the prominence of Levites in the
Davidic tradition. It therefore seems possible that at the
accession of David some of the Levites fought against their
brethren, the priests at Bethel and Dan, destroyed the golden
calves, and accepted the ark as the symbol of Yahweh. It would
then be easy to understand why Jeroboam should not only
restore the calves, but use non-Levites as priests in their service.
That at Bethel the calf was a Yahweh symbol is confirmed by
a name on one of the ostraca found at Samaria, Egli-yau,
which means either Calf of Yahweh or Yahweh is my Calf.
It is not, however, clear whether the calf should be connected
with the young bull with sprouting horns who, at Baalbec,
was the symbol of the youthful sun-god, or with the bull of
El at Ras Shamra. If Egyptian influence had been present
we should have expected a live bull as incarnation of the
god, but probably the calf was thought of as the throne or
representative of Yahweh, just as was the ark in Jerusalem (Jer.
iii. 16f.) ; and in both places, though the symbols of the
worship were different, the empty throne made possible the
growth of a more spiritual religion.

The third change—the alteration of the date of the Feast

of Tabernacles—broke the whole sequence of the festivals of
the agricultural year which gathered round the king-cult and
the fertility rites, and which probably linked the sacred marriage
rite at the autumnal Feast of Tabernacles with the slaughter of
firstborn in the Tammuz month of midsummer. Such an
alteration involved the repudiation of the Davidic king-cult and
probably a return to the more promiscuous fertility rites
practised at Shiloh.

Jeroboam's reforms did not limit worship in the north to
the two sanctuaries of Dan and Bethel. Excavations at Shechem
show that he restored Shechem as his capital and rebuilt there
the temple of the Lord of the Covenant, placing a base for a
statue against the north wall in the open courtyard. He also
rebuilt Penuel (1 Kings xii. 25), which, like Bethel, was the
scene of a theophany to Jacob.[10]

One other result of the disruption was that Judah—sometimes with the little tribe of Benjamin—became a small com-
pact kingdom around Jerusalem. The contrast between the
lavish wealth at the temple in the capital and the poverty of
the country around naturally tended to increase the importance
of this temple as the centre for religious festivals of the southern
kingdom ; but the burden of supporting such worship must
have widened the gulf between institutional religion and the
life of the common people, making it easy to understand the
ready acceptance of the later prophetic message that Yahweh
required not thousands of rams and ten thousands of rivers
of oil, but justice, mercy, and humility (Micah vi. 8).

§ ELIJAH AND JEHU

In the northern kingdom another great landmark in the
religious development was Elijah's fight against the Tyrian
Baal, to whom, according to 1 Kings xvi., Ahab reared an
altar, built a house at Samaria, made an Asherah, and set up
pillars. If we may judge from the name of Jezebel and from
the story of the god whom her son sent to consult when he

fell from the palace window, this Tyrian Baal was Baal-Zebul (2 Kings i.)—the Lord of the lofty place—whom we know from the Ras Shamra tablets. Later Jewish writers have altered the name contemptuously to Baal-Zebub—Lord of flies—but the story shows that he had a shrine on Mount Carmel where he could be consulted, and thus was no stranger to Israel. Jezebel, however, appears to have wished to make the paramount god of her own people the national god of her adopted home. The conflict on Carmel then takes on a new significance. The prolonged drought had raised the question as to whether this Baal or Yahweh was the real rain-giver. In the Phœnician records of this same drought it is Baal who gives rain at the request of Ethbaal, who in the Bible is spoken of as the father of Jezebel. Elijah challenges this Baal at the very centre of his worship in Israel—on Mount Carmel where the Yahweh altar had been allowed to fall into ruins—and he asserts that Yahweh, not Baal, is the rain-god.

Elijah's victory was followed later by a political triumph in the northern kingdom, and a priestly revolution in the south. Jehu, an army captain, was incited by the prophet— probably Elijah, not Elisha—to revolt, and overthrew the dynasty of Ahab and murdered Jezebel (2 Kings ix.). In Judæa the high priest led the movement, which ended in the death of Athaliah the queen-mother, a daughter of Jezebel, and the temporary defeat of her foreign god (2 Kings xi.). It is obvious that Baal worship did not cease in Palestine, for the seventh- and sixth-century prophets still condemn it, but in these events we see a move toward making Yahweh supreme in the land and the nation, not only as the God of battles, but also as the God of nature. The story of Jezebel's treatment of Naboth (1 Kings xxi.) is evidently intended to show that social justice was one of the motives of Elijah's fight, and by his victory an important step forward was taken toward the union of religion and social justice, which, through the work of later prophets, became a distinguishing mark of Israel's religion.

These stories are also of interest as revealing the direction whence came the impetus toward the strengthening of the

worship of Yahweh. Jehu's assistants were the Rechabites
(2 Kings x. 15), who, we learn from Jeremiah, were uncompromising nomads, with a deep opposition to all the civilization
of Palestine—houses, vines, and agriculture—and whom the
genealogies link with the Kenites and Moses. The Chronicler
records a tradition that at this same time the south of Palestine
and of Judæa was overrun by tribes from the Arabian desert
(2 Chron. xxi. 16f.). It was at this time, too, that Moab destroyed the Yahweh temple at Nebo, and Moab's conquests
may have caused a fresh invasion of nomads into Palestine,
and a new emphasis on the nomadic God, Yahweh. Elijah
himself is regarded as coming from Tishbe in Trans-Jordan,
and after his temporary defeat by Jezebel he fled to the desert
to Horeb, thus connecting his traditions with those of Moses
and the wandering Hebrews, before their settlement in Palestine (1 Kings xix.).

§ THE MOABITE STONE

We have already mentioned the Moabite stone, but for
the development of religion it merits further notice. The
stone was discovered in A.D. 1868 at Diban in Trans-Jordan,
and is written in a script and language practically identical
with ancient Hebrew. Mesha, the king of Moab, as we know
from the Old Testament, had paid tribute to Israel—100,000
lambs and 100,000 rams with the wool—but revolted after
the death of Ahab (2 Kings iii.). In his stele he records the
success of his revolt. To commemorate it he made a new high
place for Chemosh his god, because "he saved me from my
assailants and let me see my pleasure on mine enemies." The
long oppression by Israel had been possible because Chemosh
was angry with his land, but now his anger had gone. Two of
the places captured by Mesha in his revolt were Ataroth, a city
of Gad in Trans-Jordan which had been rebuilt by the Israelite
king Omri, and Nebo, where was a Yahweh sanctuary. From
Ataroth Mesha took captive the altar hearth belonging to the
Dod of Ataroth and dragged it before Chemosh. To capture

Nebo and defeat its god more care was necessary ; Mesha vowed that everything, including women and children, would be devoted to the goddess Ashtor-Chemosh ; after a night march and a dawn attack the city fell, seven thousand men and women were slaughtered to the goddess, and the cult objects dragged away to the Chemosh temple.

The account reflects the same relationship between Moab and Chemosh as we have seen between Israel and Yahweh, after the settlement in Palestine. The land is the land of Chemosh, and the fortunes of Moab are controlled by Chemosh, a fact recognized by words put into the mouth of Jephthah in the Old Testament : "Wilt not thou possess that which Chemosh thy god giveth thee ? So whomsoever Yahweh our God shall drive out from before us them will we possess" (Judges xi. 24). When Chemosh is angry the Israelites can conquer, but when he has punished his people and again shows them favour, he is stronger than the Yahweh or Dod of Israel. He, too, is a god who reveals himself through historic acts.

The cult object dragged before Chemosh from the Israelite temple at Ataroth is given the same name as that used by Ezekiel to describe part of the new altar to be set up in Jerusalem, in the new temple which should be built after the Babylonian exile ; and the word is used in Isaiah xxix. 1—Ariel—as a synonym for Jerusalem. It appears to have been a large altar on which incense was burnt, and having four horns to make it a place of refuge for those who sought the protection of the god ; 2 Samuel xvii. 13 suggests that most cities had such altars. On the stone Mesha describes it as the Ariel of the Dod of the city, and the word Dod is, in the usual unvocalized Hebrew, indistinguishable from the name David. In a Ras Shamra tablet Dod is the name given to Aleyn-Baal, the young son of Baal who dies and rises again. In the story of Saul the Bible mentions a living Dod who was head of Gibeah—it is translated Uncle in the English version (1 Sam. x. 14ff.), and in Hebrew the word comes to denote a kinsman—but it is possible that it was used there and in the name of David for the human priest-king who represented Aleyn in the annual religious festival.

The mention of Yahweh at Nebo gives the earliest external writing of the name in the form in which it occurs in the Hebrew Bible. We should like to know more of the cult objects dragged away from the temple, but they are described only by a general word meaning vessels, furnishings, or even weapons. The prominence given to the women slaves, and the sojourning there of protected men and women, suggest that at Nebo, as at the temple in Jerusalem, there were holy men and women who formed part of the temple personnel. The word translated as women slaves becomes in Hebrew the general word for Mercy—it means literally " womb "—and is often applied to Yahweh's attitude to his people. Is it not possible that the presence of women in the cult, and of the mother-goddess alongside Yahweh, has given to the idea of God something comparable to fuller humanity, womanhood as well as manhood, tenderness and love which it would have lacked if the idea of God had developed solely from a male god of storm and battle ?

§ THE FALL OF THE NORTHERN KINGDOM

The northern kingdom fell in 722 B.C., before Sargon of Assyria, and to the later biblical historians the fall of Samaria marked the final end of the northern kingdom and of its connection with Yahweh (2 Kings xvii.). They themselves were southerners, and their aim was to prove that the small band of southern Jews who returned from the exile in Babylonia was the true Israel and the sole inheritor of the nation's religion. According to these writers, the north, after 722 B.C., became inhabited by foreigners and heathen, with no legitimate share in Israel. But not all the people in the north were carried away, and although we are told that the new inhabitants worshipped their own gods and served their graven images, they and their children and their children's children down to the time of the writer, yet we are also informed that, because of a plague of lions (2 Kings xvii. 24ff.), a priest of Yahweh was sent back from Assyria to Bethel to teach the new inhabitants the true worship of Yahweh, the God of the land. We know, too, from Zechariah vii. that after the destruction of Jerusalem, when Mizpah became the civil centre, Bethel was the religious centre for the whole country, and there the annual fasts to commemorate the fall of Jerusalem were held during the seventy years of exile, from 586 to 516 B.C. More important still, a century after 722 B.C., the great prophets Jeremiah and Ezekiel treated the northern kingdom not only as in existence, but as an equal partner with the south in the worship of Yahweh. To them Israel was the elder sister of Judah, like her, married to Yahweh and false to her vows ; but she had been punished and now has shown herself more righteous than her southern sister (Jer. iii., Ezek. xxiii.). Neither prophet gives any indication of a real break in the continuity of the religion of the north. There appears to be no evidence to suggest that the religion of the northern kingdom after 722 B.C. was essentially different from the religion of the previous period ; it is possible that the golden calves may have been re-made ; but, on the other hand, it may have been thought that Hosea's prophecy had come true—that the people shall mourn over them because they shall be carried away to Assyria (viii. 6, x. 5). Much must have depended on the personal religion of the Yahweh priest who returned to Bethel as the official head of the religion of the province ; he could certainly not risk the continuance of the plague of lions by altering the old religion, but he may have been strongly influenced by Amos and Hosea, who had prophesied shortly before the catastrophe. If so, this would account for the favourable verdict passed on the northern religion by such good judges as Jeremiah and Ezekiel, and for the fact that Bethel became the centre of Yahweh worship during the exile.

CHAPTER 9

PROPHETIC CONSCIENCE

§ Emergence of the Prophets

THROUGHOUT the history of the early monarchy we find emerging from the national life men whom we call prophets,[1] and who appear either as individuals, or in groups or bands. They are men of very different character, and the word prophet needs to be given a very wide meaning to describe all of them. A glance at some of the outstanding figures will reveal the variety covered by the term.

We have already noticed the contrast between Samuel and Saul ; Samuel was the head of a community of prophets, he officiated at the high place, used his gifts to aid men in the ordinary affairs of life, and heard God speaking as Moses had done, face to face ; Saul was not a professional religious man, but as he was going away from the sacrifice at the high place he met a band of professional prophets—probably some of Samuel's own men—who were inducing a state of religious ecstasy by the help of music and, catching the contagion, he became another man possessed by the same ecstatic frenzy (I Sam. x. 11). The possession did not result in any message being received from God, but Saul became a national leader similar to some Moslem dervishes. Apparently he remained subject to spiritual possession, although later, judged by the actions which resulted from the possession, the spirits were spoken of as evil, and had to be charmed away by the music of David.

One of the earliest examples of this ecstatic possession in Syria occurs in the autobiography of the Egyptian, Wenamon, who in about 1100 B.C. was sent to Byblos to obtain cedar for the sacred barque of the god Amon. The king of Byblos refused even to see him, and robbed, disappointed, and in danger of his life, he was attempting to return to Egypt from a futile journey when suddenly, while the king was offering sacrifice, one of the noble youths in attendance on him was seized by a spirit, fell to the ground in convulsions, and demanded that the Egyptian envoy should be called, treated with respect as the messenger of the god Amon, and dismissed with honour. The king accepted the demand as coming from his god, and reversed his previous policy. In this example, too, the prophet was an ordinary individual like Saul; and possession was connected with sacrifice, it was not something apart from the official cult ; but here there was no band of prophets, nor music, and the possession, which lasted throughout the night, was simply for the purpose of delivering a message.

It appears to be possible to distinguish between professional and amateur prophets, and between ecstatic men and the man who, to quote Paul " speaketh unto men to edification and exhortation and comfort " (1 Cor. xiv.). Nathan, like Gad, was a professional prophet attached to the court of David, and probably, like the prophets maintained under Ahab's patronage, his duty was to give oracles to the king for military or political ventures ; at the end of the reign of the king he took a prominent part in the political manœuvre which placed Solomon on the throne instead of his elder brother (1 Kings i.), but he also regarded himself as guardian of the king's morals. His method of telling a story in order to draw the king's judgement and to lead to the dramatic statement, "Thou art the man " (2 Sam. xii. 7) was followed by other prophets. Haggai used the same means with his priestly questioners (Haggai ii. 14) and so also did Jesus when he completed the story of the Good Samaritan with the words, " Go thou and do likewise " (Luke x.). Ahijah, the prophet from Shiloh, who incited Jeroboam to his revolt against Solomon's idolatry and oppression, was probably ecstatic as well as professional (1 Kings xi.). He used an action to make clear his message, and the action was regarded not only as symbolic but as functional, it made the event he foretold come true. Clad in a new garment he met Jeroboam alone, and rent his garment into twelve pieces, giving ten pieces to Jeroboam as his share of Solomon's kingdom (1 Kings xi. 29). It is not likely that either the prophet or his hearers thought of the action as coercing God ; the purpose which was being achieved was God's, his word had gone out, and the prophet by his action began the fulfilment of God's revealed will. A similar use of prophetic action is seen clearly in the stories of Elisha, who was also leader of a band of ecstatic prophets. When the king of Israel visited Elisha, the prophet was dying, but he bade the king take a bow and arrows, and placing his hands on the king's hands, he made the king shoot an arrow through the open window, and said, "The arrow of the Lord's deliverance from Syria." He then told the king to smite with an arrow on the ground, and he smote three times, "and the man of God was wrath with him and said, Thou shouldst have smitten five or six times, then hadst thou smitten Syria till thou hadst consumed it ; whereas now thou shalt smite Syria but thrice" (2 Kings xiii. 14ff.). Elisha, like Saul, became a national leader. Although at first a staff captain described him as a madman, and children laughed at him as he passed, later we find him with the troops on the battlefield, and at his death he is called " the chariot of Israel and the horsemen thereof." Stories that have gathered around his name relate how he could sweeten brackish waters, make iron swim, multiply food, heal the sick, and raise the dead.

Another example of symbolic action from a prophet is seen in the story of the four hundred Yahweh prophets at Ahab's court. In answer to the king's inquiry whether he should go to war against Ramoth Gilead, one of the prophets "made him horns of iron : and he said, Thus saith the Lord, with these shalt thou push the Syrians until thou have consumed them" (1 Kings xxii. 11). But the great interest of this story is that it introduces us to a distinction between true and false prophets. All the prophets are inspired by Yahweh, but only one gives a true message, for the God who does evil as well as good, wishing to entice Ahab to his doom, sent forth a lying spirit to inspire the majority of the prophets. Jeremiah later felt that Yahweh had treated him in the same

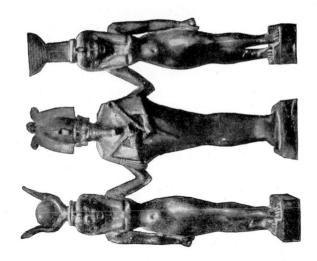

EGYPTIAN DEITIES

(Cairo Museum)

Sculptured Relief of a Six-winged Goddess
or Seraph

(Illustrated London News)

Pottery heads of Ashtoreth, Queen of Heaven

(Illustrated London News)

way, and in a startling manner burst out at God, "Thou hast seduced me, and I let myself be seduced ; thou wast stronger than I, and hast prevailed ; I am become a laughing stock " (Jer. xx. 7ff.).

Elijah is more difficult to fit into any of the types we have seen. He came from Trans-Jordan, wearing the desert garb of a coarse hair garment and a leathern girdle, which became the recognized dress of a professional prophet. He shows no opposition to sacrificial practices, but like Samuel sacrifices at the altar. Almost like an ecstatic prophet, he can gird up his loins and run before Ahab's chariot (1 Kings xviii. 46). As to Moses or Samuel, God speaks to him direct, not through visions or dreams, telling him where to meet Ahab, or intercept the messengers of Ahaziah, or at Horeb giving him the message of absolute destruction. He stands out as an individual in the same way as the great prophets who followed him and whose teaching has been preserved in the books that bear their names, but he differs from them. The emphasis is still on the man and his doings, rather than on his teaching ; his primary concern is not with the character of God, but to assert that Yahweh is the rain God and the fire God, and to oust Baal from his position in the fertility cults ; he calls men to a decision for or against Yahweh without pleading or entreaty, and is very jealous for Yahweh, God of Israel. It is interesting to remember when we look at this man that he of all the prophets was the one who Jewish tradition said would return to herald the New Age ; and the one to whom a later generation of Jews compared John the Baptist and Jesus.

A clear distinction is usually made between these earlier prophets and the later ones who are known as writing prophets. But the two kinds have much in common. Most of our information about the earlier prophets appears to have come from oral traditions, preserved by such guilds as gathered around Samuel or Elisha, or from the records of the kings at whose courts they lived, or whose dynasty owed its position to them. There are traces that similar oral traditions may have grown up around the names of the writing prophets, but the biographical or autobiographical material which has been preserved was collected early enough to prevent the formation of many legendary stories. Of the eighth-century prophets whose message we have, two worked in the northern kingdom before its fall and two in the south.

Amos, the first of the four, was like Elijah, a stern, uncompromising desert preacher, and not a native of the north. A casual labourer, he spent part of the year with flocks in the poor hilly pastures around the Judæan town of Tekoa—a town renowned for the wisdom of its inhabitants—and part helping with the fig crops in the richer lands of the Shephelah and Samaria. The contrast between his own simple, frugal life and the careless, inconsiderate luxury of the wealthy upper classes in the north roused his protest, and with a fearlessness born of the conviction that God had laid hold of him, he proclaimed his message even at the royal sanctuary at Bethel. To Amaziah, the high-priest, there was nothing to distinguish him from the professional ecstatic prophets who earned their bread by prophecy, but Amos indignantly repudiates any connection with other prophets—" I am no prophet nor a member of any prophetic guild " (Amos vii. 14)—and predicts the destruction of king, people, and priest.

Hosea belonged to the north, and knew the religion against which he spoke from the inside. Probably he had, like Samuel, been brought up at one of the holy places, and as much as the priests, was part of the professional religious life. He gives us many pictures of the religious life of the north, showing the attachment of the people to their golden calves, the worship on the high places under green trees, and the mirth of new moon and Sabbath festivals. He shows too his own attitude to the externals of religion, when he predicts that as a temporary punishment Israel will be made to live without king, princes, sacrifice, stone pillars, ephod, and teraphim (iii. 4), eating bread in an unclean land, and with no possibility of festive gatherings (ix. 3f.). Amos had protested against social injustice, but Hosea was roused by religious abuses. The priests, by their lying, stealing, murder on the road to Shechem, and snares at Tabor and Mizpah (v. 1), had set the tone for the whole nation—like people, like priest. The cult-pattern had degenerated into immorality and sexual vice. Brides, who of necessity had taken part in the fertility rites, were encouraged to be unfaithful to their husbands, and to return to commit adultery with the priests, and the people were made to believe that their corn and wine and oil were dependent on such practices. Hosea shows a depth of human affection unknown to Amos and Elijah. He knew those whom he condemned; his own wife was one of those who had been unfaithful, and he loved her. His patient efforts to win her back gave him a new insight into the persistent love of God; continually the people cried, "Come let us return unto Yahweh," but their goodness was like the morning cloud or the early dew that passeth quickly away (vi.); yet as a father with a child he has held in his arms and taught to walk (xi.), so God cannot sever completely the bonds of love that bind him to his people.

B. H. Streeter wrote [2] that it is "part of God's plan from time to time to raise up individuals of exceptional insight, whose words or actions may serve to provide more ordinary persons both with a criterion of value and a stimulus to progress. In other words, there is an inner coherence between the belief that God has a plan for mankind and the fact of the emergence in history of the exceptional individuals to whom we give the name of 'prophets.'" If we listen to their own explanation of their power and the origin of their message, we hear them saying that God has laid hold on them, that they have heard the voice of someone crying aloud in the wilderness, that God has spoken and they must needs prophesy, or that by taking the true from the false they become God's mouthpiece. In no sense is the message given as the prophet's own discovery. He has been commanded to speak and so prefaces his words with the phrase, "Thus saith Yahweh." It is God's word which he proclaims, and that word, once uttered, endures for ever; it never returns void to God, but has power to accomplish God's purpose (Is. lv. 11).

Probably most of these prophets, particularly the earlier

ones, were part of the political and religious system of their time, but their importance is due to the fact that though they remained within the system, they revolted against it. From our modern standpoint we think of them as evidence of the regenerative conscience [3] at work in society, and so far as we can trace development in the religion of the Bible, they prove the possibility of direct communion between God and man, and that human conscience can become the voice of God.

The two prophets in the south stand in complete contrast to each other : Isaiah was a courtier at Jerusalem, Micah was a peasant farmer from the fertile Judæan hills. To the former God is the great king, majestic, holy, and unapproachable (vi.), so holy that the city in which his temple is must be inviolable —no enemy can enter it nor can an arrow be shot into it (xxxvii. 33). His court life taught him of political intrigues, of attempts to retain national independence by political sagacity and duplicity, not by trusting God ; God was ignored in practical life, so men lacked the confidence and peace which flow from trusting the power of the Holy One of Israel. Some of his prophecies were enforced by symbolic actions which were probably still thought of as having magical power to influence the future. We see him walking naked and barefoot through the streets of Jerusalem to implement his prophecy of the destruction of Egypt ; and he has children by the unnamed prophetess to proclaim the limit of the time of the oppression by Syria and Israel. The names of his children, " A remnant shall remain," and " Spoil shall hasten, plunder hurry," (viii.) reveal the same type of prophecy. Like earlier prophets he gathered round himself a band of disciples, but there is little evidence of ecstatic conditions.

Micah had a countryman's distrust of the great cities, and regarded Jerusalem, Samaria, and Lachish as the cause of the people's sins (i.). He appears to have suffered under the oppression of wealthy landowners, who " covet fields and take them by violence, and defraud a man and his household, a man and his inheritance " (ii. 2). A peace-loving peasant, he longs for the day when wars will cease, swords be beaten into ploughshares, and spears into pruning-hooks, and every man shall sit under his own vine and fig tree, and none shall make them afraid (iv. 1ff.).

§ THE BACKGROUND OF THE PROPHETIC MESSAGE

Matthew Arnold wrote [4] that, for any great creative epoch in literature, two powers are necessary: the power of the man and the power of the moment. This is equally true of the eighth-century prophets, whose emergence marks a new epoch in the development of biblical religion. We understand the contribution made by these men better when we have looked at the religious, social, and historical circumstances in which they lived, and through which their message gained a hearing.

Our survey of nomadic religion and of the early religion of the settled people has shown that the Israelites appear to have thought of their God as a God of war and of thunderstorms, and that the nearest approach to a national religion came in times of danger, when the people were fighting for their national existence. This God soon found a place in the religious life of Palestine, for he had many points of contact with gods already in the land. There were already war-gods like Resheph with their warlike consorts such as Anath. Yahweh, too, was given a similar consort—we find the name Anath-yau among the Jews at Yeb—and he continued to lead the hosts of Israel. There was also a well-defined type of weather-god in the land, worshipped under such names as Baal, Teshub, Hadad, or Rimmon. Yahweh was not essentially different from them, and although at first there was a tendency to worship him alongside them, we find, for example in Elijah and Hosea, the demand that he should supplant them, and be worshipped alone as the giver of rain and corn and wine and oil (Hosea ii. 8ff.). The nomads in the desert had used magical fertility practices. The Bible speaks of Ashtaroth of the flocks, and possibly the well-known story of the way in which Jacob increased his own flocks at the expense of those of his father-in-law, Laban, may show

some of the customary rites (Gen. xxx.). It would thus be
easy for the Israelites to understand and enter into the myth
and ritual of the fertility of the land and its crops. But to the
common people the worship of such a nature god did not
involve the belief that religion affected moral life. Robertson
Smith says of Semitic religion at this time: "Except when the
nation was in danger, it called for no self-denial, and rather
encouraged an easy, sluggish indulgence in the good things
that were enjoyed under the protection of the national god.
The evils that slowly sap society, the vices that at first sight
seem too private to be matters of national concern, the dis-
orders that accompany the increase and unequal distribution
of wealth, the relaxation of moral fibre produced by luxury
and sensuality, were things that religion hardly touched at all,
and that the easy indulgent god could hardly be thought to
take note of."

It was easier to take over the gods of the conquered land
than to make the transition from a nomadic form of society
to the settled life of an agricultural people. Among the nomads
men were equal; there was very little that could be called
private property, and their means of subsistence—flocks and
pastures—were held as common possessions. Such a system
could be adjusted to the cultivation of land, and we find
traces in the Old Testament of land being allotted in strips,
as among our own forbears. Whether this method was introduced by the Aryan Hyksos or by the Semitic nomads we
do not know, but probably it was the basis of the priestly
laws of Sabbatical and Jubilee years. Such common phrases
as " the measuring lines have fallen to me in pleasant places"
(Ps. xvi. 6) witness to the same practice. To a writer in the
book of Leviticus the land and the people belonged to God
(xxv. 23, 42), and could never be permanently alienated from
him by passing into private ownership ; but from the same
book we learn that the system broke down in walled cities
and within the confines of the ever-increasing property of the
great temples (xxv. 29ff.). That an effort was made to transfer
this communal form of society even to the industrial life of

towns is shown by excavations at a number of sites in Palestine. Whole towns appear to have been devoted to particular trades, such as weaving or dyeing, and all the houses were of the same size, suggesting that the inhabitants lived on a guild basis, perhaps with communal buying and selling. Evidence for this can be seen also in the biblical name of a town, Kirjath Sepharim—the town of scribes.

Not only were the new-comers in a state of transition from one form of life to another, but the social life of the land into which they came was itself in a process of disintegration. The control of the Hyksos and Egyptian empires, with a manner of government comparable to the feudal system, had passed away, leaving no effective central authority to administer justice, and " everyone did what was right in his own eyes." Judges and elders could not be trusted to give impartial justice; the powerful used their opportunity to get wealth by any means, and their oppression widened the gulf between rich and poor. The Israelites fell easily to the temptations of such a society, and were only too prone to follow such an example as that set by Queen Jezebel, when she obtained Naboth's vineyard by having him falsely accused and executed. These conditions can clearly be seen in the prophecies of Amos and Micah.

Because, as we have seen, Palestine had no natural frontiers and was on the highway of the nations, the Israelites were not left for long undisturbed by international affairs. The idea that God revealed himself through historic events was already current by the ninth century, as we have seen from the book of Judges and the Moabite stone. It was natural, therefore, for the prophets to seize upon a particular historical event as showing the working of God, and as proclaiming his message to their contemporaries. Such historic events gave rise to the activities of each of the great prophets, and where we have a story of his call this can be clearly seen.

The visions of Amos show that the land had suffered a locust plague, severe drought, and a great earthquake (iv. 6ff., vii., ix.). Military success in Trans-Jordan had given false confidence to the nation (vi. 12ff.), but Amos saw the western movement of the Urartu kingdom from Lake Van, and interpreted it as God coming to judge his people. Hosea lived when the northern kingdom was in anarchy after the death of Jeroboam II, whose reign had lifted Israel to heights of prosperity, and brought the ease and security so dangerous to religious life. Within the kingdom kings followed each other in rapid succession by murdering predecessors, but from outside came the news that Assyria had broken the power of Urartu, and irresistibly was sweeping toward the Mediterranean. This Assyrian advance appears, too, to have roused Micah to the imminence of national destruction. Isaiah, the young courtier, felt keenly the death of Uzziah who, though a leper, was a great king and warrior, and whose biography we are told Isaiah wrote (2 Chron. xxvi. 22). The death of his hero sent the prophet into the temple to gain his vision of the enthroned God, high and lifted up, whose train filled the temple and with whose glory the whole earth was full. Many of his prophecies were occasioned by particular international events, arising from the rivalry between Assyria and Egypt, or revolts within the Assyrian empire. These historical occasions for the prophetic messages make readily intelligible the emphasis placed in them on the revelation of God through historical events.

§ Its Common Content

It is not always easy to decide how much of any prophetic book contains the teaching of the prophet whose name it bears. It is generally recognized that the books contain many additions, but there is no agreement as to the extent of the additions, nor do there appear as yet to be adequate criteria by which they can be distinguished. There is a distinct type of religion in the Bible which we can recognize as " prophetic " —it is monotheistic, imageless, non-ritual, moral—and this religion is taught mainly through the prophetic books, but it is not possible to assert with confidence how much of this religion can be attributed to either the eighth- or the sixth-century prophets and how much is a later development. It is possible to discern, within all the eighth-century prophetic books, common features which spring naturally from a re-action to the background we have described, and it seems best to summarize the common content of the teaching in terms of that background.

The mingling of nomadic and Canaanite culture had given rise to a religion in which men worshipped " Nature, not the God of Nature," and found him represented by a very human and imperfect king. The prophets recognized the inadequacy of this religion, and preached a message which eventually resulted in the transformation of both the fertility rites and the king-cults.

While men took part in the fertility rites they were im-pressed by the processes of nature—growing corn, dying vegetation, fertilizing streams, or the virility of the bull. This religion had affected all man's relationship with the forces of nature, and to that extent had entered most of his daily life, even his married and family life. He expressed this by paying to God his dues: the first of his corn, wine, and oil, the firstlings of his body and of his cattle, and probably a tithe of his produce to support the sacred temple or the royal court.

But the god of nature was totally different in character from the tribal deity worshipped by nomads, who was a parent-god and part of the family circle—a god of humanity rather than of nature : a god who could be thought of as like man who had been made in his image. His worship, too, was part of daily life, but affected a man's social relationships rather than his dealings with nature. A complete antithesis between the two types of religion would be false, but, broadly speaking, in nomadic religion the human rather than the natural element predominated. The clearest example is seen in the prophetic condemnation of the fertility rites. As Professor Hempel[5] points out, the prophets continued to speak of communion with God in terms of sexual relationship, God can " seduce " a prophet, or " take him," and man must " know " God, but to the prophets the sexual relationship itself was not an impersonal expression of communion with a god of nature, nor a means of affecting great natural forces ; it was a human act which had a bearing on those who took part, and should, like other human acts, be controlled by moral laws. To the nomadic personal god also man must pay his dues. The nature worshipper had expressed his devotion by incarnating the processes of nature, and by gifts in accordance with the character of his god ; so the prophets demanded that men should express their worship by incarnating in their daily life the character of this personal God, and offering him gifts consonant with his nature. The God of justice must be worshipped by deeds of justice, the recognition of the rights of religion and of society ; the God of loving-kindness by an attitude of loving-kindness to fellow-men as well as to God. Pilgrimages to distant holy places, sacrifices of animals, offerings and ceremonies in the harvest fields, could not be regarded as an adequate expression of worship to the personal God, and we hear Hosea saying that God desires mercy and not sacrifice, an intimate relationship with himself—the knowledge of God—rather than burnt offerings. Hosea's own experience made his expression of this truth more forceful than that of the other prophets, but in Amos and Isaiah the same attitude is seen, particularly in reference to the inadequacy of the cult.

The beginning of the transformation of the king-cult was the special contribution of Isaiah. The duty of loyal obedience and humble reverence demanded of his subjects by the Davidic king was transferred to the worship of the great King. He too was holy, majestic, and unapproachable, and his worshipper must be made fit to enter his presence ; but, unlike the human king, he was righteous as well as majestic, and fitness involved clean lips and a pure heart. The Hebrew word translated "righteous" was often on Isaiah's lips, and like the word for loving-kindness used by Hosea, was a word rich in meaning ;[6] it included the recognition of rights, loyal discharge of duties within the kingdom or community, and is a social rather than a legal term. Later, because the Hebrew mind always thought in terms of the final result of an action and not of its motive or purpose, the word could be used to express the victory and peace that come from a right relationship to the community or its head, when all dues are discharged.

It is fitting that among Isaiah's prophecies should have been placed messages that speak of a complete transformation of the king-cult, by foretelling the coming of the ideal anointed king or Messiah, who shall reign in righteousness (Isa. xi.).

The thought of God as a person, rather than as a natural force, inevitably affected the prophets' attitude to social life. Their condemnation of social injustice and the oppression of the poor sprang partly from their wish to transform the cult-pattern, but also from the disintegration in their social background. Their idea of God as a righteous judge meant the transference to national life of the ethics of the smaller group. The God of the group extended his loving-kindness and care to those outside it ; God was not confined to any one particular group, and no group could be indifferent to those outside it. Within the group all were members one of another, and if one member suffered, all suffered. The group recognized responsibility for the support and protection of each member, and justice, though it was administered by the chief, was yet by common consent the concern of all, and drew its authority from the common support. Such evils as were rampant in Israel would have inevitably caused the disintegration and destruction of a small nomadic tribe, and each of the prophets saw the nation as the tribe writ large. There was no social security, no guarantee of either justice or maintenance. Wealth and power were concentrated in the hands of a few, not for the good of the community, but to be squandered in senseless and immoral luxury. There was no sense of social responsibility—the rich drinking their wine by the pailful cared not that other members of the nation perished (Amos vi.). Micah is so burningly aware that this extravagance went on at the expense of fellow-men that he speaks of it as cannibalism: "They eat the flesh of my people, and flay their skin from off them ; and they break their bones and chop them in pieces

as for the pot, and as flesh within the cauldron " (iii. 3). The
women were no better, and both Amos and Isaiah are scathing
in their condemnation of women who encourage their lords
in oppression, demanding only for themselves longer drinks
and greater pleasure (iv. 1). Isaiah's condemnation of the
daughters of Zion has a modern ring when he says, " The
daughters of Zion are haughty and walk with stretched forth
necks and wanton eyes, mincing as they walk and making a
tinkling with their feet," but in spite of their ornaments they
shall be punished and " instead of well set hair shall come
baldness " (iii.). The connections with fertility cults of many
of the feminine ornaments named by Isaiah have been made
clear from the excavations at Ras Shamra, and we learn that
even the ladies of the eighth century were neither modern
nor original.

In reaction to their social and religious environment the
prophets show themselves more clear-sighted than many
modern reformers. They could distinguish between human
failings and divine ideals, and the corruption around them only
drove them closer to their God, who hated it as much as they
did, and was trying to draw men away from it. The priests
may teach for hire, the prophets divine for money, but the
great prophet does not break with religion, nor deny God ;
he recognizes that it is God himself who is driving him on
toward reform, and so comes with a message prefaced by the
statement, " Thus saith Yahweh."

The third element which we have to consider in the prophetic message is the interpretation of historic events as acts of
God. Professor Hempel notes that the same conception of
God as God of history is found among the Aryans ; when
the Persians were lords of history they described their god,
Ahura Mazda, as Lord of History. But again the difference
made by the prophets arose from regarding God as a person.
So long as he was thought of as a natural force—storm, rain,
fertility—he was not rational but capricious. Like the wind
he blew where he listed, his anger blazed up without reason,
and man could but accept his fate or try by magic or sacrifice

to regain the favour of his god. When, however, God is thought of as the nomadic parent-God, he may at times act strangely, but he is essentially rational. There is always a reason for his wrath, and because he is the guardian of social justice and of righteousness, the reason can usually be found in some wrong human relationship or the lack of recognition of the rights of God.

How far the prophets of the eighth century went beyond the belief seen in the Moabite stone in reference to the limits of Yahweh's power, is difficult to decide. Chemosh could control the fortunes of Israel in so far as they affected Moab, and Yahweh could call Assyria or Egypt to punish his people. At the beginning and end of the book of Amos in its present form are prophecies which recognize that Yahweh is concerned with the morals of Edom and Moab, and called the Philistine as he did Israel, but there is evidence that these passages are later additions. It is obvious, however, that the inevitable outcome of the prophetic message was the transformation of the local tribal God into the universal Lord of world history. After the settlement in the land, Yahweh became the Lord of Palestine, and to Jephthah, David, or Naaman was thought of as bound to his land, but wherever the traditions of the wilderness wanderings persisted, there would be the memory that Yahweh could travel with his people, and later, when men were taken into exile or migrated into foreign lands, they might know that their God was still with them ; thus he later transcended national boundaries and was thought of as the one and only God, Lord of all history, who continually stepped out from the unseen and the eternal into the seen and temporal.

With this new idea of the rational and moral God of history went also a transformation of the beliefs concerning the end toward which God was working. Amos and Isaiah startled their contemporaries by asserting that the longed-for Day of Yahweh would not be a day of national and material prosperity, but of moral well-being, and the doom of the wicked. God's purpose was not the victory of the nation over its enemies, but the victory of goodness over evil, and even the nation might perish if it did not seek good. Amos at first believed that a national repentance would save the people from the threatening doom, but later he appears to have lost hope ; Hosea believed that the people could be led away into captivity, or into the desert, purged from their evil and restored to their land ; Isaiah preached a doctrine of a righteous remnant, that should remain as a tree that has been felled leaves a stump that can send forth new shoots.

CHAPTER 10

POLITICS AND RELIGION

§ RELIGION AS A NATIONAL AFFAIR

AFTER the reign of Solomon we hear no more of the Canaanites as distinct from the Israelites, probably because by the end
of his life Israelite new-comers and Canaanite natives had been
combined into one kingdom. A similar fusion appears to have
taken place in religion ; for in the official religions resulting
in the north and south from this fusion, institutional elements
of both Palestinian and nomadic origin had become united at
the royal chapels, provincial temples, and local high places. In
neither the racial nor the religious sphere can the fusion have
been complete ; Israelite racial exclusiveness continually arises
—we find it in Deuteronomy vii. and in Ezra ix.—just as in
religion there are revolts against Canaanite elements.

As the two kingdoms each became consolidated and unified,
this official religion took on a national character, and, though the
two kingdoms used different symbols, gradually in both it
centred round Yahweh ; through the efforts of prophets like
Elijah, rebels like Jehu and his Rechabite assistants, and the
priest Jehoiada at Jerusalem, he became the God of the land
and of the nation.

Such a statement must not, however, be taken to imply
that Yahweh was the only deity worshipped. Hosea still had
to oppose a popular belief that natural produce was the gift
of Baal ; Zephaniah in the seventh century condemned those
among the inhabitants of Jerusalem and Judah who, with their
priests, worshipped Baal and the hosts of heaven on the housetops ; Jeremiah said that Judah had as many gods as there were
cities (ii.), and gave considerable evidence of the popularity of
the worship of the Queen of Heaven (xliv.). It is probable
that, as in Assyria, where there was a strong national religion

with one paramount god, room was found for Yahweh in the myths and pantheons of local sanctuaries ; in some places the older non-Yahweh worship continued unaltered, in others an altar or temple was built to the national God, and in yet others there was assimiliation of Yahweh to the character of local deities. Amos suggests that in Samaria, Dan, and Beer-sheba, people took their oaths by local gods (ix.), and Zephaniah says that in his day men did not swear by the name of Yahweh alone, but combined it with that of other gods; from the story of Elijah we learn that an altar to Yahweh had been erected on Mount Carmel, the home of the worship of the Syrian god Baal-Zebul, but later this altar had been thrown down and allowed to fall into bad repair (1 Kings xviii.) ; Zephaniah's description of the religious customs at Jerusalem—leaping over the thresholds—and Ezekiel's condemnation of the worship in the temple at the capital, would suggest a considerable degree of religious syncretism. Despite all this, however, the as-sumption of the eighth-century prophets that Yahweh was the controller of Israel's national destinies was apparently not challenged.

These prophets brought a very different conception of the implications of national religion. They were not primarily concerned with problems of monotheism or of imageless wor-ship. The worship of the mother-goddess at Mizpah was not condemned ; Isaiah regarded the winged serpents—the sera-phim—in the holy place at Jerusalem as messengers of Yahweh (Isa. vi.), although not long afterwards the bronze serpent which was kept there, and which tradition associated with Moses, was destroyed by Hezekiah because it was an object of worship (2 Kings xviii.). To the prophets the true worship of Yahweh, the national God, was not concerned with the maintenance of the institutions of religion—its sacrifice, tithes, altars, and temples—but with the maintenance of national morality and social justice.

As we look back over the religious development we see that it is the external features of religion which demand our attention and excite controversy, but by their emphasis on

GENERAL VIEW OF HEBRON
(*American-Colony of Jerusalem*)

Ruins of the temple of Mekal at Beth-Shan
(*The Rev. C. B. Mortlock*)

MASSEBAH IN TEMPLE OF BETH-SHAN

(*From* " The Religion of Ancient-Palestine in the Light of Archaeology," *by S. A. Cook, British Academy, Oxford Press,* 1930)

conduct the prophets reached beyond all the externals and lifted religion on to a different level ; to them the national religion was concerned with the right relationship between men and God and men and their fellows. Henceforth there is a conflict between the claims of official, institutional religion and those of morality, a conflict which marked the closing period of the monarchy in Judæa. But it must be remembered that both forms of religion were equally national, and the affair of the whole community ; there was no antithesis between public and private worship, for the self-conscious individual who demanded his own private individual contact with God had not yet emerged ; it is obvious that the prophetic emphasis on the moral content of religion and the worship of a personal God would inevitably be a factor in the emergence of such an individual.

To a certain extent, of course, religion was always a private matter, as archæology has shown. Expensive votive offerings inscribed with the names of the donors, and asking for length of days, have been found in many of the early temples in Palestine, witnessing to personal religion among the wealthy ; and countless figurines and magical amulets equally prove its presence among the common people. The excavations at Lachish have shown clearly the confidence of the people in the many household gods of Egypt, who were worshipped in that city until the end of the monarchy. But, from a practical standpoint, this religion was part of the public cultus which the prophets regarded as inadequate ; moreover, the figurines of the Queen of Heaven with her doves at Lachish were of local manufacture, and presumably, like the silver shrines of Diana of the Ephesians mentioned in the New Testament, brought their revenue to the temple treasuries (Acts xix.), so that this expression of personal religion helped the maintenance of the institutions of religion.

This same mingling of personal and public religion was present also in the religion of the nomads, and when the prophets began to transform national religion by the application of principles drawn from a nomadic life, they did not

cause religious schism by urging private devotion instead of
state religion. Morals and social justice, while they were
personal virtues, were as much the concern of the community
and the nation as a whole as the old king-cult had been ; the
nation would survive only as there were national repentance
and national morality, and the prophets became champions of
national feelings by this proclamation of morality as the true
worship of the national God.

§ Influence of Foreign Domination

The fact that religion was a national affair meant that the
institutional worship of Yahweh, under the direction of the
king, was one of the means by which national unity and
independence were expressed ; while Palestine was under the
control of Egypt, Israelite religious independence had not
been interfered with ; Egypt had always been tolerant toward
the gods of other nations, because—apart from the short
period under Akhenaten—she had herself no one national god
to whom the nation owed loyalty. Native gods of conquered
peoples were identified with those already worshipped in
Egypt, and, as we have seen, successive Pharaohs built elaborate
temples in Palestine to Palestinian gods. The Assyrians were
different. A warlike people with a national god Assur, they
did not scruple to humiliate the gods of conquered nations,
either destroying their images or taking them captive to
Assyria ; so Hosea had predicted that the golden calf of Bethel
would be carried away. Assyria also appears to have demanded
that conquered peoples should recognize and worship her god.
Such a demand was not unusual, for there are many examples
in religious history of conquered peoples paying homage to the
gods of the invaders. Even foreign alliances often involved
the worship of other gods ; thus, when we are told that
Solomon and Ahab built high places for the worship of the
national gods of their wives, we are not simply dealing with
private shrines where the queens could worship, but, as is

shown by the subsequent judgement passed on Solomon by Jewish historians, with official worship of the gods of those nations with whom marriage alliances were made. A considerable measure of the success of Cyrus in his fight against Babylonia in the sixth century B.C. was due to his introduction of a policy of religious toleration, in reversal of the policy of his predecessors.

When Ahaz at Damascus paid tribute to Tiglath-pileser the Assyrian monarch, he sent back to Jerusalem instructions that a new altar should be built according to a pattern seen at Damascus, and on his return to his capital he offered sacrifices on it (2 Kings xvi.). In spite of the writer in the book of Chronicles (2 Chron. xxviii.), it seems likely that this was an act of homage to Assyrian gods. When Hezekiah felt strong enough to revolt against his Assyrian overlord, he purged the land and the temple of the altars and the religious emblems which witnessed to political submission. His successor Manasseh, in his loyalty to the Assyrians, reintroduced the forms of Assyrian worship, and when later his grandson Josiah was able finally to throw off the yoke of the Assyrian empire, which had then become decadent, his political revolt involved a considerable religious upheaval in Judah and Jerusalem.

This close connection between politics and religion must always be borne in mind when we read in the books of Kings and Chronicles of religious reforms credited to such monarchs as Hezekiah and Josiah, or of the apostasy of Ahaz and Manasseh. The contemporary prophets give us no hint that great religious changes were taking place, and we must judge the historical books by the evidence from the prophets. The fact that the two so-called "bad" kings remained loyal subjects of the Assyrians, while the "good" kings were rebels, suggests that their actions were political rather than religious in motive, and that they were primarily concerned, not to produce a pure worship of Yahweh, but to assert national independence; they did not aim at an imageless monotheism or a worship cleansed of syncretism, but at removing all evidence of foreign

religious domination and sweeping away all foreign rivals to
the national God.

This applies particularly to the account of the reform in
621 B.C. attributed to Josiah. The story given in 2 Kings xxii.f.
—with which the parallel account in Chronicles should be
compared—has been regarded as a landmark in the religious
history of Judah. To it have been traced the centralization of
worship at the one sanctuary at Jerusalem, and the production
of a pure imageless worship purged of syncretism and sex in
accordance with the requirements of the book of Deuteronomy.
But when we remember that the account comes from the
hands of Deuteronomic writers, who wished to imply that
the Deuteronomic code was put into operation at that time,
and also when we recognize that the basis of the story is an
account of the political activity of Josiah, it is easier to understand why the later writer in the book of Chronicles did not
accept the story in Kings as a completely accurate historical
statement of the facts. The truth seems to be that Josiah's
revolt coincided with the fall of the oppressing empire, and
some elements of his "reform" were permanent, for the
Assyrians were not able to reassert their supremacy and that
of their god ; in consequence the Deuteronomic writers dated
from Josiah's reign the beginning of the reforms which later
were crystallized into the Deuteronomic code. The contemporary prophet Jeremiah mentions only the break from the
worship of the Queen of Heaven—a reform to which the people
attributed all their misfortunes and from which they went back
as soon as they had the opportunity : "We will certainly
perform every word that is gone forth out of our mouth, to
burn incense unto the queen of heaven, to pour out drink
offerings to her, as we have done, we and our fathers, our
kings and our princes, in the cities of Judah and in the streets
of Jerusalem : for then had we plenty of victuals, and were
well and saw no evil. But since we left off to burn incense
to the queen of heaven, and to pour out drink offerings to her,
we have wanted all things, and have been consumed by the
sword and by the famine " (xliv.).

§ THE POLITICAL ACTIVITIES OF ISAIAH AND JEREMIAH

It has been said that compromise is the essence of politics, but has no place in morals ; such a statement strikes at the root of the problem that faced Isaiah and Jeremiah in their attempt to work out in practice the significance of the new moral conception of national religion ; and it is interesting to see how these two great prophets in successive ages and in different ways proclaimed that religion was not the handmaid of politics.

Isaiah entered politics when he met Ahaz—at Yahweh's command—by the pool outside Jerusalem, and bade him not fear the threatened invasion by the kings of Syria and Israel, who were trying to force him to join in a general revolt against Assyria (Isa. vii.). Ahaz wished to call in the aid and protection of Assyria against the conspirators, but Isaiah told him to put his trust in God, not in political intrigues : " If you do not believe you shall not be established." Isaiah was asserting the power and majesty of the national God, Yahweh the Holy One of Israel, who could deliver his people without the help of foreign alliances. There were many things in the religion of the time which later reformers attacked, but Isaiah accepted them without any condemnation ; stone pillars, asherah, ephod, teraphim, and even the official soothsayers could remain part of Yahweh worship, but strenuously he opposed the introduction of foreign religious usages and incantations addressed to foreign deities, which would inevitably result from foreign alliances.

Ahaz did not heed his advice, but when the next king Hezekiah was being drawn into revolt against Assyria and was leaning towards alliance with Egypt, Isaiah preached the same message : " The Egyptians are men and not gods ; their horses are flesh and not spirit. When Yahweh shall stretch forth his hand both he that helpeth and he that is helped shall fall together " (xxxi.). At first Hezekiah listened, but later he joined the revolt against Assyria and signalized it by a religious revolution against the forms of worship introduced by Ahaz ; the altars which the Chronicler tells us Ahaz had built in every corner of Jerusalem, and the high places he had built in every city, were overthrown. It is of interest that the Rabshakeh— the Assyrian officer who was sent by Sennacherib to demand the surrender of Jerusalem—represented these destroyed altars as part of the worship of the national God Yahweh. Perhaps propaganda is not a new weapon in warfare ! In complete contrast to the vacillating king, Isaiah taught that national policy should be based on trust in the national God. He carried the doctrine to such an extent that, when the hordes of Sennacherib were at the gate of Jerusalem and the foreign mercenaries recruited for the defence of the city had deserted, he proclaimed that Yahweh would defend the city for his own sake, and the astounding fulfilment of his prophecy gave rise to the later belief that, whatever the people did, Jerusalem and its temple could never be captured, because Yahweh dwelt therein. Jeremiah had to combat the confidence produced by this belief, and when Jesus and Stephen were put to death part of the accusation against them was that they stated that God would destroy the temple. Isaiah said that the defence of the city would enable God to preserve the national religion, by saving a remnant in which that religion would live on, and this belief too, worked out in the later doctrine that God has a chosen few elected to salvation, had considerable influence on the development of religion.

Jeremiah approached the problem from an entirely different angle.[1] He too hated foreign worship, the forsaking of Yahweh and the building of countless altars to innumerable gods, but, believing as he did that God was using the Babylonians to punish Judah's sins, he advised submission. He prophesied that Jerusalem would be destroyed (vii.), that Yahweh would sweep away the temple where he had caused his name to dwell, and that sacrifice and all the externals of institutional religion would disappear ; but to him this did not matter. In fact, such religion had never been required by Yahweh, and its destruction would make way for the true worship, which would be preserved, not in the institutional religion of even a righteous remnant, but in the individual hearts of his people : " This is the covenant that I will make with the house of Israel ; after those days saith Yahweh, I will put my law in their inward parts, and write it on their hearts ; and will be their God, and they shall be my people. And they shall teach no more every man his neighbour, and every man his brother, saying Know Yahweh ; for they shall all know me, from the least of them even unto the greatest of them, saith Yahweh, for I will forgive their iniquities, and I will remember their sin no more " (xxxi. 31f.).

More than any other of the prophets he left a record of the struggles of his own spirit with the God whose words burnt like a fire within his bones (xx. 9), and in consequence he has become supremely the prophet of individualism in religion. His " New Covenant " was introduced by a repudiation of the old proverb, " The fathers have eaten a sour grape and the children's teeth are set on edge," and the assertion that " everyone shall die for his own iniquity ; everyone that eateth the sour grape, his teeth shall be set on edge " (xxxi. 29) ; from the intensity of his own communion with God he was made to believe that religion was essentially a private affair —a relationship between an individual man and the personal God. Israel would still remain " the people of Yahweh " and " the house of Israel," though all external forms of worship had perished and the nation had lost independence or even its entity, because in the hearts of individual Israelites existed the covenant with their God. Jeremiah's belief in the place of the individual in religion was, like Isaiah's message of the localized God and the righteous remnant, a necessary stage in the development of religion, but it must be differentiated from the later use of the belief in an undue emphasis on the value of the individual as apart from the community.

It is interesting to compare the reaction of Jeremiah to the political situation with that of Habakkuk, who probably prophesied about the same time. He too believed that God

was punishing Judah's sins by sending against her the Babylonians, but when every fresh victory brought new evidence
of the cruelty and wickedness of the conqueror, he found it
difficult to understand that the God " who was of purer eyes
than to behold evil, and could not look on iniquity " (i. 13)
had used such a ruthless nation to accomplish his holy purposes ;
these methods surely brought more evil than they punished.
Bidden by God to get away alone, he was given a longer
view into the future, and saw that, though God used such
means, when his agents overstepped his limit and showed their
overbearing pride and the evil of their nature, they were
revealing the presence within themselves of the germ of
inevitable destruction ; the empire they had founded on
violence and bloodshed would certainly fall to pieces, as a
house in which the stones cried out against the walls, and the
joints against the beams (ii. 11). This long view made possible
the sublime height of the faith enshrined in the poem which
now concludes the book of Habakkuk, and which offers
perhaps the most complete answer to the political problems
of Isaiah and Jeremiah : " Although the fig tree shall not
blossom, neither shall fruit be in the vines ; the labour of the
olive shall fail, and the fields shall yield no food ; the flocks
shall be cut off from the fold and there shall be no herd in the
stalls : yet I will rejoice in Yahweh, I will joy in the God of my
salvation " (iii. 17f.).

§ Religious Conditions in Palestine at the close of the Monarchy

It is not easy to describe briefly the stage of religious
development reached by the southern kingdom in 586 B.C.,
when the country was devastated by the Babylonians under
Nebuchadrezzar. The evidence within the historical books is
conflicting and is not supported by that from the contemporary
prophetic writings.

From the book of Kings (xxii.f.) we learn that although

Josiah died young he was a good king, and carried through an epoch-making reform in 621 B.C. on the basis of " the book of the law " discovered during renovations in the temple at Jerusalem.[2] The judgement passed in the book of Kings on the sons and grandson of Josiah, who succeeded him as kings of Judah, ignores this good reputation and condemns them for doing " that which was evil in the sight of the Lord according to all that their fathers had done " (xxiii. 32, 37), and it is usually assumed that, because the early death of Josiah discredited his reforms, subsequent kings reverted to the pre-reformation practices. This assumption may account for the picture of religious life in this period given by the three prophets Zephaniah, Jeremiah, and Ezekiel ; but the fact that these prophets do not mention the reform, and that Jeremiah in his estimate of the character of Josiah does not credit him with any attempt to purify religion, but praises him only for his general integrity (xxii. 15f.), raises doubts as to the historicity of the story of the reform in the book of Kings ; the basis of the story may have been a political rather than a purely religious act.

These doubts are further strengthened by a comparison of the account in 2 Kings xxii.f. with that in 2 Chronicles xxxiv. In the former all the reforms took place in the eighteenth year of the reign of the king, in the latter they are spread over a period of eighteen years : on his accession at eight years old the king began to seek after the God of David, in the twelfth year of his reign he carried out the great reform, and finally in the eighteenth year the book was found, a covenant was made, and a great passover was celebrated at Jerusalem in a new way. The account in Kings of the reforms of 621 B.C. has much in common with that of Chronicles for 627 B.C., but it is fuller, and is marked by a particularly antagonistic attitude to Bethel which is wholly absent from Chronicles. This attitude to Bethel may possibly indicate that the account in its present form comes from the time after Haggai and Zechariah at the close of the exile, when the opposition between Bethel and Jerusalem became explicit ; but the story of the reform shows, at least, something of the opinion of a later writer as to the state of religion in Palestine in 621 B.C.

An interesting sidelight is thrown by the names of temple officials at this time.[3]   Huldah the prophetess has a name that means weasel or mole, Achbor and Shaphan, the names of the scribes, mean respectively mouse and rock-badger or coney—all three are animals which in a late addition to the Pentateuch are classed as unclean.   In the contemporary letters found by Starkey at Lachish we find, too, Hagab (or Locust) as a Jewish name.   Robertson Smith regards the names as evidence that at this epoch, when the national religion had completely broken down, " all manners of strange sacrifices of unclean animals began to become popular and were deemed to have a peculiar purifying and consecrating power."   Professor Cook rightly says that these animal-names do not in themselves necessarily imply totemism or any systematized animal-cult, but we have already noticed that Ezekiel gives evidence for such cults in the temple at Jerusalem at this time (viii.), and from Isaiah lxv. and lxvi. we know that such worship survived in this district until after the exile.   It is usually assumed that such practices were a revival of old superstitions due to the activity of Manasseh, but it seems more probable that they had always been part of the temple worship, and were first condemned by Ezekiel, who himself accepted the cherubim images as Isaiah had accepted the seraphim.   Perhaps the process of reform was very much slower than we realize, for there were family names in post-exilic Judah which mean " flea " (Parosh, Ezra ii. 3) and " swine " (Hezir, 1 Chron. xxiv. 15, Neh. x. 21).

The Deuteronomic writer in his story of Josiah's iconoclastic acts gives us a further picture of the temple worship, much of it connected with Assyrian worship.   In the temple there was room for the cult of Baal and Asherah and of the heavenly bodies, as well as for the male and female prostitutes who were part of the ancient fertility worship.   There were altars on the roofs of the royal buildings, and the horses and chariot of the sun-god were kept at the entry of the temple ; in the valley south of the city was the hearth where children were burned ; on the Mount of Olives were altars and high places erected by Solomon to his wives' gods—probably the place where, the book of Samuel mentions, David was wont to worship. Throughout Judah and Jerusalem were high places with officiating priests, and at the gate of Jerusalem stood the shrine to the worship of the Satyrs, condemned in the book of Leviticus (xvii. 7), but later continued in another form in the post-exilic ceremony of sending out the goat of Azazel.

This same state of affairs is reflected in the prophetic writings. Zephaniah, whose prophecy is difficult to date accurately, knows nothing of a reform and condemns both civil and religious leaders. Baal is still worshipped, and the hosts of heaven from altars on the housetops, as centuries before at Ras Shamra ; there is syncretism of Yahwism and king-cult (i. 5–9) ; the leaping over the threshold which elsewhere in the Bible is connected with the worship of Dagon (1 Sam. v. 5); and the prophet speaks of prophets as reckless and treacherous, and priests as profaning both temple and law.

Jeremiah's condemnations (ii.) show the same conditions. Priests, prophets, and rulers are corrupt; foreign gods replace the " glory " of Israel and are as numerous as the cities of Judah ; worship still takes place on the high hills and under green trees as in the days of Hosea, and altars are as many as streets in the capital. Men bow down to images of stone and wood, and worship the Queen of Heaven. With all the force of the eighth-century prophets he asserts that frankincense from Sheba and the sweet-smelling cane from the far country, burnt offerings and sacrifices, are to no purpose, so long as worshippers heed not the words of Yahweh. In the famous temple sermon of chapter vii. (*cf.* xxvi.), which nearly cost him his life, he rejected the belief that the temple was inviolable and predicted its destruction. More important still, he denied that God had ever demanded either sacrifices or the burning of children, but the emphatic way in which the denial is made and his later statement that " the false pen of the scribes hath wrought lies " (viii. 8) suggest that at this time claims were

being made that the written sacrificial code at Jerusalem was
the law of Yahweh. In opposition to this claim Jeremiah
proclaimed throughout the cities of Judah and the streets of
Jerusalem that the basis of the old covenant—the distinctive
mark of the national religion—was, "Hearken unto my voice,
and I will be your God, and ye shall be my people : and walk
ye in all the way that I command you." It was because this
old covenant had been broken by the worship of other gods
and by immorality and social unrighteousness that God had
to make a new covenant, which would require neither priest
nor prophet but would be written on men's hearts (xxxi.).

If Ezekiel's prophecy can be dated in this period it too
corroborates the other evidence. There is the same condemnation of worship on high hills and under shady oaks ; images
of silver and gold form part of the cult (vi.) ; magic practices
by which souls were hunted and slain with pillows and ker-
chiefs are common among the women (xiii. 18ff.). The phrase
used by Hosea—" go awhoring after your idols "—is used by
Ezekiel, there are references to fertility cults, and he accepts
the custom of burning children as a law given by Yahweh.
Chapter xviii. reveals how closely physical taboos, as well as
morals, were connected with religion, and there is an emphasis,
unknown to Jeremiah or the earlier prophets, on the necessity
of keeping the Sabbaths.

The clearest statement of the religious practices in the
temple at Jerusalem is contained in Ezekiel viii. An image—
male or female we cannot tell—stands in the inner court ;
inside the building seventy elders led by Shaphan's son burn
incense to paintings or images of " every form of creeping
thing and abominable beasts, and all the idols of the house of
Israel " ; the women weep there for Tammuz, and men
worship the sun. The lofty conception of a pure imageless
monotheism found in the post-exilic religion did not exist in
pre-exilic Palestine except in germ. The personal religion of
Jeremiah the prophet and the reforming zeal of the priestly
Ezekiel were leading men toward this goal, but it was not
until some of the nation had walked in the fiery furnace of the

exile, and the remainder had lived among the ruined monu-
ments of their religious institutions, that she found the faith
which has stood the test of two and a half millennia.

One other piece of evidence from these two prophets,
Jeremiah (iii. 6) and Ezekiel (xxiv.), should be mentioned.
Both prophets use figures of speech that represent Yahweh as
having two consorts, as being married to two sisters, Judah
and Samaria. The law in Leviticus xviii. definitely forbids this
marriage relationship, but, more important still, this representation, which seems to us so strange on the lips of real mono-
theists worshipping the lofty holy Yahweh, links the religious
conceptions of the period with the religion of the Jewish
community at Yeb as revealed in the Elephantine papyri of
the fifth century B.C. There a group of Jews, who regarded
themselves as thoroughly orthodox and deserving of help from
their co-religionists at Jerusalem and Samaria, shared their
temple dues between Yahweh and two female deities. When
their temple had been destroyed by Egyptian rioters they sent
letters to Palestine asking for assistance in rebuilding it.
Samaria sent them help. The Jews at Jerusalem, some of whom
had returned from the exile, at first ignored their letters.
Later, however, we find a Jewish envoy at Yeb attempting
to alter the religion there to bring it into conformity with the
reformed practices at Jerusalem.

BOOK IV
REFORMATION AND REACTION

CHAPTER II

THE REFORM IN PALESTINE

§ PALESTINE IN THE EARLY PART OF THE EXILE

EXCAVATIONS at numerous sites show that Nebuchadrezzar's two invasions of Palestine in 597 and 586 B.C. left the southern kingdom devastated, but had little effect on the north. Lachish, for example, was destroyed by fire on both occasions, and there are many sites which were never again inhabited except by Arab squatters. But even just over the border into the northern kingdom at Bethel there was no devastation, and Professor Albright in his account of his excavations there [1] shows that it was not destroyed for some years, until well into the Persian period. Jerusalem escaped the first destruction, but Jeremiah tells us that all the best people were taken away or killed, and that only the " bad figs " remained (xxiv.). In the second invasion eleven years later it was thoroughly and completely razed to the ground. The numbers of those who were taken captive varies in the different biblical accounts. The figures given in the book of Jeremiah (lii.) suggest that it was a very small proportion of the population ; but modern warfare has taught us that with a ruthless and unscrupulous foe the number of captives is little indication of the extent of casualties. Many Judæans would flee into the desert and the hills, where Babylonian forces could not pursue them, and gradually they would make their way back to their home-steads and farms when the deluge had passed. But the fact that cities remained uninhabited suggests that the destruction of property and life was considerable, for usually within a comparatively short time they were rebuilt with old material pulled out from the still smoking ruins. Nebuchadrezzar had evidently decided that he must prevent the possibility of any further revolt from the rebellious city and her treacherous king. Another fact which suggests thorough destruction is that the capital of Judæa was moved northward to Mizpah (Jer. xl. 8), just south of Bethel, a circumstance that led to closer contact between the remnants of the northern and southern kingdoms during the exile.

Following upon this devastation and depopulation of the south, there came a movement of neighbouring peoples into the despoiled land. We know from the southern names in the genealogies in the book of Chronicles (1 Chron. ii., iv.) and from the hatred that grew up during the exile, that Edomites pressed in from the south—driven by the advance of Nabatæan Arabs who forced them out of their rock capital at Petra. Ezekiel speaks of Edom saying to Israel and Judah, " These two nations and these two countries are mine and we will possess it," and he adds, " but Yahweh was there " (xxxv. 10, xxxiii. 24). The book of Jubilees (xxxviii. 8) contains evidence that a tomb dedicated to the memory of Esau, the father of the Edomites, was built, or perhaps rebuilt, near Hebron. Other invaders from the coastlands, Philistines and Phœnicians, also moved in like vultures swarming in to devour prey. Unlike Sargon with the northern kingdom after 722 B.C., Nebuchadrezzar made no transference of population into Judah, which would have had a stabilizing effect ; but on the other hand the propagandist view of the post-exilic Judæan writings that the country was a complete blank for the seventy years after the destruction of the temple is not true. Life went on, in spite of the devastation, for the mixed population made up of incoming invaders and native peasantry which there, as everywhere, survived the Babylonian invasion.

Casual hints left by biblical writers enable us to reconstruct in part the religious condition in Judæa at this time. The temple in Jerusalem was completely destroyed, the priests who had not fled were either killed or taken into exile, and the

high priest was killed at Riblah. There is considerable difference of opinion as to what happened at Jerusalem. The
majority of scholars believe that there was no break in the
continuity of religious life there ; though the temple had
been destroyed, the rock altar remained, and sacrifice and
worship would still take place there. This opinion is based
partly on Jeremiah's story of the eighty men from the three
northern sanctuaries who came south bringing gifts for " the
house of Yahweh " after 586 B.C. (xli.) ; but the fact that they
turned aside to the new capital at Mizpah, and were murdered
by a man who wished to restore the Davidic line and the old
order at Jerusalem, suggests that they acquiesced in the new
order and went to Mizpah to discover where the new house
of Yahweh was to be. Moreover, in 520 B.C., when Joshua
and Zerubbabel wished to offer sacrifices at Jerusalem, they had
first to rebuild the altar (Ezra iii.). Jeremiah had predicted
that Jerusalem, like Shiloh, would be destroyed and cease to
be Yahweh's chosen dwelling place (vii.), and that the prophecy
was generally accepted and remembered is seen by Zechariah's
prophecy that although God had fulfilled the threat made
through Jeremiah, now the prophecy had been reversed, and
Yahweh would dwell in Zion and would yet again choose
Jerusalem (i. 17, ii. 12). Ezekiel painted a graphic picture of
the abuses in the temple itself before its destruction ; religious
people would believe that it lay under the curse of God, and thus
it might remain unused and in ruins for many years. The
religious as well as the political centre moved away, the political
centre, as we know, to Mizpah. The nearest ancient holy place,
which excavation shows was not destroyed at that time, was
Bethel, where, as we learn even from our present Old Testament, which has come from the hands of men who appear to
have been bitter opponents of Bethel and its religious prestige,
Yahweh worship was traced back to the patriarchs. Abraham
and Jacob had both met Yahweh and built altars there. Bethel
had been the great rival of Jerusalem from the days of Jeroboam I, and the official centre of Yahweh worship under the
Assyrians. Although the southern writers urged that the

Silver gods from the temple at Ras Shamra,
wearing gold necklaces and gold aprons.
The taller is about 11 inches high

(*Prof. C. Schaeffer*)

Romans carrying the seven-branched golden candlestick, part of the spoil from Jerusalem (bas-relief on the Arch of Titus, Rome) *(From a photograph)*

religion there was corrupt, we know from 2 Kings xvii. 41 that they admitted that the God worshipped there was Yahweh. Further we learn—again quite incidentally from Zechariah vii.—that it was at Bethel that fasts to commemorate the fate of Jerusalem, and probably the murder of Gedaliah, were held from 586 to 518 B.C., until the temple again became the religious centre of Palestine. It seems likely that those who escaped from Jerusalem fled to Bethel, and that a form of religion grew up there which was a compromise between the north and the south, between the religious usages at Bethel and at Jerusalem. At neither had the religion been monotheistic, nor a pure imageless worship.

It must be emphasized again that there is little evidence of enmity between the north and south during the last days of the monarchy and the early part of the exile. No one reading Jeremiah and Ezekiel would suspect the continuance of the old enmity. The prophets speak of them as sister kingdoms, of which the north, Samaria, has proved herself more righteous than the south. Ezekiel binds the two together with the symbolic act of tying together two sticks and prophesying that they shall be one nation (xxxvii.). At Mizpah and Bethel, at least during the five years before Gedaliah's death in 581 B.C., the remains of the age-long enmity were broken down, and just as a hundred and fifty years earlier a home had been found in Jerusalem for refugees from the devastated north, so now fugitives from the south were welcomed at Bethel and in its neighbourhood—though so near to Jerusalem, yet cut off from it by hills and valleys which helped to save it from that city's fate.

§ THE INFLUENCE OF JEREMIAH

During those five years from 586 to 581 B.C., as in the years preceding 586, the strongest religious force in Palestine was the aged prophet Jeremiah. Judged by the standards of his own time, he had been proved to be inspired by God, and a true prophet, because his predictions had at last come true, and the disaster he had so long foretold had fallen. As we have seen, he protested against the worship of other gods as well as against the immorality of the nation ; his fight against syncretistic worship had made him swing to the opposite extreme of condemning all the external forms of religious cult and the sacrificial rites in clear and unmistakable language, saying that God had never commanded the sacrifice of either animals or children. He had poured scorn on the ark, which was regarded as the throne of Yahweh (iii. 16), and on the temple as the guarantee of his presence, and he foresaw the time, like Jesus six hundred years later, when all these material symbols of the presence of God would have been swept away (John iv.). Then there would be no need for man-made legal codes, for the covenant would be written on the hearts of men ; no need for priests to tell men about God, for all would know him ; no need for animal sacrifices, for God would have forgiven men their sins.

It is almost impossible to realize the enormous shock such teaching would be to the majority of the people who listened. We learn something of the effect of the great temple sermon. Priests, prophets, and people all said, " Thou shalt surely die," and brought Jeremiah before the princes for judgement. An earlier prophet Uriah had been brought back from Egypt and slain for a similar offence, but Jeremiah was saved by the intervention of some of the influential elders and the recognition that he had spoken in the name of Yahweh. The inviolability of the temple had been proclaimed by a previous great Jerusalem prophet, and no enemy had been able to shoot his arrows into the city because Yahweh dwelt there. He sat enthroned between the cherubim, and his presence made the city unassailable. For centuries the sacrificial system had been regarded as the divinely appointed means by which the covenant between God and his people was renewed, and sins were wiped away. Prophet and priest had been given a unique place as revealers of the will of God, and without them it was thought that it was impossible to please him. But, in spite of the incredulity of the people, events had proved Jeremiah right,[2] and at Jerusalem temple, sacrifice, and priests had been swept away. Ezekiel had to explain the catastrophe by saying that Yahweh went out of the temple before its destruction and left it to its fate (xi. 23). He gives us a vivid picture of the chariot borne by cherubim, the spirits of the wind, and fitted with " wheels within wheels " to allow it to turn in any direction without a shadow caused by turning ; Yahweh had come out of the eastern end of the temple, entered his chariot and moved across the Kidron valley to the Mount of Olives, and thence, after watching the fall of his city, had moved forward again to accompany his exiled people to Babylonia. The fact that such a picture could be drawn, and that it was needed, shows how firm a hold the belief that God was localized at Jerusalem had on the people, how far they had moved from the earlier idea of the nomadic God, and how long a distance they still had to travel before they could reach the idea of Stephen that " the Most High dwelleth not in temples made with man's hands " (Acts vii. 48f., cf. Isa. lxvi. 1f.).

Unlike Jesus, Jeremiah survived the national disaster he foresaw, and when the Babylonian captain gave him the choice of accompanying the exiles or remaining with the remnant in Palestine, he elected to remain with Gedaliah, the Jewish noble whom the Babylonians made Governor, and to attempt to rebuild national life, prosperity, and religion from the ruins of the past. We should like to know how much of the book of Jeremiah contains his teaching during this reconstructive period between 586 and the murder of Gedaliah five years later, and how his great influence was used. Did he find that a pure spiritual religion of the heart without institutions or symbols, or the use of any external aids, was not practicable ? It seems possible that to this period belongs the proclamation of the new covenant in chapters xxx. and xxxi., and that just as years before he had been bidden by God to proclaim throughout the cities of Judah and the streets of Jerusalem the old covenant (vii. 22ff., xi. 14ff.), in opposition to the priestly torah which demanded sacrifices as part of God's requirements (vii. 21f., viii. 8), so now he passed through the land with God's message of comfort and hope. One incident can certainly be dated just after the murder of Gedaliah by the royal Davidic prince, Ishmael : the panic-stricken leaders, fearful of the vengeance of the Babylonian king for this further act of rebellion against authority, came to the prophet for guidance (xlii.). With words that suggest confidence in the prophet and trust in Yahweh, they promised to do " according to all things which Yahweh shall send thee to us, whether it be good or evil, we will obey the voice of Yahweh, our God, to whom we send thee." Ten days passed before the prophet could obtain an answer from God. When at last the advice came that they should remain in Palestine and have confidence in Yahweh, there is little wonder that they did not take it ; the long anxious wait had made them doubt whether the God who had not been able to save his temple and could not, or would not, answer them in their need, was able to save them from the wrath of Nebuchadrezzar. The delay made them believe that the answer was the result of political intrigue, and not the guidance of God ; preparations were made for the flight to Egypt, and we see them taking with them many of those who had tried to help in the rebuilding of the ruined land, including the prophet himself, and like their patriarchal forbears, seeking the comparative security of Egypt.

Finally we see Jeremiah laying the base for a throne to be set up by Nebuchadrezzar in Egypt when he conquered also that place of refuge ; by this symbolic act he was preparing the way for the Babylonian invasion and the final destruction of the remnant from Judah, which had forsaken its land and its God (xliii. 8ff.). His condemnation is boldly answered by the women refugees, who declare that all the misfortunes have come, not through the just wrath of Yahweh, but because they and their husbands have recently abandoned the worship of the mother-goddess, the Queen of Heaven. These people had learned nothing from the teaching of the prophet, who disappears from view reaffirming his message of the impending divine punishment.

His influence did not, however, end in this scene of utter

failure and disappointment, a tragedy hardly less black than the cross on Calvary. A real spiritual religion lived on in the hearts of those who had accepted his teaching, and who became exponents of that prophetic religion which has left its mark indelibly on so much of the Old Testament literature. Such men were the forerunners of the synagogue worship which enabled Judaism to survive when at last the temple was destroyed by the Romans, the sacrificial system ceased, and the nation was dispersed. It is possible that the apathy toward the temple and its cult, deplored by Haggai (i.) and Malachi (iii. 8ff.), was partly the result of Jeremiah's teaching. The men who said that it was no time to spend money on a temple building, may have been men who believed that such a building was not essential to their religious life. Haggai had to teach them that bad crops and lack of prosperity were due to the fact that the House of God lay in ruins ; Malachi said that the arrears of tithes were heaped up outside the windows of heaven, and prevented God from opening the windows and pouring out his blessing.

Perhaps the greatest monument to the influence of the prophet survived in the moral and spiritual teaching which was combined with priestly religion in the Deuteronomic school of writers, who attempted to do for the southern kingdom, and indeed for the whole of the Israelite nation, what the Yahweh priest sent back to Bethel by the Assyrians did for the northern kingdom after 722 B.C. That priest had returned to " teach the customs of the God of the land," and how man should worship Yahweh. Naturally he would collect in written form the religious laws and ritual of the northern kingdom, and the traditions which, gathering around the various sanctuaries and pilgrim centres, justified those religious usages. Similarly the Deuteronomists collected national and religious traditions which were in danger of perishing with the destruction of the shrines and people of Judah and Jerusalem. Probably these writers were responsible for the first connected history of Israel, and, especially if it were written at Bethel, we can understand why the stories of the founders of the local northern shrines were made part of the history, probably for the first time. To Jeremiah the national history began at the exodus from Egypt, Ezekiel mentions Abraham only in a hostile reference to the people who remained in Palestine after 597 B.C. (xxxiii. 24), and none of the patriarchal names occur in the records of the fifth-century Jewish community at Yeb in Egypt. In the book of Deuteronomy, probably the first work of this Deuteronomic school, only the names of Abraham, Isaac, and Jacob occur, and then simply in a later stratum and in reference to the oath of Yahweh to give them the land ; the book itself shows no knowledge of any other connection of the patriarchs with Palestine, and all the places of worship in the land are spoken of as heathen and to be destroyed (xii.).

The Deuteronomic history is based on the prophetic teaching of the connection of God with history. Its aim is not to present an accurate account of the nation's past, but to show the presence of the guiding, controlling hand of Yahweh, and, as Peter's first sermon in the Acts of the Apostles (ii.) aimed at justifying the cross of Jesus as part of God's foreordained purpose, so the Deuteronomic writers wanted to justify the fact of the Babylonian destruction of the southern kingdom. They showed that the true explanation of the tragedy was given by Jeremiah, and not by the women refugees in Egypt ; they traced the connection between sin and defeat, the way in which the nation had been handed over to the enemy for punishment, and, when it repented, had been delivered ; they made clear that Shiloh and Jerusalem, where Yahweh had dwelt and his temples had been built, moved inevitably to ruin because of their character, like the hero of a Shakespearean tragedy.

Our information about the compiler of the first Deuteronomic law book, and about the successive writers who supplemented his work, has to be gathered from the writings themselves, but the intimate knowledge of Egypt revealed by such references as that in chapter xi. suggests that the compiler, or one of the writers, was a man who had visited that country ;

he may well have been one of those who were carried down with Jeremiah, and belonged to the "small number that escaped from the sword to return out of the land of Egypt to the land of Judah"; possibly, we may conjecture, Baruch the son of Neriah, Jeremiah's secretary.

§ THE DEUTERONOMIC COMPROMISE

The Babylonian deluge had swept the country; the temple was destroyed, and its priestly hierarchy taken captive; and there existed a unique opportunity to reconstruct the religious life of the community on a new basis, which would have been utterly impossible while a strong priesthood at the royal sanctuary at Jerusalem, as well as at the many holy cities in the southern kingdom, was ready to defend its ancient privileges and vested interests. Drastic innovations which would have been injudicious at other times could be successfully introduced when the old order had passed away. The reformers offered a religion which could be accepted by the whole community, and the book of Deuteronomy reflects the drawing together of the remnants of the two kingdoms which from the days of Solomon had fought each other : the compromise between the two forms of religion which we have seen developing— institutional religion, and the moral spiritual religion of the prophets which culminated in Jeremiah; and finally an attempt to rationalize and purify both these forms of religion. It represents one of the most fascinating efforts towards religious reunion to be found either in the Bible or outside it. It marks an epoch in religion; it crystallized and preserved much of the prophetic teaching, which might otherwise have perished; and its spiritual and literary influence lasted for many centuries, bearing fruit again in the first century A.D. in the teaching of Jesus.

Nine of the ten commandments contained in the fifth chapter of Deuteronomy, and their exposition in the following chapters, might fairly be regarded as an adequate summary of prophetic religion, but there is no reason to believe that even so late as Jeremiah the prophets would have included the tenth—Sabbath observance—as a commandment of God, for it is mentioned only in one passage in Jeremiah (xvii. 21ff.) which on other grounds is regarded as a later addition; and the law is not again referred to in Deuteronomy. When we compare the other nine with the more priestly decalogue in Exodus xxxiv. it becomes clear that the decalogue in Deuteronomy shows the influence of prophetic ideals and teaching. God's three first demands from his people are not ritual observances, but that he alone shall be worshipped, without images, in spirit and in truth ; and then that man shall love his neighbour as himself. Failure in all these three requirements was condemned by Jeremiah in his temple sermon : "Will ye steal, murder, and commit adultery, and swear falsely, and burn incense unto Baal, and walk after other gods whom ye know not ? "

Not only is the moral teaching of the prophets prominent, but their demand for social justice is expressed in the many humanitarian laws in the book which consider the poor and unprotected—again to quote Jeremiah's famous sermon : "If ye thoroughly execute judgement between a man and his neighbour; if ye oppress not the stranger, the fatherless, and the widow, and shed not innocent blood in this place, then will I cause you to dwell in the land." The summary of God's requirements in Micah vi. is echoed in the words of the law book, " And now Israel, what doth the Lord thy God require of thee but to walk in all his ways and to love him and to serve him with all thy heart and with all thy soul, and to keep the commandments of the Lord " (Deut. x. 12), but the prophetic picture of the personal moral God has been enriched by Hosea's message of the loving God, and Jeremiah's experience of the possibility of individual response to the love of God. Though the God of Deuteronomy is a jealous God, yet he is near to men, and his law is not hidden from them, nor hard to fulfil, but, like the new covenant proclaimed by Jeremiah, " is very nigh unto thee, in thy mouth, and in thy heart, that thou mayest do it " (xxx. 11ff.).

The institutional side of religion is represented as clearly as the prophetic, but in its simplest and most rational form. Two main principles can be seen at work : centralization and purification.[3]

The repeated emphasis on " the place which the Lord thy God shall choose out of all thy tribes to set his name there," makes it clear that in future the little community was to unite for some of its worship at one central sanctuary, now that God's dwelling at Jerusalem was ruined. There the annual pilgrimages were to be held and sacrifice offered. So far as the law book is concerned, the location is left undecided ; there is not the slightest hint that it was again to be at Jerusalem ; the only place mentioned is Shechem and Mount Gerizim (xi., xxvii.), the natural centre of the whole land, and the place where from earliest times covenants were made at the temple of Baal Berith—the Lord of the Covenant. There an altar was to be built and a new covenant made, and Yahweh would indicate where his permanent dwelling was to be. With this demand for one sanctuary comes the assertion, which reforming priests as well as prophets would wish to be made, that there was one Yahweh ; it would no longer be possible to have, for example, a Yahweh of Hebron to whom vows must be paid there (2 Sam. xv. 7) ; Yahweh could not be parcelled out to different shrines ; vows and offerings to the one God must be taken to the one place where he set his name. It is still not the monotheism of the post-exilic period, for it recognizes the reality of other gods (Deut. iv. 19), but there is to be no compromise in the duty of Israelites ; the death penalty was decreed by the book for their worship of other gods (xiii.), and to this end there was to be no mixing with other people or intermarriage (vii.)—the religion is definitely and decidedly nationalistic and exclusive.

The second principle was purification of the religion from all the rites that linked it with non-Yahweh religions ; the rites which were retained were rationalized.[4] It is necessary to avoid the mistake of thinking that the reform aimed only at doing away with Canaanite forms of worship. Corn and wine and oil offerings are retained, while there is an obvious and surprising omission of any reference to the lunar feasts, which are usually regarded as nomadic in origin. The reform aimed at removing all the cruder elements of institutional religion likely to lead men away from the worship of Yahweh, whether the elements came from Canaanite or from nomadic sources. The prohibition against eating with the blood also appears here to be codified for the first time, and possibly represents an attempt to prevent the nomadic rite spoken of by St. Nilus as common among the Arabs, of eating an animal raw—the Hebrew phrase is " alive." In this connection it is of interest that eating with the blood is one of the sins with which, in the Hebrew Bible, Ezekiel charges the people of Palestine (xxxiii. 25). He is the first prophet to make the charge or to show himself " blood-conscious," but even he, like Deuteronomy, allows sacrificial meat to be seethed—the English version in Deuteronomy xvi. is an obvious mistranslation ; but the later priestly law demands that it shall be roasted because the blood and the fat are holy (*cf*. Exod. xii. 9), and it is only by roasting that one can be sure that none of the fat or blood is eaten. The rational explanation of the prohibition against eating the blood in Deuteronomy is that life resides in the blood (xii. 23), but there is no suggestion that it has any cleansing, purifying, or atoning efficacy as in the priestly code. It must simply be poured out on the ground around the altar ; there is no sprinkling of it or other ritual use.

Another feature of the reform was the break that was made with the fertility cults : worship on high hills under green trees, beside asherah, and mazzeboth (xvi. 21). It was also forbidden for holy men and women attached to the sanctuaries to give the price of their hire to the temple funds (xxiii. 18) ; and the very rational attitude to the sacrifice of the firstborn shows the same total disregard of fertility rites. It is not every firstborn that opens the womb which has to be sacrificed, but only firstborn males without blemish (xv. 19). The law about the king (xvii. 14ff.) is probably not only a concession to the northern sentiment which would not want a Davidic monarch, but, like the prohibition against sacrificing human firstborn, to prevent a continuance of the king-cult.

One other feature is interesting as showing the tendency of the reformers. In the book of Kings, where the story of the reform has been read back into the time of Josiah, stress is laid on the passover that was celebrated : " Surely there was not holden such a passover from the days of the judges that judged Israel, nor in all the days of the kings of Israel, nor of the kings of Judah " (2 Kings xxiii. 22 f.). Deuteronomy (xvi. 1) insists that the feast shall be held in the month Abib, in the spring, and that it must be connected with the feast of unleavened bread. Most scholars recognize that this is the first place in the Old Testament where the two are combined. Now it is of interest that, on a generally accepted reconstruction of the text, these are two of the demands made by the priests of Jerusalem to the Jewish community at Yeb in Egypt in the fifth century,[5] to bring the worship there into line with Jerusalem practice, and this suggests that a change had taken place at Jerusalem, not yet accepted at Yeb. We have no certain information as to the date usually fixed at Yeb for the passover, but the fact that the Egyptian riots and the destruction of the temple there took place in the summer, and were probably caused by the sacrifice of rams, which were the sacred animal of Khnum the god of Yeb, suggests that the passover, too, took place at that time. If this was also the time of the feast at Jerusalem before the Deuteronomic reform, it would appear likely that the feast had originally taken place in the month of Tammuz—June, July—when children begotten at the New Year festival in the autumn were born, and sacrificed to preserve the life of the king. The change of the date did away with another item in the king-cult, and moved the passover from midsummer to spring, linking it not with the sacrifice of human firstborn, but with the agricultural feast of unleavened bread and with the nomadic spring feast when the firstborn of the flocks were killed.

It is probable that the compiler of the book of Deuteronomy, and the prime mover in the reform, was a layman rather than either a priest or a prophet. He was able to stand apart from both and see that their powers as well as their privileges were properly defined. To him Moses the great lawgiver was also the greatest of the prophets, and both prophet and priest were necessary to religion. Priests must be given a fair share of the offering, and of the communal sacrificial meals, poor priests must be treated as a charge on the community just like other needy persons, but they had no special holiness. It was the people who as a whole were a holy people chosen by God. Similarly the prophet must be listened to, but clear tests were provided to enable men to judge between the true and the false prophet : a prophet whose predictions did not come true had spoken presumptuously, was not inspired, and should not be feared ; a prophet or a dreamer who gave signs and performed wonders, however spectacular, must be put to death if he led men away from the worship of Yahweh. Perhaps from this lay influence came also the rationalizing of the worship. The boundary between sacred and profane is amazingly low in the book : animals may be slaughtered and eaten as food without any sacrificial ritual apart from the pouring out of the blood, and none of the offerings—even tithes and firstlings— is here regarded as intrinsically holy ; if the sanctuary is too far away to make it convenient for them to be carried thither, the worshipper may sell them, and, taking the money to the sanctuary, expend it on anything his soul lusteth after—oxen, sheep, wine, or strong drink—that could be shared in a communal meal. Although it might be said of the whole Bible that it is a book for the common people, yet it is pre-eminently true that Deuteronomy is written by the people and for the people, and might rightly be called the book of the people.

CHAPTER 12

EXILIC REVIVAL

§ MESSAGE OF EZEKIEL

WE have seen that as a result of the destruction of holy places and the deportation of the priests, the new beginning of religion which became possible in Palestine was largely under the influence of Jeremiah. Among those who had been taken away to Babylonia conditions were very different. There Jeremiah's influence was not so great ; his friends had been among the pro-Babylonian families, like that of Gedaliah, which were allowed to remain in Palestine ; the captives were mainly those who had been responsible for the institutional religion, and, though they knew Jeremiah's teaching, they were his opponents. During the period between the two invasions of Palestine in 597 and 586 B.C. we hear of one contact he had with the captives, and it does not suggest that they regarded him as divinely inspired (xxix.). Jeremiah sent a letter to the Jewish elders, priests, and prophets in Babylonia warning them against any hope of an immediate return, telling them to seek the peace of their new home, and prophesying that two of their prophets would be roasted alive by Nebuchadrezzar for raising false hopes. In reply the captives wrote to the acting high-priest telling him to reprove that madman Jeremiah who pretends to be a prophet, and if necessary put him in prison and in the stocks.

Among the captives the greatest influence was exercised by Ezekiel, a young priest who had served in the temple at Jerusalem, and had been deported with the first batch in 597 B.C.[1] His call came in 592 B.C. by the river Chebar in Babylonia, and for some years we can hear both Jeremiah and Ezekiel prophesying at the same time, the one in Jerusalem and the other in exile. That Ezekiel knew Jeremiah is almost certain, for he had grown up in Jerusalem during the thirty years in which Jeremiah had been preaching in the capital, but he makes no explicit reference to him. There are echoes of Jeremiah's condemnation of prophets who preached peace when there is no peace, of his new covenant when men's hearts would be changed and "God will be their God and they his people"; but he appears to include Jeremiah among the false prophets who—and he uses Jeremiah's own word—had been seduced (xiv. 9). Jeremiah had bidden the exiles settle in Babylonia, but Ezekiel preached as openly as he dared the hope of a speedy return and the belief that the exiles would inherit the land.

Ezekiel's priestly and temple background is clear in all his message. Like Isaiah, his vision is of a majestic, holy God, remote from men, a king enthroned and unapproachable. Much of his imagery came from the temple : the cherubim who bore the flying throne may show influence from Babylonia, but they were familiar figures to a temple priest. Even his message comes, not through a voice from God, but in the vision of a scroll that he must eat (iii.). His prophetic contacts were probably with the cult-prophets rather than with those who like Jeremiah had broken away from the cultus, and many of the psychological phenomena recorded of him are probably best explained as due to possession by God, in a way similar to that of the prophets before the eighth century ; his symbolic actions are very realistically worked out. But he has only partially reached the moral religious level of Jeremiah. His stress on Sabbath observances, and on the physical contagion of God's holiness, the belief that disaster was due to no clear distinction being made between sacred and profane, and his list of sins, which classed together moral crimes with physical indecencies (xxii.), are all foreign to the teaching of Jeremiah. What we have learned from the time of Amos to be the true function of a prophet has to come to him as a special revelation ; the prophet is one who blows the trumpet when danger is near, hearing God's message of doom, and warning the people that they may have the opportunity to repent (xxxiii.)

But it seems probable that Ezekiel belonged to a reforming

party in the Jerusalem priesthood. There are many elements in the temple worship that he condemns, and his vision of the new temple in the new Jerusalem contains many departures from ancient custom (xl.ff.). His visions give a picture of institutional religion at its highest, springing, not from the experience of intimate communion with a loving Father, but from devoted and humble reverence for a holy majestic King.

His teaching can be divided into two sections, before and after the fall of Jerusalem in 586 B.C. At first he proclaimed the inevitable destruction of Jerusalem, and gave a vivid picture of abuses in institutional religion as well as the sins of the common people which were the cause of the disaster. The false worship in the temple we have already noticed; the people he accuses of shedding of blood, making idols, setting light by family ties, breaking the laws of affinity, despising God's holy things, and profaning his Sabbaths. But it must be remembered that in the book as we have it this first part of his message was delivered to the exiles, not to the men of Jerusalem, and it seems clear that the prophet was condemning these sins because they were still being practised by the exiles themselves, and would equally cause their ruin. They had brought with them not a pure religion but the syncretistic worship of the temple. They set up their idols in their hearts, burned their children, went whoring after their abominations, and worshipped the Babylonian gods of wood and stone, while still bringing their gifts to Yahweh and seeking his guidance (xiv.). Like Jeremiah he clearly foresaw the imminent fall of Jerusalem, and wished not only to point the moral but to prepare the people for it. They were still under the delusion that the great deliverance which had fulfilled Isaiah's prophecy in the time of Sennacherib, meant that God would always protect his sanctuary in Jerusalem; they believed that Yahweh was confined to his own land, and to the place where his name dwelt. Ezekiel taught that he was attached not to the land but to the people, and in his first vision he had seen Yahweh leaving his temple and the doomed city to accompany his people into exile.

After the fall of the city, when he broke his silence, it was to utter a new message. Now the blow had fallen, the past was in a sense wiped out, God's holiness and righteousness had been vindicated by the destruction of the wicked place, and the sins had been paid for. Like Jeremiah he had to meet the popular proverb, spoken in exile as in Palestine with cynical despair to explain the disaster : " The fathers have eaten sour grapes, and the children's teeth are set on edge " (xviii. 2). Both the prophets made the same answer : " The son shall not bear the iniquity of the father, but the soul that sinneth it shall die." It was the logical outcome of the prophetic moral teaching as well as of the priestly ritual—a gospel that it was possible to break the entail of the past and make a fresh beginning as a nation or an individual ; the prophets had taught moral responsibility, and the priests had shown that broken covenants could be renewed and sins forgiven by a sacrificial rite. Ezekiel develops the idea of individual responsibility to such an extent that his teaching has been called religious atomism. To him the second commandment is no longer an adequate statement of the principles on which God works ; there is to be no visiting of the sins of fathers on children, and however righteous a man may be—be he Noah, Job, or Daniel (xiv.)—he can save only himself, not even a son or daughter ; Ezekiel would have repudiated entirely the belief that by Abraham's pleading ten righteous men could have saved Jerusalem, to him the modern Sodom. At any moment, by a single act, an individual can break completely with the past, a good man can sin and a bad man can repent, and his past, whether good or bad, will not count. Ezekiel ignores the cumulative effect of the past on society and on individual character ; but his primary interest lies with the society, not with the individual. No individual can transmit his goodness or his badness to the society in which he lives, but he can, if he will, turn to God and help to form a new house of Israel. This teaching has had considerable effect on religious development, because it has been applied from the standpoint of the individual, and regarded as justifying the belief in the possibility of sudden or death-bed repentances.

Ezekiel applied to the individual the principle of just retribution which the prophets had applied to the nation, and in a
modified form his teaching became the orthodox doctrine of
individual retribution, producing the theory that always sin
caused punishment and that suffering was the result of sin.
The belief persisted into the first century A.D., and we hear the
disciple of Jesus asking, " Did this man sin or his parents that
he was born blind ? " (John ix. 2). We shall see many revolts
against this doctrine, because it was opposed to much of the
experience of daily life. Ezekiel himself ingeniously explained
the survival of some wicked men by saying that God kept
them alive to show how wicked man could be and so to justify
his destruction of the others (xiv. 21ff.).

The individual played little part in the prophet's picture of
the future. There his concern was with the restored Israel, not
as individuals or as a nation, but as a religious community
centring round the temple. This community was to be built
up from the whole house of Israel which was in exile, and was
similar to the righteous remnant spoken of by Isaiah. Ezekiel
was, however, careful to emphasize that it would not survive
on account of its own righteousness, but to prove the power
of Yahweh whose name had been profaned among the nations,
and again to show his choice of Israel. Ezekiel still proclaimed
a God whose honour and future worship were bound up with
his people Israel—they were as necessary to him as he to them,
and of necessity he must restore their fortunes. Because of
this Ezekiel believed that the restoration would precede repentance. His own message had not been successful ; the
people had treated him as a popular preacher with a lovely
voice, but their lives had remained unchanged : " And lo,
thou art unto them as a love song of one who hath a pleasant
voice, and can play well on an instrument : for they hear thy
words but they do them not " (xxxiii. 32). He knew from
experience that a new heart must be a gift from God (xi. 19).
God would take the initiative, and by a great historic act would
show his forgiveness and would bring shame and repentance
to the people. In his vision of the valley of dry bones it is the

prophetic word and the spirit of God that raise the dead and make them a mighty army (xxxvii.). This belief that conversion was to be the outcome of a historic act by God is important for the interpretation of the message of Second-Isaiah and of Jesus.

In the restored community the remnant of the northern tribes will share, there will be one nation under a Davidic prince, who is spoken of as the shepherd of his people (xxxvii. 19, 24). But there is to be no bridging of national boundaries, and the restoration will include a great and final destruction of Israel's national enemies, so that God's name may be completely vindicated. The vision of the battle against the great Gog of the land of Magog and all his allies restores to the conception of the Day of Yahweh its early popular meaning condemned by Amos, and begins the long line of prophecies which ever since Ezekiel's time have foretold the final end of the age—prophecies which have been called eschatological. It is interesting to see how Ezekiel's idea of the greatness of God aggravated his nationalism. Instead of making him say that the holy God will vindicate holiness throughout the world and has no chosen people, it makes him assert that because Israel's God is supreme, he will make his people supreme. Palestine will remain his dwelling place, and Israel will overflow its boundaries and inherit the earth. His pleasure in foretelling the extermination of the Gentiles was, however, not due entirely to the fact that they were non-Jews, but that they were fighting against Yahweh, and Israel's victory would be the triumph of right over wrong. In his symbolic visions, too, we have the beginnings of a literature which eventually supplanted prophecy in Israel, and, because it claimed to lay bare the hidden things of the future by means of symbols, was called apocalyptic.

The clearest part of the visions of the future in the book of Ezekiel is that which shows the God-given pattern of the new temple, seen when the writer was transported to a high mountain in Palestine (xl.ff.). The whole land of Palestine was to be redistributed in order that the temple might be its centre ; around it were to be the domains of priests and Levites and the land allotted to the Davidic prince, and both to the south and north were the lands of six of the tribes. Everything possible was to be done to ensure that the holiness of Yahweh would be preserved. Yahweh's presence within the temple was necessary to ensure its continued existence, and after he had re-entered it through the eastern end that end was to be built up so that none might enter again through that way. An inner court was to surround the holy place where Yahweh dwelt, and in this inner court no layman might sacrifice at the altar nor eat communal meals, no prophet could speak, and no king offer sacrifice or bless the people—a complete break with pre-exilic custom. The new prince had the privilege of paying for the sacrifices and could approach the threshold of the inner court on Sabbaths and New Moons, but there his participation ceased. Minute regulations prescribed all the ritual, for here, as throughout Ezekiel's teaching, ritual observances were essential to righteousness, and to him there was no distinction between moral and ritual sins. The kind, age, sex of sacrificial victims, the material of the priests' robes, the times of the opening of the gates, and the way in which the worshippers were to walk in procession were all described.

In these regulations we see clearly the re-emergence of the primitive idea of holiness as physical and contagious ; the priests must change their robes after officiating before they come near the people, lest the contagion of holiness should pass to them (xlii. 14). The prophet believed that ruin had come because the dividing line between sacred and profane, clean and unclean, had been obliterated ; in the new temple all danger of this was to be removed. The officiating priests were to be of the line of Zadok (xliv. 15), introduced by Solomon ; and their assistants were to be Levites, whom we have seen scattered throughout the country as priests, and who in the book of Deuteronomy are classed with the poor and needy. No others could approach the transcendent holy God, who is so far removed even from the prophet that he speaks to him through intermediaries, the Spirit, or " the man whose appearance was as the appearance of brass."

One other feature of importance emerges from this vision of the temple ; it is the idea of atonement. In Deuteronomy the purpose of sacrifice was gratitude and joy. To Ezekiel the chief aim was expiation. Daily sacrifices assured a daily purification of the nation. Offerings which in pre-exilic times had been paid to the priest as compensation or fines for certain sins now became animal sacrifices with special blood rites as atonement for sin—the flesh is still eaten by the priests, and there is no idea of transferring the sin to the animal.[2] Two special national atonement days, on the first day of each half year, prevent the accumulation of unforgiven sins. Compared with Deuteronomy, the whole idea of ritual was altered by this emphasis on the atoning, cleansing power of blood and of sacrifice—an emphasis which probably, like Ezekiel's conception of holiness, had its roots in the primitive past.

His reformation of religion takes the opposite line from that of the Deuteronomists ; in the writings of Ezekiel there is no rationalization of worship or bringing God near to men, but a frank acceptance of the mysterious, the removal of God far from the common people, so that man's sin and wickedness stand out in clear contrast to the great and holy God. It is worthy of notice that from this vision of the transcendent God sprang the greatest revival and the highest vision that the Old Testament saw.

§ THE VISION AND DISILLUSIONMENT OF SECOND-ISAIAH

The revival for which Ezekiel's vision had prepared the way came through the writings and preaching of a prophet who for political reasons at first had to remain anonymous, and probably issued his pamphlets under the name of Isaiah, the great prophet of Jerusalem with whose writings he was so familiar. Living, it seems, in Syria, he heard the news of the meteoric rise of Cyrus from an obscure prince to a world conqueror, and saw in this foreigner, whom " victory attends at every step," one whom Yahweh had girded before he had known Him. Like the prophets of old this unknown prophet was called through a historic event in which he saw the finger of God, and he sent out God's clarion call both to the dispirited remnant dwelling round the ruins of Jerusalem and to the Jews dispersed throughout the world. Through him God kept saying to the dispersed community : " Comfort ye my people, tell her that her sins are paid for and the past forgiven " (xl.) ; like a desolate and bereaved woman she will again be united to her husband and surrounded by the love of children. Dramatically he calls to the exiled people, " Hark, there is someone calling in the wilderness, Prepare ye the way for Yahweh to lead back his chosen redeemed people to their homeland." The nations among whom the exiles live will need no plagues to force them to let God's people go ; astonished at the marvellous doings of Yahweh they will carry them back and themselves worship Israel's God. These three groups—the dwellers around the ruined city of Zion, the dispersed Israelites, and the foreign nations—are continually addressed by the prophet, and his words would gain in clearness if, as in a drama, stage directions were added to the poems.

There is considerable difference of opinion among scholars as to the unity of Isaiah xl.–lxvi.,[3] which contain the prophet's message, but an intelligible meaning can be given to the chapters if we regard them as in the main the work of one man, who saw his great vision and later felt disappointment because of the lack of human response to the gospel he proclaimed. Probably he began writing in about 538 B.C., and returned to Jerusalem with the first Jews under Sheshbazzar when Cyrus's edict of toleration allowed native temples to be rebuilt and deported populations to go back to their own lands (Ezra i.). In Palestine the project of rebuilding the temple appears to have been frustrated, probably by those who were well content that, as for the past fifty years, Bethel should remain the centre of their worship. In Judæa itself much of the old syncretistic religion, condemned by Jeremiah and Ezekiel, had continued to flourish ; men still inflamed themselves with idols under green trees, burnt their children in the valleys (lvii.), and committed those acts of violence, oppression, and the shedding of innocent blood which had called forth God's wrath. Among the exiles men had taken the advice of Jeremiah literally : there was a reluctance to forsake the comfort and prosperity of their new homes for the insecurity and hardship of the barren Judæan hills, and most turned a deaf ear to the prophet's glowing Zionist vision. In world affairs, too, there was disappointment. Cyrus had conquered Babylonia as the prophet had foretold, but he had not acted as the Messiah, the anointed servant of Yahweh, purging his great empire of polytheism and acknowledging Yahweh as the only true God ; so, after all, the nations had seen no sudden revelation of the power of Israel's God. The message of the prophet became modified to meet the actual situation, but the essential elements of the early vision still remained. There is still comfort and forgiveness to the faithful who seek Yahweh while he lets himself be found ; and his word is as potent as ever, it will not return to him void (lv.). The moral teachings of the prophets can be combined with ritual observances in which all can unite. Fasts must be accompanied by giving food to the hungry, receiving the poor into one's home, and clothing the naked ; Sabbaths must not be days when one seeks one's own pleasure, but days on which employees, too, are released from their labour, and delight is taken in the holy things of God (lviii.). The project of re-building the temple is abandoned : " Thus saith Yahweh, the heavens are my throne and the earth is my footstool : what manner of house will ye build for me ? " (lxvi.).

Unlike Ezekiel, the primary concern of this prophet is his love and care for his people. The God he worshipped is as lofty and transcendent as that of Ezekiel, but not so remote or impersonal. He is both cosmic and personal ; he is a shepherd caring for his flock with a divine mercy that blots out sin. True imageless monotheism has at last emerged in Israel's religion. Yahweh is the creator and sustainer of the whole universe ; other gods have no existence, and, like their stone and wooden images, are powerless. The vehemence of the prophet's attack on idolatry shows that he was fighting it not as something practised by other nations, but among his own people—and a coin found probably at Gaza dated as late as the fourth century depicts Yahweh as a bearded figure seated on the wheel of the sun chariot. Yet belief in the reality of idols could not long have survived among those who had listened to his brilliant satire on the man who cuts down a chosen tree, makes fire to warm himself with part of it, cooks his food on its coals, and of the residue makes a god, fastens it in its place with nails, and falls down in worship before it (xliv.).

Second-Isaiah sees the universal creator in human history choosing men and nations for his purpose, and able to care for the smallest detail of his vast domain. The prophet proves that his God is real by the fact that he can interpret international events of the past and the future in terms of the working of his God, and can forecast accurately future events as the fulfilling of moral purposes of the same God. A statement as startling as that made by his great predecessor when he foretold that Jerusalem would not be captured is made by this prophet : " Behold I have created the smith that bloweth the fire of coals, and bringeth forth weapons, and I have created the waster to destroy. No weapon that is forged against thee shall prosper " (liv. 16f.).

Perhaps the greatest contribution made by these twenty-seven chapters of the book of Isaiah is contained in the poems concerning the " Servant of Yahweh." [4] Features taken from the characters of previous religious leaders, from the history of his nation, and from the writer's own experience, have been welded together to make a vivid personification of what Isaiah had called the righteous remnant. Humble and unobtrusive, the Servant carries the knowledge of Israel's God to the Gentiles ; undiscouraged, he fans to a flame every dim smouldering wick till the light of truth blazes forth. He himself will be a light to the Gentiles and a covenant that binds them to Yahweh. Insults and shame will not turn him from his purpose, and though in the end he is killed, like lambs slain at the altar, he will bear the sins of those who slay him, and, like the plants that every year die at summer time, he will rise again in even greater glory. The old idea of a national God who is bound to his chosen people has been transmuted. Still they are a chosen people, but chosen to serve and die for the sake of the whole world ; still Yahweh is their God, but theirs to share with the world, not to keep as a selfish possession.

§ Rebuilding under Haggai and Zechariah

The influence of Ezekiel and the anonymous prophet of the exile continued in the next two prophets, Haggai and Zechariah, and although, like Second-Isaiah during part of his life, they dwelt in Palestine, they belonged to the exilic revival. Their call came in 520 B.C., and, true to prophetic type, they began their preaching from contemporary events which they interpreted as revealing God's purpose. Haggai, like Amos, saw that bad crops, blight, and famine were due to the fact that the land lacked Yahweh's blessing : his temple was not rebuilt, and his presence was not there. Zechariah started from international affairs ; widespread revolts in the Persian empire after the death of Cambyses appeared to him to be the prelude to world catastrophe which would bring with it the freedom of the Jews and the beginning of the Messianic age, when God's anointed king should rule his people. Like Ezekiel and Second-Isaiah, Haggai and Zechariah both believed that the rebuilding of the temple was an essential condition of the prosperity of that new age, and that its vessels should be restored and nothing unclean should enter it again. Professor Albright's excavations at Bethel have shown that Bethel, which had survived the Babylonian invasions, was destroyed at about this time, and so the obstacle that had prevented the rebuilding had been partly removed.

It seems probable that when the rebuilding of Jerusalem began, men of Bethel offered their services, apparently desiring to combine under Joshua, the new high-priest at Jerusalem

(Ezra iv. 1ff. ; Hag. ii. 10ff.). Joshua may have agreed, but when Haggai was consulted he, like Nathan to David, turned the question back on his inquirers, and, by illustrations drawn from ritual laws, made the priests admit that all the people of Bethel, everything they touched, and all their offerings were unclean. The old national strife between the north and south, which had ended fifty years before, broke out again as a religious disruption, and continues with unabated bitterness to the present day. Haggai demanded a complete break with all the religion of the land to preserve the purity which had grown up in the exile. Possibly Haggai was striving to form that nucleus whose religion would be pure enough to fulfil the task of the Servant of Yahweh, and he believed that the only way to achieve that purpose was to express the religion in the external forms of temple worship and to enshrine it in an exclusive community.

Prophecy was transformed during the exile. It still represented the regenerative conscience of Israel, but in pre-exilic times conscience had revealed itself through revolt against official religion with its syncretistic ritual and institutions ; the prophets had then been national heroes fighting for the national worship of Israel's God, free from the accretions of Canaanite and Assyrian elements. Now, however, the conscience was on the side of the official religion which had in many ways been purged in the furnace of the exile, and the whole weight of prophetic influence was used for the establishment of a purified temple cultus. In spite of this inter-penetration of prophecy by ritual, Zechariah still demanded in the manner of his forerunners of the eighth century true judgement, compassion every man to his brother, and no oppression of the widow, fatherless, and the stranger : he went further and required that men should not imagine evil in their hearts against their neighbour ; but the message of doom and the demand for repentance have gone. Punishment had fallen : and as Second-Isaiah had been at pains to give the people the assurance of forgiveness, so Zechariah [5] drew his religious cartoon of the box containing the woman called Wickedness,

on which the heavy leaden lid is shut down ; and symbolizing
the removal of all the guilt of the land, the box is borne by
stork-like figures to Babylonia (v. 5ff.). In future God's
scroll of judgement will enter the homes of individuals, and
guilt will be borne by the man himself when he swears falsely
or steals, but the community will be free (v. 1ff.). Perhaps
it would be possible to describe this transformation of prophecy
by saying that it is not the rebel prophet who has continued
into this period, but the cult prophet, the professional attached
to the sanctuary. Zechariah, for example, defends the high-
priest against those who regard him as unfit to officiate (iii.),
and priests of Jerusalem and Bethel come to Haggai and
Zechariah to obtain oracles. Both men still use the prophetic
phrase, "Thus saith Yahweh," but they look back to the
prophetic period as a bygone age ; the spontaneity springing
from direct contact with God has gone, earlier prophets are
quoted, and to Zechariah, as to Ezekiel, the message comes
through intermediaries.

Equally important for the development of religion is the
teaching of Haggai and Zechariah about the Messiah. Both
believed that world events were hastening toward a crisis, that
Zerubbabel was the longed-for Messiah, and that through this
son of the house of David the kingdom of God would come.
Haggai says that Jeremiah's prophecy against the royal house
of David had been reversed, and God had again slipped on
the signet ring which he had cast away (ii. 23, cf. Jer. xxii. 24) ;
Zechariah calls Zerubbabel by a name already used for the
Messiah—The Branch—and he tells of the arrival in Jerusalem
of Jews bearing gifts of gold and silver, which, in accordance
with the oracle, were made into a crown for Zerubbabel (vi.).
The idea of a personal, human Messiah, a purely temporal ruler,
was current at that time ; Second-Isaiah had even given the
title to the Persian king Cyrus, and roused considerable opposition (xlv.). Zerubbabel probably accepted the rôle, assumed
kingly power and status, and was promptly removed by the
Persians, for in Zechariah's final prophecy in December
518 B.C., and at the dedication of the new temple in 516 B.C.,

there is no mention of him ; suddenly he has disappeared. This failure of Messianic prophecies had considerable effect, and for centuries the idea of a personal Messiah ceased to be important. Even in the second century B.C. the writer of the book of Daniel still thinks of the Messiah not as an individual, but as " the saints of the most High " (vii.).

In Zechariah we can see developing many features which later became of importance in religion. His visions provided much of the symbolism for later eschatological and apocalyptic writers ; the Day of Yahweh against which Amos had fought when it was thought of only as a day of vengeance against national enemies, returned as a day of Yahweh's triumph, although ethical elements had been introduced. Angels became more prominent as intermediaries between the transcendent God and men, and we find for the first time a heavenly being, the Satan—it is not yet a proper name—who reminds God of men's failings and acts as a public prosecutor.

CHAPTER 13

THE PRIESTLY REACTION

§ EXILIC INTERVENTION IN PALESTINE

MUCH of the history of the exilic period is covered by mist through which it is difficult to see clearly the sequence of events either in Palestine or Babylonia, or the course of the development of religion. Fortunately, as we have seen, there are peaks that stand up in clear light.

In Palestine, if we may judge from the book of Deuteronomy, there had been a strong reaction against the old persistent culture of the land; a definite antagonism had become explicit against the non-Jewish inhabitants of the country and against the surviving elements of ancient oriental cults. Although the book purports to legislate for " all Israel," it appears to be rather the code of a small exclusive community filled with strong national feelings and almost an anti-Gentile fanaticism. This people must keep itself separate in marriage, religious customs, and food laws from the Canaanite foreigners among whom it is dwelling; it must remember that it is a holy people whom Yahweh " has chosen to be a peculiar people unto himself, above all peoples that are upon the face of the earth " (Deut. vii., xiv.). This exclusiveness, and the care that was necessary to keep the land free from guilt, suggest the influence of the same priestly circle to which Ezekiel had belonged before he left Palestine, and, as we have seen, probably resulted from the fact that Jerusalem priests fled to Bethel after the destruction of Jerusalem.

If our reconstruction of the history of the exilic period is correct, this exclusive national religion, with its centre at Bethel, was sufficiently strong to prevent Sheshbazzar from rebuilding the temple at Jerusalem when he returned in 536 B.C. with Cyrus's permission. But it is probable that Jerusalem became at that time again the civil centre. From Haggai we learn that although in 520 B.C. no temple or altar existed, yet houses, some of them showing considerable evidence of wealth, had been built, and apparently not only the prophet but also Zerubbabel the new governor and Joshua the high-priest dwelt there. Perhaps Second-Isaiah's confidence in the future of Zion had had an effect. More important, however, had been this prophet's break from the exclusive nationalism of the Deuteronomic community. To him, too, Israel was a peculiar people chosen by God, but Israel's God was the only God and desired the worship of all nations : in him all the ends of the earth shall be saved, to him every knee shall bow, and by him all tongues swear (xlv. 22f.). Israel's mission as " a light to the Gentiles " could not be fulfilled by the old exclusiveness and nationalism ; there must be room in the new Jewish community not only for the eunuch but for the stranger (lvi.) and the man who could not claim Abraham as his ancestor. This preaching tended, at Jerusalem, to modify the rigid Deuteronomic laws.

§ NEHEMIAH

Whether the failure of Zerubbabel and the partial dis-crediting of Haggai and Zechariah caused renewed contacts between Jerusalem and the old Bethel community, we do not know, but the fact that Jerusalem remained an open city meant that it was dependent on the friendliness and goodwill of non-Jewish neighbours, and was bound to practise the non-exclusiveness of Second-Isaiah's teaching. But the influence of Deuteronomy did not pass so rapidly or completely. There were still people at Jerusalem who wished to build a wall round themselves, despite Zechariah's prophecy. After repeated attempts had been frustrated by Persian civil authorities who feared to allow that " wicked and rebellious city " to be fortified, it was this exclusive group who appealed to the Babylonian Jews against their own religious leaders and the Persian rulers, and it was this state of affairs that made necessary the secrecy of Nehemiah's night ride around the walls when he reached the Judæan capital (ii. 12). In the opinion of most scholars, Nehemiah's work at Jerusalem preceded that of Ezra, who probably came to Palestine in the seventh year of Artaxerxes II, 397 B.C. [1]

We have a fairly clear picture of the religious conditions in Jerusalem when Nehemiah arrived on his first visit in 444 B.C. Though the temple had been rebuilt for over seventy years, by the efforts of Haggai and Zechariah, its services were neglected, tithes were not paid, Levites had to return to their country homes to earn a livelihood, and the Sabbaths were not kept. Social injustice had produced conditions similar to those condemned by the eighth- and seventh-century prophets (v.) ; racial and religious purity was not the concern of even the high-priest. Foreign traders brought their wares into the city on the Sabbath ; an Ammonite, Tobiah, had rooms in the temple building, and a grandson of the high-priest had married the daughter of the Persian governor (xiii.).

Nehemiah was himself a eunuch, and, according to the Deuteronomic code, excluded from the assembly of Israel, but he was an uncompromising puritan and separatist, with Ezekiel's vision of the purity and holiness of the temple and its cultus. Whether he was a fair specimen of Babylonian Jewry we cannot decide ; the book of Ezekiel and the smallness of the numbers of those who were willing to leave the flesh-pots of Babylonia and return to Palestine suggest that he was not. Possibly we should distinguish between the priests and the laity, and regard Nehemiah as in this respect more priestly in his attitude ; possibly we should remember that to most of the Babylonian Jews, as to so many modern Jews, Palestine and Jerusalem were encircled with a halo of idealism, and breaches of the law which were readily excused and allowed by themselves in exile were not tolerated in their thought of the community living in the homeland.

As a result of Nehemiah's two visits in 444 and 432 B.C. the whole community in Judah was reformed ; the people bound themselves together in a new covenant to avoid marriage with non-Jews, to observe the Sabbath and the seventh year when all debts were released, to pay their temple dues and to support the Levites (x.). It seems probable that some of the reforms were forced on an unwilling priesthood which preferred its contacts with the outside world to religious purity. Certainly the grandson of Eliashib the high-priest was dismissed from the temple, and it has been suggested that the high-priest himself was replaced by his son Jehohanan. The rebuilding of the city walls enabled the community to retain its exclusiveness, and Nehemiah's reformation brought Judaism back into closer conformity with the Deuteronomic community which had existed at Bethel. It was the Deuteronomic code which was the basis of his covenant and probably, with some modifications, the law of the land.

That the Deuteronomic code was capable of modification is seen from the book of Malachi. The word means, "My Messenger," and was the name given to the writing of an anonymous prophet, who probably belongs to the period after Nehemiah's second visit to Jerusalem. He used the language of the Deuteronomic school and apparently accepted the code, but he did not approve of men who had taken advantage of the demand for racial purity to rid themselves of unwanted wives; he had caught, too, some glimpse of Second-Isaiah's vision, for he contrasts the honour which Gentiles accord to the name of Yahweh with the way in which Israel profanes it. From his book we learn that corruption within the priesthood had again caused neglect of organized religion, and the priests had broken their covenant with the Levites, who had ceased to receive their rightful dues. Happily the spirituality of Israel did not depend on the temple and its worship, and we are given a picture of the faithful few meeting together to preserve that spiritual religion preached by Jeremiah—a picture which may give us our first glimpse of the synagogue, later to become so influential in preserving Judaism when the temple and its priesthood had been destroyed (iii. 16).

§ Ezra

The next intervention from exilic Jews came through Ezra, whose arrival in Jerusalem is now generally believed to have been in 397 B.C. The memoirs left by Ezra were used by an editor far removed from the Persian period and knowing little of its history, so that there is much that is uncertain and obscure in the account. Ezra is described as a priest and a ready scribe of the law of the God of Israel (Ezra vii. 6), and the theory usually held is that he returned to Palestine with the law-book of the exilic community in his hand, and imposed legal and ritual reforms on the basis of this code. The code has been identified with the section of the Pentateuch known as the priestly code, and the accepted view is that just as 621 B.C. marks the introduction of the Deuteronomic code, so 397 B.C. was the date at which the priestly code which superseded it was accepted by the nation with tears of joy. Professor Welch [2] has rightly questioned this orthodox view, and his reconstruction of Ezra's work and place in the development of biblical religion appears in the main to be most satisfactory.

According to this view, Ezra returned with about 1,800 settlers, mainly from the professional religious classes, to attempt to bring practices in Palestine into line with those of the Babylonian exiles. The memoirs he wrote were reports made to the community in Babylonia, which had financed the carefully prepared undertaking. Most of the matters referred to in these reports are not reforms instituted by Ezra, but modifications accepted by him to bring the Babylonian laws into conformity with practices in Palestine.

Contract tablets found at Nippur suggest that the Jews in Mesopotamia, like their brethren at Yeb in Egypt, freely intermarried with the local population, and did not maintain the same rigid racial purity as had been enforced in Palestine by Deuteronomy and Nehemiah. When Ezra returned with his 1,800 males they were not careful to inquire into the ancestry of the Palestinian women they took as wives. This laxity

shocked the Palestinians, who pointed out to Ezra the " trespass
of them of the captivity " (ix.). Ezra was naturally extremely
grieved at this inauspicious beginning to his mission, called
all the men of the captivity to Jerusalem, and, after three
months' careful investigation, found that one hundred and
thirteen cases had been proved, and ordered these marriages
to be annulled—necessarily more radical action than had been
insisted on by Nehemiah.

The second modification arose from the custom which
had grown up in Palestine of reading out a translation in
Aramaic when the law, in accordance with the law of
Deuteronomy, was read in public at the feast of Tabernacles
every seven years. Nehemiah had found that Hebrew was
not understood, and as a spoken language was dying out in
Palestine. He " contended with them and cursed them and
smote certain of them, and plucked off their hair," but his
methods of encouraging the study of the sacred language do
not appear to have been very successful. Ezra was milder in
his treatment of the problem. There is nothing in the account
to suggest that the law brought by Ezra was new and unknown
to the people of Jerusalem, but many of them would not have
understood it when read in Hebrew. They were overjoyed
when Ezra—unlike Nehemiah—allowed it to be read in a
language they knew, and they wept for joy as they recognized
the old laws recodified (Neh. viii.).

The third matter on which Ezra wrote to his fellows in
Babylonia was also connected with the feast of Tabernacles
(Neh. viii. 13ff.). Here again the initiative is not with Ezra.
The heads of the fathers' houses of all the people, with the
priests and Levites, came to Ezra, and pointed out that the law
of Moses demanded that the people should dwell in booths for
the feast. The version of the law brought by Ezra apparently
did not include this requirement, so familiar to us in the modern
Jewish celebration of the feast ; but as a result of the representations made, " all the congregation of them that were come again
out of the captivity made booths and dwelt in the booths "—
a custom which their ancestors in the south had never observed.

The custom was accepted by Ezra and given his sanction, probably with the addition of an eighth day as a solemn assembly at the conclusion of the feast. Probably in pre-exilic Jerusalem the only tent erected at the New Year feast of Tabernacles was the one for the sacred marriage rite performed by the king, but evidence (Jud. xxi. 19) suggests that the fertility rites in the northern kingdom were different, and were connected not with the king-cult but with the dancing in the vineyards at the end of the grape harvest. In these northern rites the many booths erected for the harvesters in the vineyards would be used for the promiscuous unions. Apparently, perhaps owing to influence from Bethel, this northern custom had been adopted at Jerusalem, and when it was accepted by Ezra and the Babylonian community it was explained—like so many other rites in Judaism—by being given a historical basis which linked it with the early wanderings in the wilderness. Obviously, as Professor Welch points out, the wilderness was not a place where thick branches and willows could be obtained, and in any case the Jewish tradition was that during the wanderings the people lived in tents.

If this reconstruction of the work of Ezra be accepted it becomes clear that he was not an innovator, nor so important a figure in the development of Jewish religion as some theories would require, and it is easier to understand why the writer of Ecclesiasticus omitted all mention of him among the famous men of the nation's past. Unlike Nehemiah, who used his authority to enforce iconoclastic reforms, Ezra attempted to bring the two communities in Palestine and Babylonia together and to obtain a uniform type of institutional worship ; and, with no other authority than that of head of a commission of inquiry, he used the gentler method of compromise.

§ RELIGION OF THE CHRONICLER

For the remainder of the Persian period there is little reliable information about the history of the Jews until the conquests of Alexander the Great in 333 B.C. Archæology shows that at such places as Bethzur and Bethel the returned exiles were a poor struggling community until the Greek conquests ; at Lachish a large Persian palace was erected, and there was a small sanctuary apparently for solar worship, for the Persian religion was very syncretistic ; Jews must have possessed a certain amount of fiscal autonomy, for Jewish coins used in this period have been found.

Research into the books of Chronicles [3] shows that the sixty odd years from 397 to 333 B.C. were marked by the establishment of the priestly and scribal religion which from this time became dominant. The hope of restoring the Davidic dynasty and founding an independent Jewish kingdom had certainly not been fulfilled, but Jerusalem was fast becoming a religious and cultural centre for the scattered Jewish communities throughout the world ; to its temple they turned for prayer, and there sacrifices were offered for the atonement of their sins. But the elaborate temple ritual had in essence little in common with the other type of religion which had developed in the local synagogues or schools for studying the law. Various legal codes had crystallized into the present Pentateuch, which in the synagogue was studied for its own sake as the expression of the revealed will and purpose of God—his word to men. Though the two types of religion were in form and essence so very different, yet they both used the same Pentateuch, and often the piety of the synagogue as well as of the temple priests could and did express itself through the ritual of temple worship, as is seen from a study of the book of Psalms, which has been called " the hymn-book of the second temple."

Some of the steps leading to these later developments are being made more clear through recent work on the books of Chronicles by such scholars as Kittel, Rothstein, Von Rad, and Welch. There is now substantial agreement that two hands can be traced through these books, the one regarding David as the founder of the temple and its worship, and the other carrying the beginnings back further to Moses. The first writer relates how David made a tent shrine for the Ark, and later, wishing to replace it by a more worthy building, was given a pattern or plan of the new temple by God. All the services of this new temple and the arrangement of the priestly orders in like manner were mediated through David. The Ark was the essential element in the cultus and formed its centre ; for it the temple was built, and when sacrifices were offered before it, the Glory of Yahweh entered the temple ; the Levites had their place in the temple as the cult personnel peculiarly connected with the Ark, and, as in the writings of the Deuteronomic school, considerable prominence is given to them.

The revisers of this earlier book of Chronicles disagreed entirely with this representation of the history of Israelite religion. The temple to them was no novelty, but reproduced the tabernacle which had led the Israelites through the wilderness on their wanderings from Egypt. This original tabernacle had eventually been taken to the great high-place at Gibeon, and there Solomon had offered his coronation sacrifices. There was no need for a new pattern to be given to David, for God had already revealed it to Moses, and the temple was only a permanent substitute for that older tabernacle. Moses, not David, was the innovator, and the origin of all the institutions of the religion was carried back beyond David to Moses. The temple, its regulations, and its worship were traced to Horeb—the Deuteronomic name for Mount Sinai— and to the instruction given by God to Moses there. To these revisers the Ark lost its central place. It was respected because it contained the Decalogue, the tablets of the covenant between Yahweh and his people, but the sacrifices which brought God's Glory into the temple were offered on the altar and not before the Ark.

Thus we find two distinct groups of traditions : the earlier centring round David, the Ark, the temple, and the Levites ; and the later concerned with Moses, the law, the tabernacle, and the priests. The latter traditions are the ones we find crystallized in the priestly code ; the former appear to be connected with the Davidic hopes which were so strong in the days of Haggai and Zechariah. These hopes declined after the sudden disappearance of Zerubbabel, and do not reappear in strength until the rise of the Pharisees in the Maccabæan period. Such an analysis of the books of Chronicles does not solve the fascinating problem of the date and origin of the Mosaic tradition. We cannot even say that at this time the Mosaic tradition replaced the Davidic, except in the milieu in which these books were rewritten. Possibly we have here another indication of the influence of the remnant of the northern kingdom on the development of Jewish religion. David, who was a hero to the southern kingdom, was an invader to the north, and against his dynasty northerners had revolted as soon as they had the power. Union between Bethel and Jerusalem would scarcely be possible on a Davidic basis, but tradition connected the Mosaic tabernacle with Shiloh in the north as well as with Gibeon in the south, and Aaron his brother was debited—perhaps originally credited—with being the one to whom the form of the golden calf was first revealed. Perhaps, too, we have here a clue to help us understand the changing attitude to the Levites. The presence of Jerusalem priests at Bethel had secured for the Levites, whose shrines in the south had been destroyed by war, humane treatment in the Deuteronomic code ; but when the Bethel priesthood became supreme at Jerusalem under Joshua they were again neglected, and even Ezekiel, the reforming priest from Jerusalem, was not willing to give them—now that their ark had been destroyed—an equal place with the hereditary Jerusalem priesthood.

§ THE PRIESTLY CODE

The way in which the various elements of the priestly code developed is largely a matter of conjecture. There is no doubt that in both Palestine and Babylonia gradual codification of previous practices and laws went on throughout the exile. In Palestine the pre-exilic practices were continued with considerable modifications first at Bethel and later at Jerusalem.

In Babylonia it is probable that the influence of Ezekiel prevented the building of a temple, so that, while pre-exilic customs formed the basis of the codes there also, yet two main movements can be discerned, the aim of the first being to ensure the observance of certain rites which could be independent of the temple, but which were yet so characteristic of pre-exilic Jewish life that they separated the Jew from his Babylonian neighbour ; the second aimed at developing an ideal complete temple cultus for use after the restoration.

The working of these tendencies can be seen in the priestly history, which claimed to trace the origin of certain distinctive practices.[4] Sabbath observance was traced to the creation, the blood tabu to the flood, and circumcision to the story of Isaac. The story of Jacob illustrated the prohibition against marrying foreign women ; the passover was linked with the plagues of Egypt, and the sacrificing priesthood, with its tabernacle as the prototype of the temple, came from Sinai. It is important to differentiate between the practices inculcated and the stories used for the purpose. The former were almost certainly not new, because the whole aim was to conserve distinctive and characteristic features of pre-exilic life ; but this does not apply to the stories ; some are certainly based on old traditions, but others may be entirely new constructions for the purpose of teaching a lesson. This can be seen by the fact that often different reasons are given for the same custom. The Sabbath is commanded because God rested on the seventh day, or because a weekly rest day is necessary for man and beast. Similarly stories of the institution of circumcision are told about Abraham, Moses, and Joshua. A comparable reshaping of old traditions can be seen again in the later book of Jubilees.

Though the practices themselves were not new, there is often a new emphasis on their importance, and sometimes perhaps a change in their form. For example, circumcision [5] was of little importance in pre-exilic Palestine where the neighbouring peoples were also circumcised, but it had a new significance in Babylonia, where it was distinctive, and became a sign of the covenant between the people and Yahweh. The form of the rite also probably changed during the exile, when it was performed on eight-day old infants instead of being a puberty and marriage rite. The Sabbath, too, changed from a lunar feast to a regular seventh-day festival on which work ceased.

The second main tendency—the formation of an ideal temple cultus—is most clearly seen in the laws which are known as the Priestly Code, in which religious requirements were put into legal form, and traditional rites and institutions were codified in minutest detail. This tendency was present before the exile, when Jeremiah protested against making written laws the basis of religion and against believing that a book of the law was a substitute for spiritual communion with God (Jer. viii. 8). The process of codification was gradual, and it is possible to discover in the laws as well as in the history heterogeneous elements, which may represent either the amalgamation of different attempts to collect the laws, or alterations to bring laws into conformity with practice ; but in any case there is evidence in the various strata for gradual development. Such a development can be seen in the treatment of the high-priest. The laws in one part know only a priest who, though greater than his brethren, is yet *primus inter pares*, but later the high-priest becomes entirely different, he is anointed as the king had been, has the sole right to wear the implements of the oracle—Urim and Thummim—and to enter the Holy Place once a year ; his death marks an epoch, and he is superior to and gives orders to the civil leader.

Perhaps one of the most important developments is the Day of Atonement, the culmination of all the ceremonial, and " the keystone of the sacrificial system of post-exilic Judaism." Its date was fixed only after much hesitation, and was not known to Ezekiel or to Ezra. It combines two distinct cere-monies which are mutually exclusive and which both accom-plish the same purpose : the Levitical sprinkling of blood to cleanse from sin, and the sending away of the goat to Azazel in the wilderness, after sins had been transferred to it. Probably both ceremonies were extremely primitive, and were adapted for a new purpose by being brought into the religion of Yahweh. Belief in the power of the blood is known as very ancient, but there is evidence that the use of blood as a cleansing force was deliberately adopted by Judaism about the fifth century B.C.[6] The sending of a goat, bearing the sins of the people, to the demon of the desert was possibly part of the popular ceremonies which had always taken place at the New Year. It cannot be asserted definitely whether these and similar rites were due to the influence of Babylonian religion, with which they have been paralleled. Possibly they are due to developments from pre-exilic customs on lines analogous to those seen in Babylonia.

The outstanding feature of the priestly code is this revival of primitive customs and beliefs which had been rejected by the Deuteronomic reformers. It may have been a conscious return to the past, or have been due to re-emergence of earlier trends after the normal conditions of life and thought had broken down, but by it new life is given to many ancient rites which rested on tabu ideas and the fear of demons. The new moon again regulates the religious calendar, sacrifices are offered to appease an angry God, holiness has a physical contagion. Trial by ordeal is seen in the law requiring a wife accused of unfaithfulness to drink holy water (Num. v.), and there are the ancient ceremonies of burning a red heifer and sending away leprosy on a bird (Lev. xiv.). The use of amulets continues, and now the wearing of fringes, binding God's commandments on the forehead or on the doorpost, which were ancient safeguards against evil spirits, are pressed into the service of Yahweh.

Although as we read the books of Numbers and Leviticus some of these survivals appear to be crude and unspiritual, it must be realized that they all reveal the same religious attitude which we saw in Ezekiel. The prophet's teaching that sin and guilt had brought national disaster had had its effect on the common people, and they needed an assurance that guilt had been removed. By every possible means the priests tried to eliminate sin and guilt, and to produce a holy people in a holy land fit for a holy God.   They believed that Israel was still Yahweh's own peculiar people, but they recognized that the relationship was due to God's choice, and he would cast them off if they proved unworthy.   They recognized, too, that there was room in their religion for the proselyte and the foreigner, and they carried the story of Israel's origins back beyond Abraham to Adam, the father of all mankind.

This spiritual significance and inner meaning of the temple worship are seen most clearly in the Psalter. Dr. Wheeler Robinson has written: "No just view of Jewish religion can be gained by anyone who does not see the Psalter written in parallel columns with the book of Leviticus."[7]   The Psalms contain survivals from an ancient past adapted by the priests. Hymns to the sun, litanies of the king-cult, processional and pilgrimage songs, and forms of words regularly used at the temple in trials by ordeal, have all been combined to make a book of devotion unsurpassed in any literature.   They prove that Israel's priests were masters of the art of public and private worship, with a keen sense of the needs of worshippers and a deep reverence for the God who was present in the Holy Shrine of the temple.

§ INFLUENCE OF PERSIAN AND BABYLONIAN IDEAS

It is not easy to differentiate on the one hand Persian from Babylonian influence, or on the other to decide whether some of the distinctive influences from Mesopotamia usually connected with Persian religion entered Palestine at the time of the Persian conquests or were mediated later by the empire of Alexander the Great.   The inscription found at Persepolis[8] in A.D. 1935 relates how Xerxes in 484 B.C. at the command of the Persian god Ahura Mazda, destroyed Esagila the temple of Marduk at Babylon, and abandoned the annual ceremony of symbolically receiving the kingdom from the hand of Marduk at the New Year festival.   The action marked the end of the

Persian policy of religious toleration instituted by Cyrus when he conquered Babylonia ; it had considerable effect on the ancient world, as can be seen in the writings of the Greek poet Æschylus and possibly also in the oracles of an unknown Jewish prophet whose words have been inserted into Chapters xxiv.–xxvii. of the book of Isaiah. We do not know the effect on Jerusalem of this change in Persian policy, though Æschylus [9] suggests that Xerxes wantonly destroyed Greek shrines, and we know that temple property in Egypt was confiscated. Possibly Jews regarded discretion as the better part of valour, and were prepared to make certain concessions to Persian religion. In the Bible, and among the literature of the Jewish community at Yeb in Egypt, there is a tendency to avoid the use of the personal name Yahweh, and to use the more general term, God of Heaven, which was used of Ahura Mazda.

Judaism had much in common with the religion of Persia. Both were very ancient faiths which had been reformed and given deeper spiritual content. The earlier Persian religion, whose influence in Palestine and Syria can be traced from the fifteenth century B.C., was reformed by Zarathustra about the sixth century B.C., and thus became known as Zoroastrianism. Under his influence polytheism was abandoned, in its place being set the worship of the one god Ahura Mazda, the god of Light, who, like the Yahweh of Second-Isaiah, was creator of all things, light and darkness. The ethical element was stressed in Zoroastrianism as in Judaism ; both religions were based on a divinely given law-book, and as the later Jews personified Wisdom, regarding her as existing before the creation of the earth, so the Persians personified their divine law and thought of it as existing before the world. The stress on morals may perhaps be seen in the limestone altar at the Persian shrine found at Lachish and dated by Starkey about the third century B.C.[10] On opposite sides of the altar are a human hand in relief, and the figure of a man with upraised arms ; the single right hand is a recognized symbol of the deity in the act of blessing, and where these two symbols are found elsewhere they usually are associated with the Sun, as god of Justice.

Persian influence on Jewish thought can be traced most clearly in the development of the idea that a full life was possible after death, in the belief that the holy transcendent God had to be mediated to men through the activity of number-less angelic figures, and in speculation on the problems of the final destiny of the world and man.

As we have seen, archæology in Palestine has shown that from the earliest times there were rudimentary ideas of the possibility of rebirth or of life after death. Along different lines these ideas had developed among the Hebrews. Food and articles of personal property were placed in tombs to meet the future needs of the dead ; ancestor worship was based on the thought of an ancestor who was still alive and able to help or harm the members of his family group ; the story of the witch of Endor shows the belief that it was possible to invoke the living spirit of the dead in a form in which it could be recognized and could speak (1 Sam. xxviii.) ; the whole circle of ideas connected with fertility cults, the belief in the annual death and resurrection of vegetation and of the gods of vegeta-tion, could also be applied to human life and death, allow-ing the thought of the possibility of human rebirth from the womb of Mother Earth.

Another important element in the development of the Hebrew ideas of life after death was provided by the belief, found so clearly in Babylonian religion, that the dead go down to Sheol. To Babylonian thought Sheol was an underground city of darkness and hopelessness from which there was no return. The Hebrew, too, speaks of the " gates " and " bars " of Sheol to which men " go down " ; it is synonymous with the " pit " and with " destruction." But there are two important ideas connected with Sheol in the Old Testament : to the Hebrew, man was a body animated by the Spirit or Breath of God, and without a body human existence was unthinkable ; thus the disembodied shades who inhabited Sheol could not possess any real existence. The satire in the

book of Isaiah on the death of the king of Babylonia illustrates
this idea of Sheol :

> Sheol from beneath is stirred for thee, to greet thy coming ;
> It rouses for thee all the shades, all the great of the earth ;
> It raises up from their thrones all kings of the nations,
> All of them shall answer and say unto thee :
> Even thou art made weak like us, unto us thou art equal.
> Brought down to Sheol is thy Glory, the tumult of thy harps ;
> Worms are spread out as thy couch, maggots are thy coverlet.

(xiv. 9ff.).

The second point of interest is that Sheol was thought of as
beyond the presence of Yahweh. In Babylonian religion there
were gods of the underworld, but to the Hebrew there was no
remembrance of Yahweh in Sheol, none there could praise
him (Ps. vi. 5) ; Yahweh himself remembered no more those
who had gone down to Sheol, " for they are cut off from his
hand."

Belief in Sheol may gradually have replaced necromancy
and ancestor worship among the Israelites, and it is possible
that at an earlier stage even in Israel Yahweh was thought of
as having power in Sheol, for in Amos ix. 2 we find the proclamation that there would be no escape for fugitives from
God : " Though they dig into Sheol, thence will my hand
take them." This earlier belief, if it existed in Israel, may have
been destroyed by reformers who swept away a belief in real
existence after death when they broke from the myths of the
underworld and other heathen elements in religion, but it
appears more probable that belief in Sheol was deliberately
adopted by reformers in the sixth century, because it could
more easily make terms with Yahweh worship than could other
heathen cults of the dead.

The reformed Persian religion of Zarathustra appears to
have developed from the observation of natural phenomena a
doctrine similar to that of Paul in his letter to the Corinthians ;
that though at death this earthly body is dissolved, a new
spiritual body will clothe us in the after-life (2 Cor. v.). The
dark, lonely, hopeless hell is reserved only for the wicked,

whom a moral judgement at death separates from the good who go to a joyful paradise of light. The first definite proof of the influence of these ideas on Judaism occurs in passages which are usually assigned to the Greek period (Isa. xxvi. 19, Dan. xii. 2), but it is possible that Ezekiel's vision of the reborn Israel, Second-Isaiah's picture of the risen Servant of Yahweh, Job's triumphant faith and the Psalmists' belief that not even death could separate men from fellowship with God, all reflect this influence.

According to one Jewish tradition, the Jews brought the names of the angels from Babylon, but neither in Persian religion nor in Palestine was the belief in angels and demons a sudden growth. Behind it lay the polytheism of an older oriental world which could not be eradicated, some of the old gods being degraded into demons, and others becoming messengers or angels of the one true God. We saw how early tendencies toward monotheism caused the characteristics of different gods to be given to one supreme God ; here an opposite tendency caused attributes of the one God to be given a separate existence and personified.[11] In Palestine the development of the tendency belongs to the Greek period, and the traces of it which can be seen in the Hebrew Old Testament are difficult to date with certainty. We have seen in Ezekiel and Zechariah how reverence for the majestic holiness of God had created a demand for intermediaries to transmit God's will to the prophet ; this same demand is seen in the introduction of the " angel of Yahweh " into the stories of the early history of Israel, sometimes distinct from Yahweh, and at others identified with him ; and it is evident in the personification of Wisdom in the book of Proverbs. But it must be remembered that in the early pre-exilic religion Yahweh was not represented as alone ; he was surrounded by the " sons of God " and " all the host of heaven stood by him on his right hand and on his left " ; he could send out an evil spirit to torment Saul, or a lying spirit to entice Ahab to his doom. The later modification of monotheism by the growth of angelology was a return of old beliefs in a new form. The old local and functional gods were replaced by angels, and it is not possible with any confidence to assert the presence of Persian influence except in the developed forms of the belief.

The same judgement applies to the influence of Persian ideas on the Old Testament conceptions of the final destiny of the world.[12] As in Babylonian religion there had been pictured a conflict between good and evil forces, so in Persian there is developed a dualism of good and evil, light and darkness, Ahura Mazda and Ahriman, and Persian speculation was concerned with the way in which victory would be finally won by goodness. We shall find traces of this speculation in the Greek period, but, apart from those elements which Persian religion held in common with the older Iranian culture and which may have entered Judaism through Canaan in pre-exilic times, it seems probable that Persian influence was mediated by Greek culture after the conquests of Alexander the Great.

BOOK V
THE PARTING OF THE WAYS

CHAPTER 14

THE GREEK PERIOD

§ DIVERGING TENDENCIES

EXCAVATIONS in Palestine have warned us against thinking that in the whole land there was a high level of religious development, or that either the vision of Second-Isaiah or the lofty achievement of priestly religion had succeeded in stamping out all lower forms. Bousset wrote : [1]

Whenever the higher faith of a people shows signs of a break up, or threatens collapse, before newer and higher forms have crystallized—that is in the periods of transition—lower forms of belief issue again from the depths of popular consciousness. So in Judaism and all the surrounding world in the Greek and Roman period, with the crumbling of religious beliefs a rank growth of superstition luxuriated with uncanny vigour ; beliefs in demons, ghosts, exorcisms, magical spells, the power of a name, tying of knots, and numerous other crazy practices became the religious stock-in-trade of the world.

This statement is confirmed by archæological evidence. From Samaria comes proof of magical practices, in the form of figures with a right hand or leg twisted off, and at Marissa in the south, numerous little lead figures were discovered with hands and legs bound together.

The reassertion of old oriental religious beliefs which had never been suppressed can be seen in the syncretistic tendencies of the transition period. The coinage of Palestine and Phœnicia shows us old native gods reappearing in hellenic dress. Mountain gods of the Baal and Hadad type are associated with the cult of Zeus ; youthful gods like Adonis, and redeemers like Mithra, considerably increase in numbers.[2] Yahweh was identified with Zeus at least by the fourth century, probably in the very religious city of Gaza with its eight great temples. The small coin mentioned above, now in the British Museum, pictures the Solar Zeus, but the name on the coin is that of Yahu in Aramaic lettering of the fourth century B.C. The Alexandrian Jew who was the author of the famous letter of Aristeas wrote : " Greek and Jew worship the same God, Lord and Creator of the Universe, though we call him by different names." The Most High God—Zeus Hypsistos—was invoked by Greek and Jew. We have here another movement toward monotheism, recalling the one in the Persian period when, after religious intolerance under Xerxes had given greater supremacy to Ahura Mazda, the use of the phrase, " God of Heaven," showed that even in Judaism there was a tendency to worship the universal Sky-God and to regard all the great gods as different manifestations of the same deity.[3] Another factor in the movements towards monotheism must have been the dispersal of Jews throughout the whole Greek empire. The synagogues they built in almost every city brought to Gentile neighbours the idea of a God who was not bound to any one shrine or locality.

These syncretistic movements toward monotheism were in conflict with other syncretistic tendencies to revive old polytheism. Artaxerxes II, in whose reign Ezra probably returned to Palestine, was not content with the worship of Ahura Mazda ; he gave official recognition to the redeeming solar-god Mithra, and also set up throughout his empire images of the goddess Anahita. We know that such an image was erected at Damascus ; possibly there were others elsewhere in Syria and even in Palestine. Such worship would strengthen the cult of Anath, which we found persisting among the Jews at Yeb, but on the other hand it would rouse the bitter opposition of those Jews who shared the religion of Second-Isaiah, believing in the uselessness of idols and the uniqueness of Israel's redeemer Yahweh. Yet to quote Professor Oesterley : " It must be recognized that during the two or three generations immediately preceding the beginning of the Greek period (roughly 300 B.C.) a monotheistic belief was by no means yet accepted by the Jews as a whole." [4] Just as the writings of Ezekiel and Second-Isaiah contain evidence of contemporary Jewish idolatry, so the condemnation of idol worship in the Apocryphal literature shows that even so late as the Maccabæan period Jews were not free from this danger.

Many scholars find evidence for strife within Judaism in the last eleven chapters of Isaiah, which since the time of Duhm in A.D. 1892 have been generally regarded as a separate third section of the book, and called Trito-Isaiah. There reference is made to tables spread for Gad the god of luck, and to wine poured out to Mene the god of fortune ; mysterious sacrificial cults with a recrudescence of earlier pre-exilic forms of worship are also mentioned as practised in Palestine. From classical and archæological evidence we know of the fish goddess at Askalon, and of a temple at Bethshan built to the worship of Bacchus. Herod the Great not only built the wonderful temple to Yahweh at Jerusalem but an equally splendid one at Samaria to the worship of Augustus the Roman Emperor, with an altar for sacrifices to be offered before the emperor's colossal statue. In the Persian period the Jews at Yeb had recognized the existence of " The Gods " of Egypt, and had taken oaths by Sati the consort of the local Egyptian god Khnum, but now even in Palestine itself we can trace considerable influence of the worship of foreign gods—citrus fruit and branches carried at the feast of Tabernacles, and the lights used in the festival of the winter solstice, are from the cult of Dionysus ; during this period, too, the personal name Yahweh was replaced by Adonai—a word which could not but be associated with Adonis.

Another conflict which marks this period is between the vision of the writer of the Servant songs in Isaiah, and the policy of Nehemiah—the ideals of inclusiveness and the practice of exclusiveness. Haggai had rejected the help of northern Israelites, and Nehemiah's southern kingdom was small and exclusive, centring round an isolated Jerusalem, and having the nationalism of the Deuteronomic laws as its basis. Exclusive nationalism, expressed in cruel vindictiveness and fanatical intolerance, is revealed in the "ideal" account of Joshua's conquest of Canaan given in the Deuteronomic writings in the book of Joshua ; it is seen, too, in the vehemence of many of the prophetic utterances against the Gentiles, and in the book of Esther. Perhaps this intolerance was necessary to enable Israel to fulfil her destiny, but it had from pre-exilic days been opposed by the great prophets. They proclaimed that though Israel was Yahweh's child, like a father he would chasten ; that God's choice of Israel as a peculiar treasured people brought not favouritism and privileges but responsibility : " You only have I known—entered into intimate contact with—of all the families of the earth, therefore will I visit upon you all your iniquities " (Amos iii. 1). The beautiful idyll of Ruth traced the ancestry of the great hero David to intermarriage with the hated foreigner ; and the writer of the challenging story of Jonah pictures God as filled with compassion for the perishing thousands of heathen Nineveh and their cattle. Both books revolted against the self-centred exclusiveness of the new Judaism.

Second-Isaiah had seen the Jews as a missionary people with a message for the nations, a people chosen to give to the world the peculiar treasure of its law, a martyr offering life itself that the Gentile might know the only true God ; but now a compromise grew up which emphasized other elements in the prophet's teaching. Zion was to be the centre of a new religious empire, nations would flow to it, and pilgrimage thither would be a necessary condition of material prosperity, even of nature's gift of rain (Zech. xiv. 17). The vision of a people becoming great as servants of God with something of value to give the world was replaced by the dream of a world dominated by a priestly people possessing a monopoly of saving rites, and the ideal of the equality of all men gave way to the thought of Gentiles as tributaries—hewers of wood and drawers of water. Passages can be quoted from the Jewish writings of the Greek period which show that national exclusiveness was not accepted by all Jews (Ecclus. x. 2, Testament of Twelve Patriarchs, Judah xxiv. 5f.), but it received the main emphasis. Eating with Gentiles as well as intermarriage was forbidden, and the book of Jubilees (xxx. 7) repeats the Deuteronomic demand for the death penalty for the latter offence.

There was a similar divergence between those who stressed the ritual elements in religion and those who placed the emphasis on the spiritual side. This conflict, too, had its roots in the teaching of the pre-exilic prophets—perhaps even farther back, in the difference between nomadic and Canaanite religious customs. The prophets, in their revolt against all that savoured of heathenism, had probably rejected much of value which later returned in the priestly code. Amos, and perhaps Hosea, had not hesitated to regard sacrificial ritual as foreign to the pure religion of Yahweh, but by the time of Jeremiah, as we have seen, sacrifices were claimed as instituted at the command of Yahweh and as ensuring the safety of the nation ; Ezekiel regarded the profanation of the Sabbath as a major cause of the exile, and Haggai made the rebuilding of the temple his first aim. The so-called Trito-Isaiah stressed ritual observance just as did Nehemiah, and in the official religion which triumphed at Jerusalem after the exile, ritualism was dominant. This official religion, as it is reflected in the priestly code, made the institutions of religion of supreme importance —orders of the priesthood, elaborate sacrifices, distinction between clean and unclean, rites of purification, and observance of the religious calendar. This same emphasis can be seen in the descriptions of temple ritual given in Ecclesiasticus (l. 1–21), the letter of Aristeas, and the collection of Jewish teaching contained in the Mishna.[5]

But there were other influences at work. Two of these— the Wisdom literature, and the religion of the law—will be looked at later ; they played an important part in curbing the priestly reaction to the past and the concentration on religious observances. But of more interest is the fact that the moral and spiritual religion of the prophets did not die. The book of Deuteronomy places in the forefront of God's requirements the moral decalogue, and combines ritual with morality; the concluding chapters of Isaiah contain, along with a stress on ritualism, the prophecy of a religion without even a temple, and the book of Psalms—the " Hymn-book of the second temple " or the " Anthem-book of the Levitical choirs "—shows the same combination.   Though some of the Psalms, like the book of Chronicles, have been impregnated with ritualism, and it is obvious that the Psalter as a whole has been adapted for temple and cult usage, yet beneath this adaptation lies a wealth of personal devotion and private piety. Possibly this piety sprang from the worship of Jews in the Diaspora, scattered throughout the world and beyond the reach of regular attendance at the temple in Jerusalem ; possibly it reflects the religion of the laity in Palestine ; but in either case it was the lineal descendant of the religion of Micah and Jeremiah.   Even when the Psalmist was among the temple crowd his interest was in the singing of praise, in the moral rather than the ritual requirements of the law, and he rejoiced in being in the presence of God more than in offering bloody sacrifices.   That there was a conflict between the two types of religion is seen from Psalm li.   The man who wrote, " Thou delightest not in sacrifice else would I give it ; thou hast no pleasure in burnt offering," is not likely to be the same as he who wrote three verses later, " Then shalt thou delight in proper sacrifices, in burnt offerings and whole burnt offerings : then shall they offer bullocks upon thine altar."   There is ample evidence of editorial activity in the Psalter, and it is of considerable interest to find this trace of conflict surviving. It reminds us that all these diverging tendencies and the numerous revolts against orthodox doctrine were movements within Judaism itself ; there was no seceding from the main body. The prophets from Amos to Jeremiah remained inside Judaism, regenerating the religion from within.   This fact had an enormous influence on the development of biblical religion. A difference of emphasis, condemned by contemporaneous official religion, could later be incorporated, and enrich the religion against which it had revolted.

§ THE MACCABÆAN REVOLT

Among the many causes leading to the Maccabæan revolt the chief was the sudden attempt of Antiochus IV—Epiphanes —to enforce the complete hellenization of Jewish religion. Until this attempt there had been a gradual permeation of Greek influence into Judaism. This influence came through two channels, from the Jews in the Diaspora, and directly from the Greeks themselves. Since the conquests of Alexander the Great there had been a rapid spread of Jewish population outside Palestine, particularly in Egypt. From 312 to 200 B.C. Palestine and Syria were under Egyptian control and archæology reveals that strong hellenistic influence on Palestine at this time was mediated through Egypt, where, as we know, there was a large and active Jewish community. In particular the influence of Alexandrian Jewry was dominant, and formed the channel through which came much Greek influence—a fact that may explain the very large Egyptian element in the Psalms and Proverbs, as well as in other parts of the Wisdom literature.

But Greek influence also entered in a more direct way. Alexander had settled Macedonian troops and colonists in Palestine, founding some new cities, but mainly hellenizing existing ones, particularly in the maritime plain, along the frontiers, and at strategic points, so that Judæa was surrounded by Greek colonies and deeply influenced by Greek customs and ideas. When the Seleucid Antiochus III conquered Palestine in 200 B.C. and drove out the Egyptians, he won over the temple personnel by exempting them from the special poll tax. We have seen how, under Zerubbabel, and again at the time of Nehemiah, the priestly hierarchy was more open to foreign influences and freer from traditional Judaism, and here again we see the priests taking a leading part in the acceptance of hellenic ideas. But the Seleucid monarchs did not regard the high-priest as holding a hereditary office. He was the leader of the people, to be kept in office only so long as he retained the Seleucid favour and could outbribe his opponents. Consequently the high-priest became subservient to the Greek ruler, and showed little respect for the customs and traditions of his own people. Jason, a Jewish high-priest, sent representatives to the great games festival at Tyre with a gift to provide a sacrifice for Zeus. The cleavage between hellenizing leaders and traditionalist Jews widened until the outbreak of the great Maccabæan revolt in 167 B.C. From 1 Maccabees i. we learn that considerable numbers of Jews had accepted hellenistic modifications of Judaism, abandoning monotheism, observance of the Sabbath, and the practice of circumcision.

Hellenistic influence had at first been gradual, and wisely the Seleucids did not attempt to force Greek culture on the Jews, but granted it as a privilege and as an expression of royal favour. Even Antiochus IV was petitioned for permission to build a gymnasium in Jerusalem. Many Jews welcomed Greek culture as offering a more enlightened religion, bringing the advantages of Greek civilization. Just as Israelites had identified Yahweh with the fertility Baals, and later with the Persian Ahura Mazda as God of the Heavens, so now Jews were willing to use phrases which identified Yahweh with Zeus. Assimilation could be seen in dress, language, and the neglect even of such a distinctive Jewish practice as circumcision. But there still remained a large number of conservative Jews who clung tenaciously to their ancient customs. When Antiochus, for political reasons, attempted to crush what he thought to be a small conservative element, he went too far even for hellenistic Jews. They had been willing to assimilate their religion to Greek thought and practice, but they were not willing that their religion should be replaced by Greek worship, that the Zeus image, possibly with the features of Antiochus, should stand in the temple, that pigs should be sacrificed there, and that circumcision, the observance of the Sabbath, and the reading of the Scriptures should be forbidden. The whole country became united in a fight for religious freedom, and throughout the whole nation in Palestine, Greek influence was suddenly checked. Judas Maccabæus, who became the national leader, was an uncompromising traditionalist, and any hellenistic Jews who would not join in the struggle for freedom were treated as Gentiles, persecuted, and slain.

The victory which came exactly three years after the desecration of the temple, caused, however, a break in the Jewish ranks, and the emergence of opposing parties in Judaism —a prominent feature of these years. The Hasidim, or pious ones, who had joined in the fight for religious freedom, and had even obeyed the summons to fight on the Sabbath day, were not willing to continue the fight for political independ- ence. These Hasidim later became known as Pharisees. They stood for a Levitical high-priesthood and a Davidic Messiah or king, and thus strongly opposed the family of Judas when it assumed the office of high-priest and later of king.

The Hasidim were not, however, the dominant party, the fight was continued, and an important development took place at the end of the second century B.C., when on the con- quest of Idumæa in the south and Galilee in the north, the inhabitants were forcibly made to accept Jewish religion and customs. The action represented a complete reversal of the policy of Haggai and Nehemiah, which had aimed at preserving the purity of the religious nucleus, and marked a return to a political instead of a religious ideal for the national destiny, a political ideal which eventually brought ruin to the Jewish people in A.D. 70 and 132.

§ THE WISDOM LITERATURE

We have seen that Palestinian Judaism was greatly influenced by the Jews in Egypt ; there are many scholars—particularly Professor Causse [6]—who would trace to a large extent the diverging tendencies within the Judaism of this period to the large number of Jewish communities dispersed throughout the Greek empire. As fifteen centuries earlier under the Hyksos rulers Palestine had been the centre of a widespread empire, and had received fresh religious impulses both from

east and west, so now the movement of her own sons to and
fro throughout the world conquered by Alexander the Great
caused a free exchange of ideas which left considerable impression
on the development of biblical religion.   Probably it was this
widespread Diaspora which was responsible for the growth of
Persian ideas in Palestine, the rapid acceptance of the idea of
the resurrection, and the appearance of many writings containing a programme of the future and describing the end of
the age.

   The greatest monument to the influence of the Diaspora
is the writings which are called the Wisdom Literature.   In
the Hebrew Old Testament, Proverbs, Job, Ecclesiastes, and
some of the Psalms belong to this literature, while in the larger
Greek canon there are also Ecclesiasticus or the Wisdom of Ben
Sira, and the Wisdom of Solomon.   Professor Oesterley [7] has
rightly stressed the cosmopolitan character of these writings.
In the Bible it was early recognized that wisdom was universal :
Edomite and Egyptian wisdom are mentioned ;   Solomon's
wisdom is compared with that of " The children of the east " ;
and Job and his friends are represented as non-Israelites.   The
Jews were familiar with the wisdom literature of Egypt and
Babylonia ;   a passage in the Proverbs—xxii. 17 to xxiii. 14
—has been borrowed from an Egyptian writing called the
" Teaching of Amen-em-ope " ;   and a fragment of an Aramaic
version of the Babylonian wisdom book, the story of Ahikar,
was found among the Jewish documents at Yeb.   Hebrew
wisdom shared many of the characteristics common to the
wisdom writings of other nations :   cosmopolitan humani-
tarianism replaced Jewish nationalism ;   there is a cold detached
attitude to religion, and an appeal to practical experience rather
than to tradition or national history.   But it is interesting that
in Hebrew wisdom, in spite of the prominence of the inquisitive
and speculative spirit, there is never any doubt expressed as
to the existence of God or about monotheism, and also there
is little evidence of the kind of speculation we have seen in
Persian eschatology, and theories about the after life ;   it is
throughout monotheistic and confines its horizon to this life.

There is not unanimity among scholars as to the extent of direct Greek influence in Hebrew wisdom writings. Dr. Ranston, Schürer, and Cheyne [8] have claimed that the influence of the Greek spirit was strong from the second century onwards, and that it can be seen in the Psalms, and in the inquisitive attitude in Ecclesiastes and in Job ; Kennett believed that though Hebrew wisdom was stimulated by Greek philosophy it remained emphatically Hebrew, and that nowhere, with the possible exception of Ecclesiastes, are there any traces of Greek thought ; Professor Oesterley would agree that the religion of the Jews remained uninfluenced by Greek philosophy and ideas, although Greek influence can be traced in the thought of individual Jewish writers. Probably it is wiser to agree with Dr. Ranston that, although no direct quotations can be found in Hebrew writings from such Greek wisdom writers as Theognis and Hesiod, yet ideas from such men had penetrated into the circles in which the Jewish writers lived. To quote Cheyne, " There was a fertilization of the intellectual soil by new ideas throughout all the Jewish world." [9]

Three main types of wisdom teaching can be discerned in the Old Testament. The aim of the first was to present the truths of religion in a form in which they would appeal to men of the world, so that the non-religious man would accept them and live by them. The best example of this form of wisdom is the book of Proverbs, which has been described as a " popular handbook of religious instruction," carefully planned to appeal to the man who wishes to know what is the practical value of religion and how it can be applied to the ordinary affairs of daily life ; it is marked by much practical common sense. The writer believed that reverence for God is the first essential of wisdom, but that worldly prosperity is the inevitable outcome of religion. There is a prophetic insistence on the unity of religion and morality : " He that oppresseth the poor reproacheth his Maker : but he that hath mercy on the needy honoureth him " (xiv. 31). The writer was a man of simple faith in the justice of God, with deep religious feeling, honestly endeavouring to prove that " Religion is the best policy." He attempts to work out practically Ezekiel's doctrine of individual retribution in this life ; worldly success or failure follows naturally, in his view, as reward or punishment from God. There is an attempt to inculcate a scale of values which makes a man recognize that " wisdom is better than riches," " better is little with reverence for Yahweh, than great treasure with trouble. Better is a dinner of herbs where love is than a stalled ox with hatred " (Prov. xv.) ; but the reader is encouraged to believe that wisdom will bring riches and enable the righteous to flourish. Even such subtlety and cleverness as was displayed by Jacob is accepted as an outcome of wisdom, and the appeal throughout is selfish—there is great gain in possessing the wisdom that springs from reverence for God (iii. 13ff.).

The second type of wisdom found an easy contact with the prophetic conception of Yahweh as the controller of nature, particularly as it was proclaimed by Second-Isaiah. It encouraged an interest in cosmic phenomena and in the contemplation of God's work in nature. It asserted that there was no break in consistency within God's world, so that contemplation of nature became a remedy against scepticism or despair. Wisdom was personified as a pre-existent worker with God in the creation of all things—a belief which influenced the later doctrines of the " Word of God " without whom nothing was made, and of the pre-existent Messiah. In Babylonian speculations Nabu, the god of wisdom, was represented as Marduk's helper in creation, and it is of interest that the word " wisdom " is feminine in Hebrew, so that with the personification we have a sublimation of the feminine principle in deity.

This type of wisdom is seen clearly in part of Proverbs viii. and in the speeches which are put into the mouth of God in the book of Job—speeches which have been described as intended " to humble Job, but also to encourage him to step out into the picture gallery of God's world." The God who in the ancient days had thundered from Sinai, before whose march from Seir the earth trembled, the heavens dropped their rain, and the mountains lost their stability or flowed like a molten stream, was still the God whose ways were so far removed from man's ways that they were past finding out. The writers of the nature Psalms—viii., xix., xxix., lxv., civ., cxlviii.—had taught men the wonder of the creator and sustainer of all things, and the poet who wrote the speech in Job xxxviii. endeavoured to teach a faith in a God who "moves in a mysterious way," "deep in unfathomable mines of never failing skill," whose wisdom must be trusted though it cannot be traced.

Disillusionment and successive disappointments of the post-exilic age brought a third type of wisdom which was more intellectual ; it revolted against the orthodox doctrine of individual retribution, and was not content to rest on faith in an inscrutable creator, but attempted to face the problem as to whether God was friendly and his government of the world just. It is seen at its best in the book of Job. Probably the story of Job was old ; Job is mentioned by Ezekiel (xiv. 14, 20) with Daniel and Noah as a proverbially wise man. The name Daniel was known at Ras Shamra in the fourteenth century ; possibly the name of Job was equally old, and a story woven round the name was retold to show that suffering may be, not the result of sin, but the test of the reality of a man's faith. The writer of the Servant songs in Second-Isaiah had held that suffering might be a means of redeeming others from sin—an approach to the interpretation of the cross of Jesus of Nazareth. Here, in the prologue to the book of Job, suffering is regarded as the proof of disinterested and unselfish piety. Job suffers to disprove the sneer of Satan, " Doth Job serve God for naught ? "—perhaps another facet of Calvary, if we may accept the older view that there was a cry of desolation from the cross, rather than the more modern opinion that the cry was a shout of triumph introducing Psalm xxii. which ends with the note of praise and confidence.

The book does not give a complete answer to the problem of how the suffering of innocent individuals can be reconciled with the justice of God. Jesus later suggested that such suffering could be used to proclaim the power of God : in answer to the question, " Did this man sin or his parents that he was born blind ? " he answered " Neither, but that God may be glorified " (John ix.).   Job claims that suffering may be the supreme test of faith, to prove the intrinsic worth of God to the believing soul—an absolute abnegation that gives everything in worship to God, hoping for nothing in return,   We have seen the same faith in the psalm at the end of the book of Habakkuk, and it occurs again in the book of Daniel when the Hebrew youths, replying to the king's threat, expressed their faith in the power of their God to deliver them, and added, " But if not, be it known unto thee, O king, that we will not serve thy gods " (Dan. iii. 18).

The writers both of the Servant songs and of Job revolted against the orthodox doctrine preached by the pre-exilic prophets and assumed by the Deuteronomic historians, that calamity is invariably caused by sin.   Events disproved and belied the doctrine, and showed it to be inadequate for practical purposes.   In the picture of the Servant the old conception of the corporate unity of the nation is used to meet the impatience of the nationalist who asked why the nation suffered, but Job, following Jeremiah, accepts the later valuation of the individual, and finds the road toward solution along the path of individual fellowship with God.   Both have a rock-like faith in a God who is interested in and loves the individual, to whom a man can turn in distress seeking justification.   The book of Job reaches great heights of religion : chapter xxxi. contains an excellent summary of Jewish morality of that early Greek period—the same mixture of morals and ritual found earlier in the book of Leviticus, but it contains also the attempt to cleanse the soul from bitterness, the recognition that it is not enough to bear with patience any suffering, that all resentment and sense of injustice must be purged from one's life, so that when nailed to the cross of suffering it is possible to pray, " Father forgive them, for they know not what they do."

Very different is the contribution made by the writer of the other wisdom book, Ecclesiastes.   It is, as Professor Lods [10] says, a far more incisive criticism of established doctrine. The writer is a man who rejects the orthodox belief in individual retribution, and knows nothing of the fellowship with the living God which is found in Job ; under Greek influence he reaches a radically sceptical attitude. In spite of his scepticism he is no atheist ; God is in the background of all his thinking ; yet though he retains the belief in the existence of God, his horizon is bounded by the daily life of work, food, and pleasure. Often he reiterates the belief that the only thing worth while in life is to take pleasure in one's work and food, all else is to no purpose, a striving after wind, and in his disillusionment he declares that all paths lead to the grave. He rejects as unproved the newer doctrine of immortality ; no-one can be sure that at death the process of creation is reversed, and the breath that made man a living soul returns to God when the body dissolves in the dust (iii. 21) ; it is better to be a living dog than a dead lion (ix. 4). Partly his scepticism was the result of losing all social sense. The emphasis on the individual had taken from him the old nomadic sense of corporate unity, and he had not learned to put in its place a consciousness of social solidarity which recognizes the responsibility of the individual to his group—an essential element in Hebrew and Christian religion.

§ THE LAW

While all these extraneous influences were bearing on Judaism, there grew up in the religion itself a profound reverence for the written law.[11] That this began very early is seen from Jeremiah's protest against the growing belief that the possession of writings could supersede fellowship with God : " How do ye say, we are wise, and the law of the Lord is with us ? Behold the false pen of scribes hath made lies " (viii. 8). But it is clear that the work of codification during the exile in Palestine and Babylonia had given a new prominence to the law as a distinctive feature of Jewish religion, both for the priests whose temple ritual was enshrined within it, and for the scattered Jews of the Diaspora who could never participate in the sacrificial ritual, but could study the revelation of God in the sacred book.

Like the growth of personal piety and of the prophetic idea of a spiritual temple, this book religion tended to curb the influence both of the priestly return to the ritual of the past and of the movement towards hellenism. The real centre of this new religion of the law was the synagogue, an institution which appears to have been original to Judaism. The first evidence we have of the existence of synagogues comes from an inscription of Ptolemy III (246–221 B.C.) found at Shedia near Alexandria, and it is probable that they were a creation of the Jews outside Palestine, to whom the temple was out of reach. Sukenik [12] tells us that so far no remains of synagogues have been found in Palestine which can be dated earlier than the first century A.D., but Psalm lxxiv. 8 shows that there were such places of worship in Palestine by the time of Antiochus Epiphanes (175–163 B.C.). The first definite reference to synagogues in Palestine occurs in 1 Enoch (xiv. 8), but the fact that they are not mentioned in the book of Maccabees suggests that there was no regular worship in synagogue buildings; possibly, like the Christian churches, buildings came later than assemblies for worship in private houses. The object of the weekly assemblies which took place in these synagogues was twofold—worship and instruction. At first the synagogue was called a " House of Prayer "—a phrase used in Isaiah lvi. to describe the temple—but every meeting included, in addition to public prayer by one of the worshippers and responses by the congregation, a reading from the Pentateuch and from the Prophets, with a translation into the vernacular Aramaic and an exposition. In its inception it appears to have been " a cult without clergy," the only officials being those who had been chosen to maintain order, and to take charge of the finances. There was a minimum of symbolism or ceremonial; as in the pre-exilic prophetic religion, the appeal was made primarily to the conscience, will, and intellect rather than to the senses; in many ways it was a movement toward that pure adoration "in spirit and in truth" which Jesus foretold (John iv.). It cannot, however, be emphasized too strongly that this worship in the synagogues was bound by indissoluble ties to the temple cult, for both accepted the same law-book ; to both, though it could not be practised in the synagogue, the sacrificial priestly cultus was an essential part of the true religion demanded by God in his will revealed in the law ; both stressed the moral as well as the ritual requirements of God. Jewish literature contains a story of how on one occasion the choir of Levitical singers walked from the temple to a neighbouring synagogue, thus taking part in both services.[13] The difference was that the one could exist so long as there was a law to be studied, the other of necessity ceased when the temple was destroyed.

Very soon a group of officials arose, however, in the synagogue, particularly the class known as Scribes. Most of them belonged to the section of Jews who during the second century B.C. had become called Pharisees (cf. 1 Macc. vii. 12f.), and were opposed to the Sadducees or priestly aristocracy. These Pharisees appear to have been the spiritual descendants of the Pious Ones or Hasidim, who separated themselves from the Maccabæans when the latter began their fight for political independence ; their name may mean " those who were separate," or, it has been suggested, though without much acceptance, that it may be formed from the word "Persian," and be a reference—from opponents, like most such nicknames— to the fact that they were willing to accept certain Persian modifications of the old religion, such as, for example, the belief in the resurrection. They were, however, men who were willing to give their lives in unflinching attachment to the sacred scriptures and the customs handed down by tradition ; their influence dates from this heroic time. After the destruction of the temple in A.D. 70 and the consequent abolition of the temple cultus, the Sadducees lost their position of administration ; spiritual power and authority passed to the Scribes and Pharisees, who appear to have been more concerned with the synagogue and its worship. It was their decisions that had legal force in Judaism. It is of interest to notice that though these Scribes and Pharisees stood for the law and the traditional customs, they were not the conservatives in thought, for the priestly Sadducees, as we know from the New Testament, were far less ready to modify their views by accepting the Persian belief in life after death, or by accepting the traditional oral law.

Even during the Old Testament period the Scribes had been organized into guilds (1 Chron. ii. 55), and high praise was given to them by Ben Sira (Ecclus. xxxviii. 24) as men who searched out wisdom, meditated on the law, occupied themselves in prayer, and, like the ancient prophets, stood in the councils of God.

The duty of the scribe was to interpret the law, because the simple believer was not regarded as competent to decide for himself as to the interpretation of a particular passage. Among scribes divergent views were settled by a majority vote. Every decision had to be based on an interpretation of a biblical passage and on the oral law which, it was claimed, had been handed down in unbroken succession from Moses and which had a validity equal to that of the written law.[14] Though some of those interpretations were forced and far from the original meaning, and the whole method was extremely cumbersome, yet it offered the possibility of development and change. These decisions were collected, and along with oral law were given the same value as Old Testament writings; it must be remembered that Jesus's condemnation of this religion of the law arose from the emphasis placed on the later casuistical rules, which often, in both spirit and letter, contradicted the older law (Mark vii.). This casuistical type of law can be seen most clearly in the Mishna, where there is considerable discussion as to what the Law allows and forbids. Much of the discussion contains admirable teaching, but some can be described as a " mosquito swarm of little things." Professor Oesterley has written of it :

Pharisaism had created the oral law to be a fence for the protection of the pious against sin, and the nobler side of Pharisaism so regarded it.

Ruins of the synagogue at Capernaum

Stone from the ruins showing bunch of grapes and star

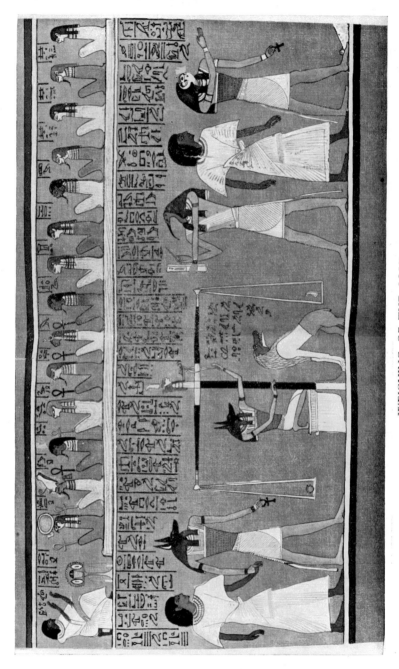

WEIGHING OF THE SOUL

(From " Papyri of Hunefer and Anhai," by Sir Ernest Budge)

To the less noble side of Pharisaism the fence had become an all-absorbing interest, transcending that which it guarded—the fence of imprisonment rather than the fence of protection.[15]

Professor Lods sums up this religion of the Law in the following words :

To the law the preservation of Judaism is due. Every hour of life it controlled men and stopped assimilation to surroundings. It inculcated in successive ages the prophetic principles : the unity of God and the high moral demands seen in the Pentateuch. But it linked for ever Judaism with many archaic practices originally inspired by most primitive ideas of Semitic paganism. The law tried to spiritualize some of them by new interpretations, but often it perpetuated the naturalistic and magical beliefs which had given birth to such rites. The law juxtaposes without any real synthesis ancient and modern, material and spiritual, individual and national, and is characteristic of the new stage which Judaism represents in the evolution of the religion of Israel.

§ THE APOCALYPTIC WRITERS

Though the Pharisees predominated in later Judaism and established in it the central authority and importance of the Law, in some writings of the Greek and Roman period, from 200 B.C. to A.D. 100, the Law is almost disregarded. These writings—called apocalyptic—occupy a considerable portion of the Apocrypha and Pseudepigrapha, the literature which, as we have seen, was included in the Greek Old Testament, but not in the Hebrew ; all are written under assumed names. Like the book of Daniel, some of the books are given the names of great men of the past—Enoch, Esra, and the Testaments of the Twelve Patriarchs : others are edifying popular tales more akin to the book of Jonah, such as Judith and Tobit.

These apocalyptic writings have much in common with those of the prophets of pre-exilic Israel. All contain evidence of considerable religious enthusiasm and claim direct divine inspiration (1 Enoch i. 2) ; the moral element in their teaching is strong, there is a demand for uprightness of character, truth in dealing with one's fellows, and an attitude of love and forgiveness. As historical events had played a part in the rise of the prophets, so war, persecution, and national unrest were the spring of these writings and procured for them a more ready acceptance among the common people. Like the prophets, these writers proclaimed doctrines which differed from the official religion of their time, but although the prophetic books became part of the canon of the Jewish Old Testament, the apocalyptic writings were never accepted by orthodox Judaism.

Burkitt [16] and Professor Oesterley rightly stress the importance of the writings to help us understand the attitude and religious background of the multitudes who listened to Jesus, and it is probable that Jesus, and to a greater extent his disciples, and the New Testament writers were influenced by them. Most of the writings have come to us through Christian hands, and they contain many prophecies on which Christians would naturally and readily seize as fulfilled in Jesus ; but Moore has shown that they represent tendencies outside the main stream of Jewish life and thought, and, because they are cast in a highly imaginative and visionary form, ought not to be used as a basis on which to build theories of the development of normal Jewish doctrine :

It may well be doubted whether the exegetical and juristic studies of the Rabbis, and under ordinary circumstances the hard realities of life for the people, let them get more excited about the end of the world and afterwards than either scholars or the mass of Christians to-day over the cabalistic combinations and chronological calculations of our own millenarians.

Much of the material contained in the Apocalypses probably came from popular Jewish traditions which gathered round the idea of the Day of Yahweh. This idea in its popular form was, as we have seen, rejected by the eighth-century prophets, but returned again in new forms in Ezekiel and post-exilic biblical writings. In the apocalyptic writings these traditional beliefs were mingled in confusing and irreconcilable contradictions with material from outside Judaism, and nowhere are external influences—especially from Persia—so clearly seen in Jewish literature.

The two subjects around which most of the thought of the writings clusters are the kingdom of Heaven and the life beyond death. The first term included all the joys of the return of the golden age under the rule of God. In the Old Testament the scene of the kingdom had been this earth with Jerusalem as its centre, and some of the writings of the Greek period retain this picture (Ecclus. xxxvi.), but the viewpoint of the apocalyptic writers is usually less national, the kingdom being set in the supernatural world where it was easier to conceive of God's rule as absolute (1 Enoch xlv.). Signs and wonders by which the coming of the kingdom could be recognized had been given by Old Testament prophets (cf. Zech. i., Joel ii., Ezekiel), but under Persian influence these were greatly elaborated, and the language used is, in many cases, identical with that of New Testament writers.

The picture drawn of the ideal ruler varies.[17] Sometimes the thought is theocratic and God himself is king, at others there is to be an anointed " Messiah " who may be a human figure—a Davidic prince from the tribe of Judah or a priest from Levi—or a supernatural divine being—the Son of Man coming on the clouds of heaven, and the object of man's worship (1 Enoch xlvi., lxii.).

Perhaps the most important development in Judaism during this period was in reference to life beyond death.[18] We have seen some of the movements toward belief in resurrection and a future life reflected in later writings in the Old Testament, but, under foreign influence, these beliefs grew and became systematized. The thought was not uniform. There were differences of opinion as to whether all would rise or only the good; as to the nature of the risen body which would be reunited to the spirit; and as to when the final judgement would take place. The removal of the bounds of human horizons from this world to the next affected the theories of retribution. No longer need the punishment for sin be sought in this life ; as there is to be an abode of bliss for the righteous, an earthly or heavenly paradise, so the wicked will be condemned to a hell combining the horrors of Sheol with the unquenchable fires of the valley of Hinnom where the rubbish of Jerusalem was burnt and where, in the sixth century, children had been sacrificed. Calamities, which to Jewish thought remained a sign of divine displeasure, had given to men in the Greek period a deep consciousness of sin : there was a stress on the need of repentance and the possibility of God's forgiveness. But, despite their religious fervour, apocalyptic writers did not offer the assurance of forgiveness which had been brought by the later prophets ; their hopes and aspirations centred in the Messianic kingdom which would intervene between the end of the present age and the final consummation of the world, and much of their enthusiasm was expended in arid wastes of curious speculation.

CHAPTER 15

THE PROPHETIC RENAISSANCE

§ PROPHETIC ELEMENTS IN THE TEACHING OF JESUS

THE story opens with a message from God, not to a prophet, but to a priest officiating in the temple. The priest's son, John the Baptist, became what in the Old Testament we should call a professional prophet, proclaiming a message of doom and judgement. He wore prophetic garb like Elijah—a camel-hair garment and a leather belt (Mark i. 6)—a garb which had previously been so discredited that a late edition to the book of Zechariah (xiii. 4) says that anyone wearing the hairy garment to deceive should be thrust through and slain by his parents. Like Amos, he proclaimed the near approach of the Day of Yahweh or the Reign of God, when all the wicked —Jew and Gentile—would be destroyed ; but he offered escape from the wrath of God to those who repented of their sins and by the symbolic act of initiation prepared to enter the Kingdom. This initial act was baptism, a Jewish rite of total immersion in water demanded of proselytes on entering Judaism, and possibly of priests after ceremonial defilement.[1] John, in true prophetic style, applied the rite to Jews themselves ; they needed the same cleansing to enter the Kingdom of God that was demanded of Gentiles entering Judaism, for descent from Abraham would not save them on the dread day. According to Luke's gospel there do not appear to have been any national boundaries to John's kingdom, and he baptized alike Pharisees, publicans, and soldiers (iii.).

One of those who were baptized was Jesus, a cousin of John, six months younger, whose birth had also been heralded by a divine message. Further stories were told about the birth of Jesus which, whatever may be their historical value, must be seen in their Jewish setting. God's part in all birth was recognized by Jewish thought : Eve said of Cain, " By the help of Yahweh I have gotten a man child," prophets spoke of God as forming them in the womb, and angels announced the coming of outstanding personalities ; there was thus little foreign to Hebrew thought in the story of the birth of Jesus. It should be remembered, however, that the genealogies showing the descent of Jesus from David trace it through Joseph, his earthly father.

Jesus, like his prophetic predecessors, did not break from the institutional religion of his day ; he attended and took part in the synagogue worship each Sabbath day (Luke iv. 16), and he taught in the temple, calling it " My Father's House." But like the prophets he condemned abuses in religion and lack of spirituality ; and, like the apocalyptic writers, he demanded as essentials of worship love of one another, forgiveness and the putting away of hatred and bitterness (cf. Testaments of the XII Patriarchs, Gad vi. 1–3). He challenged equally both forms of institutional religion which had grown up in Judaism, the priestly religion of the temple, and the scribal religion of the law. Although the temple was his natural centre in Jerusalem, yet his teaching was unaffected by its animal sacrifices, which he mentions only to condemn in Hosea's words, " I desire mercy and not sacrifice " (Matt. ix. 13, xii. 7). The prophets had been national leaders who made their appeal to the whole nation, often over the heads of rulers and religious leaders ; perhaps even more than they, Jesus went beyond the institutional religion of his day and made a direct appeal to outsiders to turn to God and enter his kingdom, seldom asking them to take part in synagogue or temple worship. One of the unproved charges made against him was that, like Jeremiah, he foretold the destruction of the temple. But the dogmas and practices that had grown up around the written law were also condemned—they are like straining your soup to keep out a gnat while letting a camel slip through, or carefully washing the outside of your cup and leaving the inside filthy (Matt. xxiii.). Even the Mosaic laws, which by that time were regarded as intrinsically holy because they were thought of as the final revelation of God's will, were treated by him as a stage in development to be completed by fuller revelation (Matt. v.).

Some religious practices, such as the observance of the Sabbath, fasting, and the rules of ritual purity, were at times deliberately broken by him, perhaps as a protest against the emphasis placed upon them. It would be difficult to find a more deliberate challenge to Sabbath observance than telling a healed man to carry his bed home through the streets of Jerusalem on the Sabbath (John v.)—but often there were Old Testament grounds for his action. He appears to have been widely read in the Scriptures and in contemporary Jewish literature. He appealed, for example, to the Mosaic law when he condemned oral traditions which allowed a man to make light of his duty to his parents (Mark vii.) ; and used the Deuteronomic version of the Sabbath law when he claimed that the Sabbath was made for man, and that God works every day of the week (Mark ii. 27 ; John v. 17).

Professor Wilson Knight says, " Jesus speaks in parable to awaken, rather than inject, the thought required ; to release an automatic recognition " ; in this Jesus follows the prophetic method used by Nathan. Another prophetic element, as Professor Dodd shows,[2] is his use of symbolic acts. Two of these were also a direct challenge to the authorities, and appear to have been largely responsible for his death : these acts were the triumphal entry into Jerusalem and the cleansing of the temple. The first aroused popular enthusiasm by publicly proclaiming that he was the Messiah, but at the same time it defined his conception of the Messiah as the same as that of the Pharisee who wrote the prophecy in Zechariah, which he was symbolically fulfilling : " Rejoice greatly O daughter of Zion ; shout O daughter of Jerusalem ; behold thy king cometh unto thee, he is just and bringing salvation ; lowly and riding upon an ass, upon a colt the foal of an ass." By the second act he symbolically cleansed the temple from its priestly corruptions and vested interests, and established the new order in which the building should no longer be a den of thieves, but a house of prayer for all peoples (Mark xi.).

A third symbolic act was performed alone with his disciples. The way in which he had said grace at meals was so characteristic that he could be recognized by it (Luke xxiv. 30), and he made this characteristic act a symbol of his death. The broken bread and poured-out wine were his broken body and his shed blood, and his disciples, by sharing the meal, became pledged to his sacrifice and entered the New Covenant, which, like Jeremiah's new covenant, brought forgiveness of sins and knowledge of God. Perhaps, like the older prophets, he regarded the actions as more than symbols and as themselves acts which began the fulfilment of God's purpose.

Like Isaiah, he gathered around him a body of disciples for special teaching, and it is probable that, like Jeremiah who had a secretary called Baruch, Jesus too had among his followers men who could commit to writing some of his words —a fact of considerable importance when we are studying the historicity of the stories and recorded teaching of Jesus.

But in many ways he went beyond the prophets. He does not use their phrase, "Thus saith Yahweh," but instead says, "I say unto you." Partly this was a revolt against contemporary rabbinical teachers who always quoted authorities or the chain of oral tradition for every statement, and partly it was due to his consciousness of authority derived from the indwelling of the Spirit of God (Mark i.). He also went farther by the way in which he lived out his teaching. Though many stories are told of him comparable to those of Elijah and Elisha—raising dead, multiplying food, controlling natural forces—yet we have also stories which illustrate his practical concern for the outcast, needy, and sinners, his way of breaking down class and religious barriers. Beyond the prophetic condemnations of abuses there was a new positive element, a kindliness and sympathy which gave to Hosea's word "Hesed" a richer, more personal meaning, so that men later coined the phrase, "The Grace (or Graciousness) of Jesus"; this new element was seen pre-eminently in the act in which—to quote his own words—he gave his life a ransom for many (Mark x. 45).

§ His Teaching about the Kingdom

From the Gospel records we learn that the idea of the Kingdom was central to the teaching of Jesus as it was to the apocalyptic writers, with whom in some ways he appears to have had more in common than with some forms of orthodox Judaism. He began his public ministry by proclaiming, as John had done, that the Kingdom was near, and he was executed under the superscription, "King of the Jews." There was much in common between his teaching of the Kingdom and that of Judaism. Under Persian influence, apocalyptic Judaism had developed the idea that there were periods in which the world was under the control of Evil which would be overthrown by the final victory of God. These eschatological hopes had modified the old popular idea of the "Day of Yahweh" by permanently embodying in it moral considerations ; the Kingdom would come in the future through repentance and a strict adherence to the law. These hopes were seen especially in times of persecution, but the date at which the consummation was to come was continually altered as each prediction failed. Jeremiah's "seventy years" became "seven times seventy" in Daniel, and was altered again in Enoch.

In this connection it appears possible to trace development within the teaching of Jesus himself. At first he preached that the Kingdom men had long hoped to see was coming, was near at hand (Mark i. 15), and would be seen by his disciples (Mark xiii. 30). Later he spoke of the Kingdom as already come, a present fact among men, so that men could now enter it. Like Ezekiel, he taught that its coming was independent of repentance ; neither indifference nor hostility could prevent it, they could only hinder men from entering it, and one of his charges against the Scribes and Pharisees was that they neither entered it themselves nor allowed entrance to those who wished to go in (Matt. xxiii. 13). It has been suggested [3] that this change in Jesus's teaching took place at Cæsarea Philippi, when Peter made his great confession, " Thou art the Messiah, the son of the living God." Rabbinical teachers had spoken of the Kingdom as coming as soon as any human being acknowledged God as King ; Jesus probably had a similar idea, and thus Peter's confession meant that the Kingdom had come. It is an interesting confirmation of this that on another occasion Jesus called Peter Satan, saying that Satan had desired to gain the allegiance of Peter, and when he described the sudden coming of the Kingdom he exclaimed, " I beheld Satan falling as a star from heaven "—Peter's declaration had caused the defeat of Satan.

Later in his life Jesus spoke of the Kingdom as about to have a sudden and final public inauguration ; and he preached in a way that made his followers expect the speedy end of the present world, and the introduction of a new age (Mark ix. 1). When tried before the high-priest, for example, he said, " Ye shall see the Son of Man sitting at the right hand of power and coming with the clouds of glory " (Mark xiv. 62), quoting the vision of Daniel, " I saw in the night visions and behold, there came with the clouds of heaven one like unto the son of man, and he came even unto the ancient of days and there was given him dominion, glory and a kingdom " (vii. 13).

The ethical teaching of Jesus can best be summarized as a description of life in the Kingdom of God, and like the teaching in the book of Micah it can be regarded as incarnating in daily life the character of God. The Levitical law-book demanded a holy people because God is holy ; Jesus demanded a loving, forgiving people because God is love and forgives ; those who became members of the Kingdom must live in accordance with the divine will. Both proclaimed, " Be ye perfect as your Father in heaven is perfect " (Matt. v. 48). Perhaps the outstanding feature that distinguished his Kingdom from the kingdoms of this world was that its basis was giving, and not getting, and its aim or motive service, rather than security, self-advancement, or authority (Mark x. 42f.). That he stressed the value of the individual—particularly the child (Matt. xviii.)—in the sight of God has often been emphasized ; the God who fell to the ground with every sparrow was a God who attached an immeasurable value to every individual creature—of more value than many sparrows (Matt. x. 31) ; but it should be recognized that, like Ezekiel, he lays no emphasis on the rights of the individual as apart from the community ; each man's importance comes as he enters the Kingdom, or accepts his responsibility as a member of the family of God. In a famous verse in John's Gospel (iii. 16) we are told that God so loved the world that he sent his son into the world, and the aim of his coming is not simply that individuals who respond shall have everlasting life, but that the world through him may be saved. It might almost be claimed that in the teaching of Jesus there is a revival in a new form of the old nomadic conception of corporate unity ; if we receive a " little one " we receive Jesus, and receiving him we receive God ; in clothing the naked, feeding the hungry, and visiting the prisoner, we are really doing these acts to Jesus (Matt. xxv.). The demands of the Kingdom are as absolute as to the old nomad was the duty of blood revenge ; family ties must not interfere with it, for the love of our most intimate kin is secondary, even life itself is of no account compared with that first loyalty to Jesus and the Kingdom of God (Matt. x. 37). We know that we are in the Kingdom and have passed from death to life because we love the brethren ; " By this shall all men know that ye are my disciples, because ye have love one for another " (John xiii. 35).

It is significant that in the Gospel of John the term, " Kingdom of God," is replaced by the phrase, " everlasting life "— a phrase which appears to mean not quantity but quality of life. In the later parts of the Old Testament the earlier Hebrew idea, that blessedness lay in length of days, had begun to be replaced by the belief that even death could not sever man's fellowship with God, so that it was possible to begin a kind of life here which transcended death and the dividing line between life here and hereafter (Ps. xvi.). The Kingdom of God has not only been given to men and has come upon them, as Professor Dodd says, "in the series of historical events which unfolds itself in the ministry of Jesus," but that Kingdom is also in the world beyond this, in the heaven where from all eternity God has reigned as King. In that Kingdom the patriarchs are alive and many will come from east and west to sit at meat with them, but we here and now can enter the same Kingdom. Though Jesus uses, as he was bound to, the symbols of space and time, and the imagery of the eschatological writers of the past, they are inadequate to express his idea of God's Kingdom. The contrast is not between life here and hereafter, but between life in the Kingdom and outside it, for the crisis of the coming of the Kingdom and of the individual's entrance into it far transcends that of physical death. As the prophets had proclaimed a religion which transcended the differences of ritual and ceremonial, by insisting upon obedience to the moral will of God and fellowship with him in spirit, so Jesus pierced the highly coloured exterior of eschatological speculation in reference to this world and the world to come, by asserting that the powers of the world to come had broken down the wall of partition and invaded this world. The story of the angelic choir breaking through the starry vault of heaven to proclaim the coming of the Messiah is symbolic of the entry of the eternal Kingdom into the temporal world, of the eternal God, who to the prophets had revealed himself in history, stepping out into the world of time.

The fact that to Jesus it was of supreme importance that the Kingdom of God had already come affected his view of judgement. As he swept aside the speculation about successive ages of good and evil which under Persian influence had entered Judaism, so he took the essential truth from all those theories of future judgement which we found in the ancient Egyptian religion, and which had developed in Judaism through contact with Persian thought. The judgement was not an event which happened either at the death of an individual, or at the end of the age. Judgement came with the Kingdom, and men passed judgement on themselves by their attitude to it. Here again it appears that the writer of the Fourth Gospel has retained the clue to the permanent message of Jesus, stripped of its temporary parabolic dress : " Now is the judgement of this world. . . . And this is the judgement, that the light is come into the world and men loved the darkness rather than the light : for their works were evil " (iii. 19).

§ ABOUT GOD

His teaching about God can be summarized under two terms, King and Father ; both ideas had their roots firmly fixed in the Old Testament, and in contemporary Jewish teaching, where in prayer God was addressed as " Our Father, Our King."

Professor Manson has written :

The eternal and absolute sovereignty of God was an integral part of the religious heritage of the people among whom our Lord lived and worked. . . . This vision of God as King, which had been the inspiration of the great prophets, had in the days of Jesus become an article of faith to every pious Jew.

How early God was addressed as King in Hebrew religion we do not know ; it was not until the time of the Chronicler that the " throne of David " became spoken of as the " throne of Yahweh," but probably from the beginning of the kingship of Israel the king was thought of, to quote Riehm,[4] as " the visible representative of the invisible divine king." When Israel was given a human king like other nations, it took over the idea that the king was the visible embodiment of the divine Lord. We have seen how this idea of the king as God was transformed by Isaiah into that of God as King. He appears to have been the first of the eighth-century prophets to speak of God in that way ; in his inaugural vision he exclaimed, " Mine eyes have seen the King, the Lord of Hosts." This theocratic idea was read back into the history of the past,

and we have the stories of Gideon declining the title of king
on the ground that "Yahweh shall be king over you"
(Judges viii. 23), and Samuel resisting the people's demand
for a king because it meant the rejection of Yahweh as
King (1 Sam. x. 19).   The idea became an integral part of
post-exilic Judaism, particularly after the fall of the Davidic
dynasty, and the failure of Davidic hopes of a restoration.
Ezekiel pictured the divine King as enthroned on the cherubim
in unapproachable holiness, and in the Psalms Yahweh is
addressed as King.   It is probable that in post-exilic Judaism
the annual pre-exilic ceremony of enthroning the king became
one of enthroning Yahweh as King, and probably as "King
over all the World," and that this ceremony was responsible
for the increase in the references to God as King ; but it
must also be recognized, as Kennett suggested,[5] that the use
of the title may have been in conscious opposition to the claim
of Antiochus IV to be both God and King.

The idea that kingship was real only where there were
loyal, obedient subjects, made possible the development—
particularly under the influence of Persian dualism—of the
thought that there existed opposing kingdoms of good and
evil, warring against each other, the one loyal to God and the
other subject to the prince of devils—Beelzebub, Satan, or, to
use the Persian name, Asmodæus.   Beelzebub was a degenera-
tion of the name Baal-Zebul, the Phœnician god worshipped
by Jezebel's son ; Satan is a word which first occurs in the
Old Testament in the book of Zechariah, where it is not a
proper name but, as in the prologue to Job, the title of a
servant of God comparable to the "King's eye" among
Persian court officials, whose business it was to keep the king
informed of events happening throughout the kingdom ;
later, in the book of the Chronicler, the word becomes a proper
name, used for the supernatural tempter of David ; and in
later Judaism, as in the New Testament, it is the name of the
prince and leader of the forces of evil.   In the teaching of Jesus
the conflict is recognized, but there is never any doubt expressed
as to where victory will lie.   The coming of the kingdom

involved the defeat of the prince of this world, and Jesus could exclaim, "Be of good cheer, I have overcome the world" (John xvi. 33). The loving power of God made any permanent or thorough dualism impossible to conceive.

The character of God as King can be seen from the picture of the kingdom which would result from his kingly rule in the hearts of men. When we listen to the parable of the Good Samaritan (Luke x.), or to the cry, "I have not found such faith, no, not in Israel" (Matt. viii. 10), there can be no question that the Kingdom had no national boundaries, and that the kingship of God was thought of as universal. Though Jesus did not stress this universal kingship, yet it appears from the developments that followed immediately after his death that he thought of God as ruling, and gathering his subjects from, Jew and Gentile—he accepted the vision of the Servant of Yahweh, rather than that of Ezekiel. His assertion of the kingship of God carried with it the recognition of the two sides of the relationship between God and man : on the one side God was the God of history overruling all the affairs of men and the world to accomplish his purpose ; and on the other he had laid on man the duty of absolute loyalty and active co-operation with his will. The prayer Jesus taught his followers was, "Thy will be done," and in Gethsemane as he faced death he himself prayed, "Not my will but thine be done" (Mark xiv. 36).

The characteristic term Jesus used for God was, however, "Father." Again, like "King," this term was no new departure as a name for God. The symbolism of physical fatherhood with which primitive man had crudely expressed his sense of connection with God had receded into the background —a fact which has a bearing on our understanding of the story of the virgin birth—and in its place had grown the idea of a moral relationship expressed in God's fatherly care and love, and man's devotion and moral likeness to his Father (John viii. 33ff.).

In the Old Testament God had been thought of as the Father of Israel, or of the anointed king who became his "son" at his coronation. Prophets spoke of God as bringing up his son Israel out of Egypt, and teaching him to walk. It is possible that even in the Old Testament this relationship was thought of as conditioned by the son's response, and that in a peculiar sense God was one who pitied like a father those who feared him (Ps. ciii. 13) ; but in the second and first centuries B.C. God became first the Father of the righteous in Israel, and later the Father of all the righteous everywhere, Jew or Gentile. This development may owe much to the universality of the wisdom literature, in which there is a tendency to equate the wise and righteous in contrast to the fools and the wicked ; but in any case it was a movement toward a new universalism. In Jewish teaching of the time of Jesus the thought of God as Father was prominent, expressing, as Moore wrote : " a personal relation to the people collectively and a summary of the whole relation between God and the religious man." [6] God was often spoken of as " Our " or " Thy Father in Heaven " ; perhaps the best-known saying is that of Rabbi Judah in the " Sayings of the Jewish Fathers " : " Be strong as a leopard, swift as an eagle, fleet as a gazelle, brave as a lion, to do the will of thy Father which is in heaven."

Words, especially words often used, like ritual acts, are symbols into which vastly different meanings can be put by different persons ; the fact that the use of the title " Father " for God became so peculiarly characteristic of Christianity suggests that to Jesus, and through him to his disciples, there was a warm wealth of personal relationship in the term which it had not in Judaism—a fact that is confirmed when we remember that one of the few Aramaic words used by Jesus and preserved by the New Testament writers was Abba—Father ; it appears that all such original sayings were retained because, to the hearers, they contained an intonation or meaning which could not be adequately expressed in translation : Talitha cumi (Mark v. 41), Ephphatha (Mark vii. 34), Eloi, Eloi, lama sabachthani (Mark xv. 34). Professor Manson suggests that the relationship was so intimate that Jesus spoke directly of God as Father only to his disciples, and then only after Peter's

"YAHU" AS A SOLAR ZEUS

(From "The Religion of Ancient Palestine in the Light of Archaeology," by S. A. Cook,
British Academy, Oxford Press, 1930)

The Garden of Gethsemane and its new church at the foot of the Mount of Olives

(*The Sphere*)

THE GARDEN TOMB

(*From* "The Garden Tomb, Golgotha," *by A. W. Crawley-Boevey, Committee of the Garden Tomb Maintenance Fund*)

confession. God the Father was the central fact in the teaching of Jesus, as it was the supreme reality in his life.

As Father God takes the initiative in dealing with his family. He is kind to the evil and the ungrateful ; like a shepherd he goes out to seek and save the sinner ; he runs to greet his returning prodigal son, and equally leaves the music and dancing to go out and entreat the sulky elder boy. He has time for, and interest in, each one of his children ; and there is no smallest detail of individual life that is not his care—even the hairs of your head are all numbered—and he asks from his children that they will trust him for all the common things of daily life, make his Kingdom their primary interest, love him with their whole being, and recognize to the full their obligations to the other members of the one family. It has rightly been said that all the teaching of Jesus on the fatherhood of God was summed up in the family prayer he taught his disciples ; a prayer which has brought to countless thousands of worshippers the restful peace of being at home with the loving Father, the inspiration of a vision of co-operation with the will and Kingdom of God, and confident trust in the one to whom belongs all power.

§ About Himself

Old Testament prophets began their career with inaugural visions which set the tone for their whole ministry. Sometimes, as with Amos and Jeremiah, the vision was concerned with the message to be delivered by the prophet or the task to be performed ; sometimes, as with Isaiah and Ezekiel, it embodied a new conception of God. The inaugural vision of Jesus came at his baptism, and consisted of three main elements. First he heard a voice saying, " Thou art my beloved son " ; steeped as he was in the Old Testament and contemporary Rabbinical literature, the idea that he was in a peculiar sense God's son meant also that he was the Anointed One or Messiah —perhaps his apprehension was not uninfluenced by his Davidic descent and the remembrance of the litany of the king-cult in Psalm ii. The second element was the realization that the Messiah was to fulfil the picture in Second-Isaiah of the Servant of Yahweh; the phrase, "In whom I am well pleased," is a quotation from these songs, and shows that in his vision Jesus recognized that as Messiah he must suffer like the Servant, and perhaps be killed.[7] The third element was the knowledge that the Spirit of God had come upon him as it had upon the Servant, filling him with the power of God. The three temptations which followed the vision spring out of these three elements, and they set the tone for his life and work.

The consciousness that the Spirit of God was upon him was pictured in the symbolism of the descending dove that rested on him; it was early seen in the authority he assumed; and it was explicitly claimed when, before his rejection by the people at Nazareth, he identified his mission with that of the spirit-filled messenger portrayed in the book of Second-Isaiah (Isa. lxi., Luke iv. 21). Old Testament thinkers had frequently expressed their experience of contact between man and God by saying that the wind or Spirit of God invaded human personality, and thus they had accounted for new or abnormal powers manifested in human life, whether it was the strength of Samson, the madness of Saul, or the changed heart which Jeremiah and Ezekiel had believed would begin the new Israel. The content of the term, "Spirit of God," had developed as the idea of Yahweh grew; all the amoral and unspiritual elements went from it; "take not thy holy spirit from me," became the earnest prayer of the penitent sinner; and the prophet proclaimed that the Kingdom of God would be ushered in by the outpouring of the Spirit on all men (Joel ii. 28)—a vision that Jesus and his disciples claimed to have been fulfilled in their time (Acts ii. 17).

The realization that he was the Messiah appears to have been kept secret by him lest popular uprisings, by their political repercussions, should speedily end his work.[8] He defeated the temptation openly to proclaim his Messiahship by the fulfil-ment of one of the many expectations which in contemporary

Judaism had been associated with the coming of the Messiah ; when he did avow it, after Peter's confession, he used the ambiguous phrase, " Son of Man." This is the ordinary Aramaic phrase for " man," and was so used by Jesus when he said that the Sabbath was made for man, and man is lord of the Sabbath, and when he proclaimed that man has power on earth to forgive sins (Mark ii.). In Ezekiel it was the title with which God's messenger addressed the prophet. In Daniel it was used as the name for the saints of the Most High—an interesting communal use of the term ; in Enoch the phrase becomes the title for the personal supernatural king who judges men and acts as God's vice-regent, and there is little doubt that both Peter and later the Jewish high-priest knew that when Jesus used the phrase of himself he claimed to be the Messiah.

That to Jesus himself there was a distinction between the Messiah as Son,⁹ and others as prophets, is clear from some of his parables, particularly that of the wicked husbandmen (Matt. xxi.). It is seen, too, in his claim to possess a peculiar and intimate knowledge of God which could be mediated only through him, and which enabled him to act as an intermediary between God and man, so that coming to him one came to God, and found refreshment when tired and overburdened (Matt. xi. 25ff.). Perhaps the clearest indication that, although often he spoke of himself to men as *primus inter pares*, yet he was conscious that he was not like other men, is shown, as we have seen, by his use of the word Father, and the depth of religious experience which is there visible, and it is in the Fourth Gospel that we get the clearest picture of the intimacy of Jesus with God.

The element in the baptismal vision which appears to be new was the connection of the Messiah with the suffering Servant and the interpretation of his life and work in terms of that vision. Contemporary Judaism had not applied that vision to the Messiah, and had no conception of a suffering Messiah. Professor Oesterley has noted that, in Jewish interpretation, whenever the humiliation of the Servant of Yahweh is mentioned it is interpreted as a reference to the people of

Israel ; but when the glory of the Servant is spoken of it is interpreted as in reference to the Messiah. Jesus appears early to have recognized that as Messiah he must suffer ; his forecast of his death and resurrection, his foretelling of insults and rejection, and his interpretation of his death as " a ransom for many " were all the outcome of his identification of the Messiah with the suffering Servant, and his acceptance of that rôle for himself. Probably, too, his silence in the judgement hall can be explained as a conscious fulfilling of the description of the Servant as the lamb dumb before her butchers and the sheep before her shearers ; and similarly such a phrase as " I, if I be lifted up, will draw all men unto me " suggests the picture of the nations repenting in astonishment when they recognize that " by his stripes we are healed." The triumphal entry into Jerusalem was partly an attempt to make the general public see something of that vision which he had found so difficult to convey even to his disciples. There he linked Messiahship with the meek and lowly ruler who, in contrast to a bloody warrior like Judas Maccabæus, or the Zealots who believed in using violence to remove the Roman conqueror, would bring joy and peace as well as justice and victory when he rode into Jerusalem ; the king who would speak peace to the nations and whose dominion would be from the River to the ends of the earth.

CHAPTER 16

CHRISTIANITY AND JUDAISM

§ APOSTOLIC INTERPRETATION OF JESUS AND HIS TEACHING

THE primary task of the apostolic preaching after the death of Jesus was to interpret the fact of that death. That Peter had learnt the lesson Jesus taught is shown by the fact that he used the figure of the Servant of Yahweh as his explanation. The test of a prophet for Second-Isaiah was his power to interpret historic events as the working of God. So in the Old Testament the three great national events—the exodus from Egypt, the exile to Babylon, and the return from captivity—had all been explained by prophets, and the recognition of God as present in human history had brought a revival in religion. God became recognized as active in the affairs of men, and could not be ignored. So too the apostolic preaching, by its interpretation of the cross, brought new revival and a rapid increase in the number of Christians. Peter proclaimed that, though wicked men were responsible for the death of Jesus, it was in accordance with the foreknowledge and determined counsel of God (Acts ii. 22f.).

An interesting development seen in the early chapters of the Acts of the Apostles is the interpretation of the life of Jesus as a new giving of the law. Jesus had apparently put himself on an equality with Moses, and the writer of the account of the giving of the Spirit at Pentecost worked out that idea. Pentecost was the season when Jews celebrated the giving of the law on Sinai with wind and fire, and often the law was spoken of as wine. Now the law was superseded. With unusual natural phenomena, before representatives not alone of Israel but of the whole world, men were filled with the new wine which Jesus had predicted would burst the old wine skins. As Moses had said, " Would to God all Yahweh's people were prophets" (Num. xi. 29), so now all the disciples were seized by the Spirit, and, like the prophets of old, spoke in ecstatic language—" speaking with tongues " occurred again in the Church at Corinth. We find evidence of further working of the old prophetic spirit among Christians, as, for example, when the prophet at Ephesus by symbolic acts predicts Paul's arrest (Acts xxi. 10ff.).

Most of the developments were, however, nearer to the teaching of Jesus than this. There was at first a clear and vivid expectation of the speedy consummation of the Kingdom of God, when Jesus should return with power and publicly inaugurate the new age. This hope, apparently shared by Jesus, played a large part in the life of the early Christian community. It is clearly stated in the opening of the Acts as a message given by angels when Jesus ascended, and it was strong in the early teaching of Paul. It was revived again under persecution, and can be seen combined with Jewish eschatological teaching in the book of the Revelation ; it has often been revived in the history of the Christian Church, modified by the fact that what was regarded as imminent in the first century is still regarded as speedily to come in the twentieth.

A more normal development is seen in the creation of the Fellowship of the Church, which both in doctrine and in fact took the place of the conception of the Kingdom of God as already realized. At first without organization, gathering in each other's houses for the breaking of bread and prayer, the Church enjoyed a corporate life of happy and intimate fellowship, with a self-sacrificing devotion to the common cause even to the point of an experiment in communal living (Acts iv. 32). It grew rapidly, and of necessity—especially in the face of persecution—became more fully organized and disciplined, placing a larger emphasis on order. Under Paul's influence it was called the Body of Christ, and the metaphor of a body with many limbs and a common indwelling life or spirit was thoroughly worked out (1 Cor. xii.). Here we see the re-emergence of the old nomadic corporate idea in a new form due to Paul's own experience. His inaugural vision on the road to Damascus, when the voice said, "I am Jesus whom thou persecutest," made him realize that Jesus was one with the disciples whom he was seeking to destroy (Acts ix.). This Body of Christ was thought of as the new Israel, inheriting the promises made by God and replacing the Righteous Remnant of older Judaism. In the past God had selected certain individuals and left others ; Isaac and Jacob had been chosen, and Ishmael and Esau left ; so Jesus had been chosen and had founded the new Israel.

The new community used two symbolic acts, one of initiation and the other of fellowship. The baptism which John had practised, and which had constituted the call of Jesus, ceased to be thought of as an act of entry into the Kingdom of God, and became a personal act of surrender to Jesus, in which the initiate, by being covered with water, was buried with Christ, and rose again to a new life with him, thus sharing his death and resurrection (Rom. vi.). The Communion meal became a fellowship act, in which the Church remembered Jesus, renewed its oath of allegiance to him, proclaimed the meaning of his death, and looked forward to his second advent (1 Cor. xi.).

Beliefs about Jesus himself also developed during this period. At first he was spoken of as God's servant, and it would appear that the earliest form of creed asserted that he was the Messiah—" Jesus is Christ " (Acts xviii. 5). Emphasis was placed on his death and resurrection, as can be seen by the large amount of space devoted to the events leading up to the cross and to the cross itself in the Gospels. The early Church interpreted that death, as Jesus had done, by the imagery of Isaiah liii. and the suffering Servant—" Jesus died for our sakes according to the Scriptures " (1 Cor. xv.). The cross thus gave to the followers of Jesus their assurance of forgiveness, taking the place of the successive attempts we have already seen in the Old Testament. It was the proof of the forgiving love of God ; his viceroy, his anointed one, had died that forgiveness might come to men ; God had taken the initiative as Ezekiel had prophesied, and, as Jeremiah had foretold in his vision of the new covenant, men could know God because he had forgiven them their sins. Paul put it that God commended his own love toward us in that while we were yet sinners Christ died for us (Rom. v. 8) ; and he preached a Messiah crucified, to the Jews a stumbling block, to the Greeks foolishness, but to those who responded to the call the power of God and the wisdom of God (1 Cor. i. 23).

It is abundantly clear from history that the early Christians did not doubt the reality of the resurrection and that the centre of their worship was a living heavenly Christ, but Christians have always recognized that there are difficulties in the stories of the resurrection both in reference to historical facts and as to the relationship of the risen Christ to God. Both difficulties still remain, but the stories, like those of Jesus's birth, must be seen in their Jewish setting. To the Jew, personal immortality of the spirit was inconceivable, for the spirit existed only as embodied : Blake put it the other way : "man has no body apart from his soul, for what we call body is but that part of the soul discerned by the five senses." The Jews thought in terms of the resurrection of the body, and hence the importance to them of the empty tomb, a fact for which any theory of the resurrection must account. Paul accepted the fact of the risen Messiah, and without mentioning the empty tomb moved slightly toward the Greek idea of the immortality of the soul, when he spoke of the body as transformed, and like a new growth from an old seed, rising not the same natural body but a spiritual one. He remained, however, still firmly anchored to the Hebrew belief that a spirit needed a body (1 Cor. xv.).

The relationship of the risen Messiah to God was still more difficult to express. To Jews it was sufficient to speak of him as Messiah, but to Gentile Christians and in hellenic thought the word Messiah had not the same connotation. There the earliest creed (1 Cor. xii. 3) appears to have been determined by Paul's inaugural vision and his spontaneous address to the figure who appeared to him; *Kurios*, or "Lord," is the word used in the Greek version of the Old Testament for the Hebrew word Yahweh, and accepted by the Aramaic-speaking community who translated it as *Marana*, " Our Lord " (1 Cor. xvi. 22). The use of the term made it natural from the beginning to ascribe to Jesus the nature of God. But the later history of the Church shows that the New Testament writers did not achieve any conception which approached a systematic or complete Christology. Many attempts were made : for example, the statement that Jesus was appointed Son at the Baptism, and that he was miraculously born without a human father ; Paul used the Hebrew idea of Wisdom as the pre-existent helper of God at the creation as a metaphor for Jesus, and equated him with the Spirit of God—" the Lord is the Spirit," he said (2 Cor. iii. 17). In the Fourth Gospel there is a clear distinction between Jesus and the Spirit which would come after Jesus had gone (*cf.* also Acts i. 8), and the writer uses the " Word of God " with which to equate Jesus. Both Paul and the writer of the Prologue to John's Gospel make use of the tendency in Judaism to treat as separate persons such attributes of God as Wisdom or Spirit and the Word which had inspired the prophets of old. Perhaps the most satisfying attempt is seen in the phrase used to the Corinthians : " God was in the Messiah reconciling the world to himself " (2 Cor. v. 19). It takes up the thought characteristic of the Maccabæan Psalms, which picture God as stepping out into the world to deliver his people.

The influence of Greek thought is seen most clearly in the Epistle to the Hebrews, and in the Gospel of John. The former uses the Platonic theory that the actual is a type of the heavenly real or ideal—the Levitical laws were but the type foreshadowing the real priesthood of Jesus—an interpretation which has had considerable influence on later Christian thought. The Gospel of John reinterprets the whole life and teaching of Jesus in language which could be understood in hellenic circles. Jesus was the Logos or Word of God ; he gave men power to become sons of God and to enter, not the Kingdom of God, but a new quality of life called Eternal Life. All life, including the historic life of Jesus, was seen in the setting of an eternal realm. Just as in the teaching of Jesus the Kingdom of God transcended our categories of time and space, so to the author of the Fourth Gospel, as to Paul, Jesus himself could not be thought of as having beginning or end. Paul had used the Greek idea of heavenly patterns when he spoke of Jesus as the heavenly man, and asserted so emphatically the pre-existence of Christ ; in the prologue to the Fourth Gospel the same assertion is made by the use of another term—the Logos or Word of God—equally at home in Greek and Hebrew thought, and like the Pauline idea of the Heavenly Man developed by the Alexandrian Jew Philo. Paul had called Christ " the image of the invisible God, the firstborn of all creation ; for in him were all things created " (Col. i. 15), and the Fourth Gospel described the Logos in words that recall the opening phrase of the Hebrew Bible, " In the beginning was the Word, and the Word was with God, and the Word was God. The same was in the beginning with God. All things were made through him ; and without him was not anything made " (John i.).

All these successive interpretations of Jesus and his work are a sign of the vitality of Christian experience, before it was crystallized into a book or dogmatized into creeds.

§ THE CONFLICT BETWEEN JUDAISM AND CHRISTIANITY

Many Jewish and Christian scholars have thought that it is possible to distinguish between the teaching of Jesus and the Christianity which resulted from the work of Paul, and the Rev. E. Levine [1] states that " the Jew is drawn to the conclusion that the divorce between Judaism and Christianity could not have been consummated without the abrogation of the ceremonial law which was the work of Paul." A study of the religion of the Old Testament would suggest that Professor S. A. Cook is nearer the truth when he writes that " although there is an entirely new development, there is no break with the past " ; it is rather the religion of Second-

Isaiah that is " the end of one series of stages and the beginning of another which leads on to the rise of Christianity." [2] The separation in the first century A.D. had its rise in the diverging lines that ran out from the zenith of Israelite religion in the sixth century B.C.

It is unfortunate that Jewish Rabbinical literature was not collected in its present form until the second century A.D., so that although many of its sayings and traditions must be contemporary with the rise of Christianity, it cannot with confidence be used to illustrate the condition of Judaism at that time. There are, however, features of the contemporaneous religion of the Jews known to us from other sources which enable us to understand partly the reason for the break between that religion and Christianity. These features can be summed up under two heads : the divergence of sects within Judaism, and the growth of nationalism.

We have already mentioned the opposition between the Pharisees and the Sadducees. The latter were probably named after Zadok—either the priest who in the time of Solomon replaced Abiathar as chief priest at Jerusalem and whose descendants were regarded by Ezekiel as the only legitimate priests of the temple, or a later leader of the same name. They were priests, careful for the ritual and ceremonial laws of the Pentateuch, and so devoted to it that at the destruction of the temple they were slain in hundreds, unarmed and unresisting, while faithfully performing their temple duties ; they represented the conservative element in ritual, but they continued the priestly trait which we saw so pronounced in the time of Nehemiah and the Maccabæan revolt—they were willing for considerable compromise in order to maintain their contacts with secular authorities and their own position as recognized national leaders. Their opposition to Jesus and his followers was due to their fear of the dangers of enthusiasm in religion and of the political results of a popular messianic uprising, and to the fact that Jesus so openly challenged some of the forms of temple worship and practice. After the death of Jesus their objection sprang from a refusal to accept the fact of his resurrection or to believe in an after-life (Acts xxiii. 6).

Diverse judgement has been passed on the Pharisees both in the New Testament and since. Jesus warned his disciples against the leaven of the Pharisees, scathingly condemning their meticulous rules of ceremonial purity, their love of display in religion, and their devotion to their own man-made traditions, with which they modified to their own advantage the rigours of the Mosaic code (Mark vii.) ; they were whited sepulchres, hypocrites whose appearance was excellent, but who inside were foul and corrupt. But he also called them the " righteous that need no repentance," the " whole who have no need of a physician " (Mark ii. 17), and uttered to them words of the most amazing tenderness which in God's name he spoke to anyone, " Son, thou art ever with me, and all that is mine is thine " (Luke xv. 31). Research during recent years—particularly by Jewish scholars—has increased our knowledge of Pharisaism [3] and raised considerably our estimation of it ; and it seems possible that the vehemence of Jesus's attack was caused not only by the failure of individual Pharisees, but by elements in Pharisaism which prevented it from rising to the spiritual ideals of religion which they professed and which were so close to his own.[4] The late Herbert Loewe [5] has pointed out that many of the controversies between Jesus and the Pharisees were echoes of debates within Pharisaism itself, and that the Talmud differentiates seven kinds of Pharisees : the " shoulder Pharisee " who bears his good deeds on his shoulder ; the " Wait a little Pharisee " who says " Wait till I do my good deed " ; the " Bruised Pharisee " who has hurt himself against a wall to avoid looking at a woman ; the " Pestle Pharisee " with his head down in mock humility ; the " Reckoning Pharisee " who casts up his account of sins and virtues ; the " God-fearing Pharisee " like Job ; and the " God-loving Pharisee " like Abraham. Many of these criticisms of Pharisees by themselves correspond to Jesus's condemnations, and it is probable that similar types might be found among Christians, and would be equally severely judged by him. Pharisees attempted to bring all life within the orbit of religion; to them we owe the canon of the Old Testament; the synagogue with its emphasis on prayer rather than animal sacrifice was their creation; and the Pharisaic brotherhoods, open to all God-fearing Jews and proselytes, combined social service with an encouragement of public and private worship. They were more nationalistic and more pious than the Sadducees, and condemned Jesus for his association with publicans—Jews who collected taxes for the Romans—and irreligious men and women, and because he regarded so many of the traditional rules of conduct and forms of religion as unnecessary to salvation. The offer of the free pardon of a gracious Father to men and women who did not observe the law nor take part in the accepted institutions of religion seemed to the Pharisees to sweep away the very basis of faith. To them, sin was transgression of the laws of God, and, to obtain his forgiveness, repentance must be linked with observance of the rites God had appointed in the Mosaic code.

Another party in Judaism at this time was the Essenes. These men were organized into ascetic groups, wearing white robes, and living a communal life without any private property. They supported themselves by agriculture and handicrafts, and the centre of their life together was the communal meal eaten as a religious ceremony. Like the Pharisees, they had a great veneration for the Mosaic law, for Sabbath observance, and for rules of purity; but they repudiated all animal sacrifice.

A similar group of which all knowledge had been lost, and whose date is keenly disputed, has become known through the discovery in A.D. 1910 of an old Hebrew fragment at Cairo. The writing relates to a party of Jews who migrated to Damascus and bound themselves under a " New Covenant." Their rules of ceremonial purity were even more rigid than those of the Essenes, but there was no repudiation of animal sacrifice. They stressed the need for human kindness, and held strongly the hope of the coming of the Messiah.

Besides these more orthodox Jewish communities there were among hellenistic Jews some who, in their desire to commend their religion to cultured Gentiles, modified that religion considerably and departed further from traditional Judaism. Philo had attempted to explain to the Gentile world many of the Jewish practices—circumcision, Sabbath observance, dietary laws—as allegories, though he claimed that it was necessary to observe them literally. But there were Jews, called by Dr. E. R. Bevan[6] "Liberal" Jews, "who declared that laws of circumcision and keeping of the Sabbath were not literally binding ; all that God required was that men should have the virtues which these external things typified." These liberal Jews were probably kin to the hellenizing Jews of the Maccabæan age, who also repudiated many of the distinguishing marks of Judaism.

A further link between the Jew and Greek was provided by " those who feared God " ; Gentiles who were connected with the synagogue took part in its religious and social activities, and kept much of the Mosaic law though without being circumcised. It was among these adherents of the synagogue that Paul made many of his early converts to Christianity.

It is obvious that among these varying shades of Jewish belief the new Christian community for a time would pass almost unnoticed. Jesus, like the prophets before him, lived and died a Jew, but it must be remembered that he was brought up in Galilee where Jewry differed from that in Judæa. He attended the synagogue "as his custom was," and at the great feasts could be found in the temple at Jerusalem. Christian thought at first developed in close contact with Judaism, and the fellowship of the early Church was a closely knit religious group within Judaism, not easily distinguishable from the many other self-contained Jewish groups and brotherhoods. Christians met for worship in the temple, they did not repudiate the Mosaic laws, and among those who joined the fellowship were priests as well as Pharisees, Palestinian Jews as well as Jews from the Diaspora who had closer affinities with Greek culture.

It was apparently among the hellenistic Jews that the ferment grew which eventually burst the old wine skins of Judaism and spilt Christianity throughout the world, but it was the growth of nationalism which made the skins lose their elasticity. It might have been thought that the Roman tolerance of religion would tend to quieten nationalist feeling, but in fact the Maccabæan revolt had left too large a legacy of aspirations for political independence. Although in the Diaspora hellenic influences continued to modify Jewish national exclusiveness— Paul could speak Greek, and the New Testament writers quoted from the Greek version of the Old Testament—yet in Palestine itself Greek influences received a strong and sudden check. Eschatological writers had fanned the flames of nationalism to a fire of fanaticism by raising hopes of God's sudden imminent intervention to win freedom from the hated Roman rule, and the establishment of the long-expected Kingdom. The hopes were confused and varied, but they were central to all Jewish thought in the time of Jesus, and ran through all grades of society ; everyone was in a state of collective expectancy, and, because there is always hope in catastrophe, most people looked for catastrophic happenings.

Bound up with this nationalism was the fact that any claimant to be the Messiah was sure of a following, particularly from the more revolutionary elements of the population. Five thousand Galileans attempted to force Jesus to declare himself king and lead them in revolt against Rome (John vi. 15) ; Zealots and Assassins were pledged to murder Romans or pro-Roman Jews ; and in the temple even the gentle Simeon who dedicated Jesus was " looking for the consolation of Israel." It was this nationalism which caused the destruction of Jerusalem, and was largely responsible for the breach between Judaism and Christianity. To quote Professor S. A. Cook :

There can be no more impressive crisis than that nineteen centuries ago when, amid conflicting religious impulses, widespread disaster and ruin came through the passion of self-confident fanatics, and a new direction was given to the history of thought by a Christianity which did not grow out of, but in opposition to, them. Right and wrong ideas of God and Reality were in conflict, and the rise of Christianity is really a unique cosmic event.

At first, conscious that they were adherents of one who had been handed over by Jews and executed by Romans, the Christians remained behind locked doors " for fear of the Jews " (John xx. 19) ; but the Romans took no action against them and the Jews made no denunciations. Peter began the conflict. He openly proclaimed that the Jewish leaders were murderers, won large numbers of followers, and by a conspicuous act of healing proved the power of the Name of Jesus (Acts iii.). The Pharisaic leader Rabbi Gamaliel, when the Sadducean priestly leaders wished to check this new fire that threatened to sweep through Judaism, counselled caution, suggesting that if this movement were like other Messianic risings it would come to naught, " but if it is of God ye will not be able to overthrow it ; lest haply ye be found even to be fighting against God " (Acts v.).

The next opposition to the young Christian sect came from hellenic Jews. Stephen—perhaps originally one of themselves —became a Christian and proclaimed a spiritual religion, objecting to the stress laid on the temple and its cultus, the casuistical regulations by which the Mosaic law had been interpreted, and the neglect of the prophetic element in the Pentateuch ; a riot followed in which he was killed and many of the Christians were scattered. Conversions were made among the Samaritans, and after an inquiry by the Christian leaders at Jerusalem had confirmed that the converts possessed the same spiritual phenomena as had been seen in the first converts at Pentecost, they were accepted into the fellowship (Acts viii.).

A further step was taken when a Roman centurion was converted (Acts x.f.). The man was a Gentile adherent of the synagogue but not a proselyte. Peter visited him in response to a dream vision, and after being " amazed that on the Gentiles also was poured out the Holy Spirit," gave orders that he should be baptized and so recognized as a full member of the Church. The action was questioned at Jerusalem, because its approval meant that in principle the break with Judaism had already taken place—a man could become a Christian

without being a circumcised member of the Jewish nation or
faith. Peter maintained that God had shown him that he must
not call any man common or unclean, and that the criterion
was whether God gave his spirit to a man—a criterion
apparently easy to use. The conversion of Gentiles continued,
and these converts began to be called Christians rather than
Jews (Acts xi. 26), but the position was not accepted by many
of the Judæan Christians.

Later, after the wholesale gathering-in of Gentiles during
the missionary journeys of Paul and Barnabas, a conference
was held at Jerusalem (Acts xv.). Peter, Paul, and Barnabas
related their experiences, and it was finally agreed that the
Mosaic law did not apply to the Gentile converts. There were
still " those of the circumcision " who tried to persuade the
converts that the observance of Jewish regulations was necessary
if they were to fulfil all righteousness, and even Peter was
made to believe that it was unwise to share in the common
meal with non-Jews (Gal. ii. 11f.), but in principle the battle
had been won, and it was left to Paul to justify the decision
and lay the foundations for Christian, as distinct from Jewish,
theology. The break between Jew and Christian was completed in A.D. 132, when nationalist Jews, rallying round Bar
Koziba, a military leader, recognised him as Messiah—a recognition no Christian could share, however strong his nationalist
feeling.

The conflict was in essence that between Deuteronomy and
Second-Isaiah. The book of Deuteronomy was responsible for
post-exilic and modern Judaism ; the book of Second-Isaiah
provided the religious outlook which was continued and developed in Christianity. A modern Jewish writer [7] claims that
the secret of the strength of Judaism lies in its separation.
" The work of Israel in the world is to disseminate the knowledge of God, and to mediate the truths that have been com-
municated to them. This can be done only by a stringent
adherence to the conception of Israel as a people distinct from
other peoples with a mission to the rest of mankind." It was
" ceremonial which bound the nation together and helped

them to understand what their mission was." The observance of the Sabbath as a covenant between God and Israel, the Festivals as divinely ordained commemorations of the great events in the history of the nation's past, circumcision as the sign of the covenant people, the dietary laws, " the total abrogation of which would mean a speedy end to Jewish separatism, and the beginning of the end of Judaism," all these are still the differentiating features of Judaism, giving the Jew the consciousness that he is part of a people holy unto the Lord his God, chosen to be a peculiar people out of all the peoples that are on the face of the earth.

The faith which it is his mission to proclaim could be adequately stated in words drawn from the fifth to the eleventh chapters of Deuteronomy : imageless worship of the one true God who had revealed himself completely through Moses ; serving him with humble love and reverent fear ; doing justice and mercy even to the stranger ; teaching this worship to his children. Even the modern Zionism, which binds together so many Jews who have ceased to observe much of the ceremonial law, might be expressed in words drawn from Deuteronomy xi. 23ff.

The teaching of Second-Isaiah was essentially different. Because there is only one God the creator of all things, all men can call him Father, and he is bound not only to Israel but equally to all nations. Israel has been chosen to be a covenant between God and the nations, a light to the Gentiles, to take to waiting peoples the glorious truth of God. There is no longer the static conception of remaining apart and by separation and distinction witnessing to the truth, but the motion of a venture, breaking down the walls of partition and going out to proclaim a message. The truth is all important, not the nation ; Israel does not labour to maintain her separation and her purity or even her national existence, she is willing to suffer and to die if by her death she can win the ends of the earth to look unto her God and be saved. Worship will not be confined to Jerusalem or to a temple made with man's hands, for Heaven is God's throne and the whole earth is his footstool.

For centuries these two ways of thought had remained together within Judaism, as during the life of Jesus and for years after his death they continued to do, and one cannot help asking—speculating—whether the break was inevitable. The genius of Jewish religion and the secret of its development had been its power of regeneration from within through prophets and priests. Prophets might be slain, but their message lived on within the parent religion and, becoming incorporated within it, caused continual renaissance—rebirth from the old. Perhaps there comes a stage when the old body can no longer contain the growing spirit, and must be discarded so that the spirit may become incarnate in a new body better fitted to be the instrument for that spirit's expression of itself. But history seems to make abundantly clear that Nemesis follows all schism. Schismatics overemphasize the particular truth they see, so that being out of proportion it ceases to be in any real sense " truth " ; the parent body rejects the truth which has been the cause of the break, and becomes stunted in growth. When the schism came between Judaism and Christianity, those highest elements in Judaism which had been embodied in Jesus tended to be rejected or at least accorded second place by Jewry. The essential of Judaism was in reality not its ceremonial, nor the symbols of the covenant between it and God, nor the festivals which proclaimed the history of its past, but the character of the God worshipped through that ceremonial, expressed in the covenant, revealed through the mighty acts of redemption in its history. Early Christianity having no symbols, ceremonial, or festivals of its own, and one supreme act of history—the Cross of Calvary—tended to emphasize the character of God revealed in the Grace of Jesus Christ; and the elements in his character which were stressed were those that had been revealed in the highest reaches of Old Testament faith—the loving-kindness of Hosea's God, the universal care of Jonah's, the redemptive adventure of the God of Second-Isaiah—elements which ceased to receive primary stress in Judaism. It may be true that, from the standpoint of future development, Christianity became Christ-centric rather than

Theo-centric, but it is also true that Judaism became law-centred and even self-centred, and ceased to impress the non-Jewish world with a character that embodied the highest attributes of God in the Old Testament, attributes embodied in the life and death of Jesus, who in self-sacrificing love gave all, even his life, to commend God's love to all men. Herbert Loewe once said to the present writer that he remained a Jew because he believed that Jews had something to give to the world ; if the Kingdom for which Jew and Christian both pray is to be spread in the world both must learn, like the Servant and like Jesus, to count all life in terms of service, not gain.

BOOK VI

LINES OF DEVELOPMENT

CHAPTER 17

REVELATION OF GOD

§ God's Will declared through Priest, Prophet, and Law

In the beginning, among Semitic peoples, priests appear to have been custodians of shrines and their treasures, particularly the sacred implements through which oracles were obtained from the god, revealing his will on questions too difficult to be decided in ordinary tribal councils. In the Old Testament these implements were called Urim and Thummim, and were probably two stones kept in the pocket of the Ephod —possibly a linen apron or sporran worn by an image or by the priest—and, whatever forms of divination may have been used, this form of oracle supplanted all others among the Hebrews. From the books of Samuel we learn that only yes or no could be answered to the questioner (1 Sam. xiv. 41f., LXX.),[1] and that sometimes the oracle did not work, so that no answer could be obtained. Other methods of obtaining oracles, as found in other religions, may have been used in Palestine ; and from the double caves at Gezer it seems likely that a human accomplice was employed in some forms of divination.

It is of importance to notice that the Hebrew name for a priest suggests that his primary duty was to reveal the will of God ;[2] from this custom grew the Law, which contained the instruction or direction given by priests ; and it was long before this priestly function was superseded by the performance of ritual acts. In the song called the " Blessing of Moses " in Deuteronomy xxxiii. the blessing of the priestly tribe of Levi includes first the possession of the Urim and Thummim, the power to teach Jacob God's judgements and Israel his law, and then finally the offering of incense and whole burnt offerings. Reforming prophets, who deprecated the value of ritual acts, accepted the teaching function of the priests and condemned only the fact that this power had been abused for private gain.

At first the presence of a priest was not essential to sacrifice. This was performed by the offerer himself or by the head of the family or group which brought the gifts, and even after Israel had come into contact with the more elaborate ritual of Canaanite sanctuaries, the natural head of the group rather than the priest continued to offer sacrifices. At Shiloh Eli and his sons did not slay the beasts, but merely collected a share of its flesh, and Elijah himself offered the bullock on Carmel without the aid of priests. But a settled state made sanctuaries grow in importance, ritual became more complex, and the custodian of the shrine, who knew better than anyone the manner and character of the particular god and how he should be approached when his help and guidance were needed, became so indispensable that even for private offerings his help was necessary. He alone could properly perform the ritual acts required in man's approach to God. Thus from an early period his function would be not only to reveal God to man, but also to lead men to God. There can be no real antithesis between the two functions, for obviously one who opens the way for man to approach God must also be one who thereby reveals God, like the Egyptian priest who every morning opened the doors of the little shrine and, using a figure of Ma'at the goddess of truth and reality, disclosed to the adoring gaze of worshippers the golden divine image.

Both these aspects of priesthood are clearly seen in the New Testament Epistle to the Hebrews. There Jesus, called our great high-priest, reveals God's will in the sacrifice of his own life as the supreme act of doing the will of God, but he also leads his followers into the holy place of the presence of God ; to use the daring figure of that writer, he opens the way to God through his torn flesh as through the rent veil that once separated the inaccessible holy place from the tread of laymen's feet (Heb. x. 20).

We may perhaps say that the priestly revelation could be more objective and less mediated than some other forms of revelation. Like a doorkeeper the priest opened the door, showed men how to approach God, and then stood aside ; he made known God's character and put men into contact with him ; the oracle could answer without any reference to the personality of the priest, and the seeker could obtain his dream oracle in the sanctuary without any mediation. But later—perhaps through the influence of Ezekiel in the sixth century B.C.—the ancient ideas of the physical contagion of God's holiness were revived with wider application. The priest who dwelt in God's domain partook of his holiness, and was thought of as alone fit or able to approach him, and the doorkeeper became the attendant who was the only person to enter the presence of the unapproachable holy God ; he brought back God's message and mediated between God and man. Special rules of conduct were required of him, and though Judaism never demanded celibacy of its priests, they became men apart, and the Deuteronomic ideal of a holy people became replaced by that of a holy priesthood. The cause of the exile was thought to have been the lack of distinction between sacred and profane, and a fence had to be made around the holy dwelling of God. The altar, where for centuries laymen had offered their sacrifices, was placed beyond their approach ; priests alone could offer sacrifice and handle the sacrificial blood so rich in atoning power. As the oracle became a powerful weapon in the hands of priests, so the altar and its blood, through which alone men could gain forgiveness and reconciliation with God, became equally a means of increasing their own importance. They grew into a powerful priestly class with strong vested interests in maintaining institutional religion, and throughout the priestly history—to quote Robertson Smith—the " highest developments of priestly influence are hardly separable from something of magical superstition."

Jeremiah, in his vision of the reconstruction of religion, pictured a day when priests would no longer be required ; religion would still be an affair of the community, but each man would have entered into intimacy with God, because God would have broken down the walls of sin and forgiven men their trespasses (Jer. xxxi.). Priests would not be necessary to teach men to know God, nor to obtain forgiveness by ritual acts ; and in Judaism, for all practical purposes, the prophecy came true. At the final destruction of the temple, the ritual of the temple ceased, and the teaching function of priests passed into the hands of legal experts—those who knew the law of God. In spite of the growth of synagogue worship, the centre of religion was the home, and the father of the family became again the natural religious leader in the many domestic rites and blessings, the prayers and the instruction of children. Groups of families could voluntarily associate themselves together for corporate worship, choose their " Chief of the Synagogue " or even set aside one of their number for full-time religious work as minister, although the earlier rule was that there were to be no professional religious leaders—a rabbi earned his living at his trade, and followed Hillel's command never to make worldly use of the Law.

A similar development appears to have taken place in Christianity, but it soon became recognized that " a labourer is worthy of his hire," and in most parts of the Christian Church there is now a paid professional ministry. The priesthood grew up in the Christian Church and was accorded powers and privileges denied to the laity ; the same care as was taken in the Old Testament to prove the genealogical descent of the priesthood has been used to assert the possession of an unbroken Christian tradition, and to maintain order by the theory of apostolic succession. In the Christian priesthood the two functions seen in the Jewish conception of the priesthood, those of teacher and of ritual celebrant, have also been combined.

§ THROUGH PROPHET

The prophet was from the beginning always a mediator between God and man, but he differed from the oracle-giving priest by the fact that his revelation was given with physical accompaniments of supernatural inspiration, excitement, and frenzy. Even more than the priest he was a peculiar person in a special relationship to God, and differentiated from ordinary people. Sometimes, like the priest, he was part of the cultus, and revelation came to him during sacrifice or in the temple—it is significant that at Jerusalem there was a priest whose duty it was to control prophets who prophesied in the temple courts (Jer. xxix. 26). These professional prophets were maintained, too, at the royal court to give guidance on state affairs. But there were also unprofessional lay prophets. A man might be seized by the Spirit of God while taking part in a religious service, at the sound of music, or while following his flocks. Afterwards he might become a professional prophet, recognized as a spirit-possessed man, or he might, having delivered his message, return to his ordinary occupation. Primarily, however, the status and influence of prophets in religion were due to the fact that they had given evidence of being possessed or seized by the Spirit of God, evidence which was probably always attested by abnormal psychical or physical conditions.

To Hebrew, as to much primitive, thought, human personality was open to the invasion of external spirit forces, particularly that of the Spirit of God. This invasive force might have many consequences : it rushed on Samson, enabling him to rend a young lion ; it clothed itself with Gideon, giving him the power to fight against Baal worship ; it made Joseph a man of affairs, and Joshua a military leader. It did not necessarily produce results that were either religious or moral, but always the effects were in some way abnormal or unusual, whether shown in words or deeds. Ecstatic utterance may at first have consisted of sensible words or of ravings that needed to be interpreted ; Paul's letters to the Corinthians suggest that often speaking with tongues under spiritual inspiration was of the latter type (1 Cor. xiv.).

Always, however, the real prophet spoke under a sense of compulsion. When God utters his voice the prophet must speak ; God takes Amos from following the flocks ; God's word is an uncontainable fire within Jeremiah's bones, and though the message be one of doom or of the death of a beloved wife who was the " apple of his eye " to Ezekiel, the prophet has no option but to speak. In this compulsion lay the evidence of divine inspiration : no man chose to be a prophet nor decided on his message ; the message came to him with an irresistible spiritual force and he had to proclaim when and what he was told, even though he felt that he was being deceived. He was equally helpless to obtain a message as to resist it. Music or the society of other prophets might help to induce a state of ecstasy, but, like the priest with his oracle, there were times when no answer came from God to his messenger.

As prophecy developed it ceased to be the ecstatic ravings of a possessed person whose mouth God used, and became the outcome of direct fellowship with God. The prophet knew himself to be in the presence of God ; God used his thoughts, his conscience, and his power of moral judgement to give through him a moral and spiritual message which by its intrinsic worth showed that the speaker was not deceived when he introduced it by the phrase, " Thus saith Yahweh." The prophet did not thereby claim that there was no human element in his message, nor that his inspiration was verbal. The more we study the prophetic utterances the more obvious it becomes that the circumstances and character of each particular prophet intimately affected his message ; it was always—to use Phillips Brooks's definition of preaching—truth through personality. The prophet would equally have repudiated the suggestion that the moral judgement was his own, or that the insight into the purposes of God or the events of the future came from his own power of prediction. He had stood in the councils of God and had heard the word of God ; whether it was fulfilled or not mattered nothing to him; it carried with it its own inherent proof of divine origin, and its power, like that of curse or blessing to most primitive people, to bring about its own ultimate fulfilment.

The transition from an earlier form of prophecy in which the prophet was the passive recipient of a message, or an instrument in the hand of God, is recognized in the reference to Moses in Numbers xii. 6—other prophets had been spoken to by vision or dream and in dark sayings, but Moses face to face, mouth to mouth. As Cheyne[3] said, " the frenzied dervish-prophet of Saul's time could not satisfy an age of higher religious culture "; but—to use the words of Robertson Smith —we must seek " the true mark of the prophet in something higher than passive ecstasy—in the personal sympathy between himself and Yahweh, by virtue of which the God-sent thought approves itself to him inwardly and not by external authority." Mediation through a human personality left open the possibility of error and made it necessary to find criteria by which to distinguish between true and false prophets, but the variety of individuals enriched the revelation of God, the continual action of inspired consciences prevented the religion of either priest or prophet from becoming stereotyped and sinking into a series of meaningless words and symbols.

Before the great prophetic renaissance of the first century A.D. prophecy had been replaced, partly by guilds of temple singers whose work was spoken of as prophesying and whose antiphonal answer to the people's songs was regarded as the message of God, and partly by the writers of apocalyptic literature. These latter added to the older prophetic pictures of doom a vision of the bright Messianic future kingdom, often fanatically nationalistic. To some extent, with his proclamation of the Kingdom, John the Baptist was in the line of succession from these writers, but Christian writers thought of the prophetic office as culminating in the supreme revelation of Jesus. Prophecy which is only partial is done away with when the perfect fulfilment comes, said Paul to the Corinthians

(1 Cor. xiii.), and the writer to the Hebrews contrasts the revelation through Jesus with that through the prophets : " God, having of olden times spoken unto the fathers in the prophets in fragments and in a variety of forms, hath at the end of these days spoken unto us in a Son." Prophecy which had begun in men who were capable of being filled with the Spirit of God, continued in men who lived in intimacy with God, was fulfilled in one who was to such an extent " one with God " in spirit and character that men called him " a Son."

J. Armitage Robinson writes :

The ultimate triumph in the primitive Church of the ministry of office, over what we may call the ministry of enthusiasm, has made it difficult for us to realize that there ever was a time when bishops, presbyters, and deacons were not the prominent figures of the ecclesiastical community. The highest authority was accorded to the itinerant spirit-filled prophet, who was above criticism and had to be supported by the community. So long as administration was quite subordinate, and the prophets were true expounders of a divine message, all would go well ; but the expansion and general settlement of the church gave a growing importance to the official class and a dual control was inconsistent with the church's unity.[4]

Robinson also suggests that even in the New Testament period immorality cloaked itself with the prophetic mantle, that it was difficult to differentiate true and false prophets, and that prestige and " the emoluments attaching to the prophetic gift made it worth while for unworthy persons to simulate the possession of it."

In any modern attempt at reconstruction it seems probable that it may be necessary to differentiate between the teaching function of the ministry and spiritual leadership. The teaching function of priest or prophet is needed, religious education is required from properly trained teachers, and such training is possible. Biblical languages and literature, theology, the history and philosophy of religion, and Church history can be taught, and young men and women can be trained to impart it ; but the priestly power of leading worshippers into the presence of God, whether with or without symbols and ceremonial, and the inspiration enabling a prophet to proclaim the message of God to his generation, are both the gift of God. They cannot be implanted by academic training ; like religion itself they must be " caught not taught," and should not become the prerogative of a professional class. The history of Judaism and of the Christian Church shows abundantly that such spiritual leaders have existed within and outside the ranks of regular officials, and that there is nothing more basic than the fact that the Spirit of God can lead any man into " all truth," making known his will and purpose, and guiding all those who seek his presence and listen for his word. In all the creative epochs there has been a democratization of priestly and prophetic functions. Moses exclaimed, " Would that all the Lord's people were prophets." Israel is depicted as a nation of priests, and the New Testament speaks of all believers as being " Kings and Priests unto God." Perhaps we should cease to think of spiritual leadership in terms of a professional class, and be more ready to seek it among the rank and file of the Church, and, more important still, we should not regard the call of God as an act which permanently sets a man in a class apart from his fellows. The men or women thus called by God should be encouraged to deliver the word of God given to them, but we should not expect God always to use the same agents to deliver messages from himself whenever there are meetings for worship. Such expectation leads to-day, as in the days of the Old Testament prophets, to the passing of counterfeit coin—human visions instead of the divine word.

Experience has shown all too clearly that the incentive of private gain, and still more of personal authority, is one of the most subtle temptations which professional religious leaders have to face. A higher standard in regard to selflessness is rightly required of those who have been set aside by the Church and chosen by God for spiritual leadership. To them applies to some extent Amos's message from God to Israel : " You only have I known of all the families of the earth, therefore I will require of you your sins." It might be well in the light of the experience of all branches of the Church to attempt so to modify our organization that this temptation is removed or reduced to a minimum. Although in a specialized world the practice of the Jewish Rabbis is no longer possible, their unselfish spirit is essential ; what Jesus called the Gentile conception of greatness must be abjured by Christian leaders and rejected by the Church in its thought of leadership (Mark x. 42f.). Dr. Garvie used to tell his students that ministers were not chosen to lord it over God's heritage, though they might have to see that no one else did. Men must enter the ministry not because there is authority to be exercised or a profession to be followed, but service to be rendered.

§ Law

The legal revelation of God's will resulted from both priestly and prophetic revelations and crystallized them into written forms. Its centre was formed by civil and religious laws and established customs and practices. As many of these had been given originally through priestly oracles, it formed a collection of priestly precedents ; but the word Torah—the Hebrew word for the law—means far more than our word law. It was instruction or direction given by the priests, and included guidance as to God's will and instructions as to his requirements and character. It was also, however, the technical name for the five books of the Pentateuch ascribed to Moses, and these books included a rich variety of literature and human experience. In its present form it was written down after the activities of the great prophets, and much of the prophetic teaching has been embodied in it, so that laws have been modified, stories, myths, and legends retold, and new lessons inculcated. The regenerative conscience of the prophets worked on the conservative system of priestly instruction and custom to produce the law ; but it must be remembered that it was the priest who, although he revived so much of the past, yet preserved the prophetic message—a fact that should always correct the common tendency to regard prophet and priest as in opposition. The true prophet was in opposition to every religious abuse, whether in priest, people, or fellow prophet, and the true priest, accepting the criticism, modified his ritual and customs when popular demand permitted.

To the Jew no part of the Bible equals the Torah in authority, although later the Prophetic books, the Writings, and the Mishna are all regarded as Scripture. This Torah, which is the result of successive editing of different codes and a long rich development, was regarded as the work of Moses, and was thought of as having been given once for all through him. It was thus treated as the written and final statement of the revealed will of God given for all time. No other revelation was possible or necessary. Fortunately this book revelation was saved from becoming too dogmatic or static by the growth of a body of oral law, by the belief that the written law needed to be interpreted, and by the fact that it contained such a wide range of ideas and contents that it was always possible to find a passage which, without too much exegetical trickery, could be made to support almost any decision or opinion.

Despite this possibility of reinterpretation, however, the conception of a written law-book did in fact put revelation into the past ; God had revealed himself to Moses, and his revelation was complete and final. The same theory was applied to the prophetic revelation. This too was put into the past, and the prophetic age was thought of as over, so that in future God's will could be known fully through a diligent study of the Law and the Prophets. There was a tendency to remove God a stage away from contact with man ; fellowship with him was gained through the written word.

There are Christians of whose beliefs the same may be said : their religion too is founded on an infallible book through which alone God has revealed himself once for all and completely. It must be emphasized that both to Jews and Christians who hold such views, those written pages are no dead letter. Some of the Psalms and much Christian writing show that the Torah and the whole Bible can mediate the presence and the Spirit of God, filling the reader with warm enthusiasm and sincere devotion. Just as a new Judaism was created through the Law, when the temple had been destroyed, the nation scattered, and the native land trampled by foreign conquerors, so to Jew and Christian the written word has been a source of strength and an inspiration to new life. But it is doubtful whether Jesus regarded his spoken word—or even his life—as the final revelation of God : though he claimed to be the promised Messiah, and taught that men would gain access to God and knowledge of him through himself, yet he was equally emphatic in his assertion that his followers would do greater things than he had done, and that the spirit of God would lead them into all truth. In a much quoted and often mutilated passage he scathingly remarked to those who stressed so strongly the importance of studying the written word: "Ye search the scriptures because ye think that in them ye have eternal life ; and these are they which bear witness of me ; and ye will not come to me that ye may have life " (John v. 39). Not only will new light and truth spring forth from the word of God as it has done ever since that word was written, but God did not cease to speak when the human ear ceased to hear the voice of Moses and of Jesus ; through history and human life he continues to lead men responsive to his spirit onward into new visions of his will and character. Advance in religious truth is a reward of careful study of the written word of God in the Bible, an unprejudiced mind that eagerly accepts and sifts new knowledge from whatever source it comes, a life of reverent humble companionship with the God of Truth ; and, as Jesus said, he who willeth to do shall know.

§ CHARACTER OF GOD SEEN IN HISTORY AND HUMAN LIFE

We have seen how to Hebrew and primitive thought human personality was considered as open to the invasive power of the Spirit of God, and that he was regarded as being able to reveal himself directly to chosen individuals. There are stories in the Old Testament that speak of him revealing himself through human figures called angels or messengers, but it is interesting to discover that in the Pentateuch, whenever he thus speaks to man, at some point in the story the messenger is identified with Yahweh himself, so that, even in the revised form in which the story has reached us, we can recognize that to the earlier story-teller it was Yahweh himself in human form who walked with men in their garden when the evening breeze was blowing, appeared as traveller at the door of their tent, listened to their pleading on behalf of a doomed city, and accepted their offerings of food and sacrifice. In the visions of Ezekiel and Zechariah the angel, or heavenly messenger, gives God's message to the prophet and mediates between him and sinful man ; in later Judaism and Christianity the world is full of these angelic hosts, some of whom are known by name and have special functions—Michael is the Guardian of Israel, Gabriel the revealer to Daniel and to Mary—others are " ministering spirits sent to minister to those who are heirs of salvation."

Stories were also told of God's revelation through nature. To Second-Isaiah and the Psalmists nature revealed the work of the creator and sustainer of all things ; to Job the " picture gallery of God's world " revealed unfathomable wisdom ; to Jesus rain, sunshine, and the beauty of flowers spoke of the loving care of the Father. To writers in the Old Testament God came through the storm to Moses on Sinai and to Deborah and Samuel on the battlefield ; to Elijah, when he ran away to Horeb to meet the God of Moses, he came through the silence of utter desolation. His voice spoke from a burning bush ; his presence was in the pillar of fire that guided his people in the darkness, and his glory was seen in the luminous cloud—the glory that later was spoken of as the Shekinah Glory, the glory dwelling among men. The writer of the prologue to John's Gospel takes up the same thought when he uses the Greek word similar in sound to express the idea that in Jesus God had taken flesh and " dwelt among men," so that they could behold his glory.

The New Testament idea of God becoming incarnate in a human form—so common in other religions—was thus not foreign to Hebrew thought ; it became the way in which Christians expressed their belief that God had again taken the initiative in entering the world in Jesus ; and Paul too used it to explain his experience of an indwelling Christ : " It is not I who live, but Christ Jesus who lives in me." In the loftiest visions of the Old Testament true religion was seen to be the incarnation of the character of God in human life, in Paul it became the incarnating of the Messiah in daily life, as the Messiah himself had incarnated the spirit and character of God.

Perhaps the most objective revelation of God in the Old Testament is that which was thought of as coming through historic events. In its simplest form it was guidance through a particular event, like the dry and the wet fleece of Gideon, or the sign given by a prophet to substantiate his message. Later an outstanding event in Israel's history, like the deliverance from Egypt at the Red Sea, was interpreted by prophet or singer as an act of God revealing his character and purpose. Such revelations needed to be interpreted by one who like a prophet had stood in the council of God, and the interpretation of history became an outstanding feature of the work of the prophets, who believed that God would do nothing without revealing it to his servants, and that in all his government of the world he was consistent. They believed that consequently the past and the present could be interpreted and the future foretold in accordance with principles springing from God's moral character, and that even without a special revelation it was possible to apply those moral principles, and so understand history and current happenings, in the unshakable confidence that Right and God would triumph over evil, so that God's purpose could not finally be thwarted.

The prophet lived in a small world ruled by a great God. We have pushed the bounds of our world to infinity without being able to enlarge our conception of God beyond the limitations imposed by the idea of personality, which is, after all, anthropomorphic. We can see God's activity in the past—

Israel's history, the Cross of Calvary—but if religion is to be again the vital force it was to prophets and early Christians, we must conceive of God as active in the modern world ; as working out his purpose both in the intimate personal affairs of daily life and in national and international happenings. To Second-Isaiah his God was distinguished from all others by his power to enable his prophets so to understand the past and present that they could fearlessly and accurately foretell the future. The God who used Assyria and Babylonia still uses the aggression and cruelty of nations, the selfishness of individuals, and the cross of injustice and social evil to which humanity is nailed, as stepping-stones to salvation and as the revelation of his will. Both as Jews and Christians, we need to move on from the past with its revelation of God to previous generations, and, by bringing their rich experience to bear on the life we live and the world in which we are, make the character and will of the living God plain to our generation through contemporary events.

Such an interpretation becomes possible only to a monotheistic faith. Monotheism is not negative, the denial of the existence of other gods, nor the worship of one solitary God. Both Jew and Christian have in many ways moved from such an idea of the Godhead. The rich background of angelic figures, the personification of the attributes of God, the anticipation of the coming of the One who above all others could be called the " Son of God," all modified the stark monotheism of Judaism, and led to the Christian picture of a social Godhead of Father, Son, and Spirit—a picture true to the genius of the religion we have been studying in that it gives a new form to an ancient belief, the belief we found in early nomadic religion. The essential element in monotheism would appear to be the assertion of the unity of will and consistency of purpose in the government of the world and of men, and the recognition that any fresh revelation must be in line with the highest revelation that yet has been vouchsafed to us.

CHAPTER 18

WORSHIP

§ CORPORATE RITES

WORSHIP has been defined by Miss Evelyn Underhill [1] as the response of the creature to the eternal ; at its heart we find the adoring response of spirit to Spirit, and on its circumference every action or attitude of man that expresses his movement Godwards. But, to quote the same writer: " The character of worship is always decided by the worshipper's conception of God and his relation to God : that is to say, whatever its ritual expression may be, it always has a theological basis." The strong sense of social solidarity—the belief that an individual and his God were both members of a larger community—meant that man's earliest response to God was through corporate rites.

These corporate rites were enacted at places which had a special holiness, either because the dead were buried there or because God had taken the initiative and revealed himself at that particular place. At first there were many of these holy places, some connected with private dwellings, whether painted caves or the " house of gods " made by the young Micah and his mother in the period of the Judges ; altars stood on high hills, under green trees, or at the corners of the streets, open-air pilgrim shrines, and later elaborate temples at provincial centres ; last of all, to the Jews sacrificial rites were legitimate only at the one central sanctuary at Jerusalem. This centralization of corporate worship removed much of religion from contact with the daily life of men, and very soon there sprang up local sanctuaries, replacing the former sacrificial altars and shrines as places where men met for prayer and instruction.

It is of interest to find that in the first century A.D. these local synagogues were not only places where worship took place when the temple was too far distant, but even in Jerusalem itself there were synagogues which were the meeting-places for people with particular views or associations—there was a synagogue for the hellenists to which probably both Paul and Stephen belonged. But there was apparently no opposition between temple and synagogue worship ; the times of meeting were deliberately chosen to synchronize with the occasions of sacrificial services at the temple, and we find those whose ordinary religious life was fed, instructed, and disciplined in the synagogues, present at the great festivals in the temple and probably contributing much to the rich devotional worship there. Both synagogue and temple had a place in the corporate religious life of the Jewish people, in much the same way as the priest and prophet had had in pre-exilic Israel.

In Jewish religion, too, the family and the home were, and have always remained, a centre of corporate worship. Perhaps from the days when the family tombs were within the home certain religious rites took place in the family circle. The Deuteronomic attempt to purify religion by centralizing it at one sanctuary could not break down the family character of such a festival as the Passover, and to-day many religious acts in Jewish homes testify to a more lasting influence exercised by the Deuteronomic reformers: " these words which I command thee this day shall be upon thy heart : thou shalt teach them diligently unto thy children and shalt talk of them when thou sittest in thine house . . . and shalt write them upon the doorposts of thy house, and upon thy gates." Thus, when the temple had been destroyed, the corporate worship of the family as well as community worship in the synagogue remained.

From early times, too, there were sacred seasons when men could especially approach God—the seasons of the agricultural or the nomadic year; spring and autumn, seed-time and harvest, the phases of the moon and the Sabbath. The character of these festivals reflects fairly accurately in successive periods the meaning of religion and of worship to the particular age. In the early days, and still to the Deuteronomic reformer, the essential character was joyous fellowship with one another and with God. In Deuteronomy there is a loud, emphatic note of thanksgiving. The gatherings were communal feasts in which men brought their gifts to God as an expression of gratitude for all his benefits, and, sharing the gifts with God and their fellow-worshippers, rejoiced before the Lord in a common meal. In the post-exilic age, exile and disaster had left their stamp on religion, and atonement, penitence for sin, and the need for forgiveness formed the dominant motive in the corporate worship. The note of joy can still be heard. Worship in the temple and the study of the law in the synagogue enabled men to enter into a fellowship with God which brought deep satisfaction and made them say: "A day in thy courts is better than a thousand ; I would rather be a doorkeeper in the house of my God than dwell in the tents of wickedness."

It is interesting, too, to see how the conception of God as the God of history entered into corporate worship. Both Jew and Christian connected religious festivals with historic occasions. Whether the festivals were taken over from the older framework of the religious year or were newly instituted, the Jew connected them with events in God's redemptive history of Israel, and the Christian made them commemorative of successive events in the life of Jesus. This connection has not only an educative value, but it asserts continually the supreme reality of religion to both Jew and Christian—that though God is transcendent, holy, and distinct from the world and men, yet he is a present reality, active in the realm of time and space, revealing himself in historic events.

The centre of these early corporate rites appears to have been originally an animal—or human—sacrifice. The original meaning to the Semitic peoples of this sacrifice is uncertain ; the human sacrifice appears to have had as its basis the principle of giving life to gain life, as so much animal offering had in Assyria and Babylonia ; but the animal offerings may originally have been communal meals shared between the people, their dead, and their god, in which the common eating of flesh and drinking of blood was the means by which the common life was shared. In later times there was a fully developed ritual in which the worshippers shared by liturgical responses, singing of psalms, and bringing of offerings, and there were certain acts which the priests alone could perform. Since the destruction of the temple, the centre of Jewish public worship has been the Scroll of the Law through which God is revealed.

Christian worship developed in a similar manner. Prayer and worship took place, both for Jesus and his disciples, in the temple, and even after the death of Jesus disciples gathered there for the hours of prayer, and to make and fulfil vows like other Jews. They also used the synagogues for teaching and preaching, and knew the more intimate house fellowship, and the family worship of the " Church in the Home." The centre of corporate worship was " the breaking of bread," which in some branches of the Church remains a simple act of fellowship, thanksgiving, and commemoration around a communion table. In other branches the altar has returned to replace the table, and at the altar the sacrifice is offered. The central object of worship to most Christians is Christ, regarded as the supreme revelation of God through whom God can be approached and known.

§ Symbolism

Corporate worship always involves some form of ritual and the use of symbols. Miss Underhill defines ritual as " an agreed pattern of ceremonial movements, sounds, and verbal formulas, creating a framework within which corporate religious actions can take place." By means of this agreed pattern the worshipper can lose his individuality and completely share in the common worship ; and because this is the aim, Dr. Marett is right when he says that in true ritual the tune matters more than the words. Worship involves the whole of man's nature, and it must find social expression in acts that can be done together ; such ritual acts not only express worship but they stimulate it ; they bring into play the elements of feeling and habit which are as necessary to worship as will and attention.

But it must not be forgotten that the primary purpose of religious ritual is not the same as that of community singing. It aims not simply at producing a certain emotional atmosphere, but at bringing the worshipper into communion with God, and the constituent elements of ritual must be so blended as to further and express this aim. In the orgiastic dances of the priests of Baal on Mount Carmel, or the nude dance of David before the Ark, the form and significance of the dance were probably as important as its rhythm, and, to quote Miss Underhill: "It is only too easy for the best and most significant cultus to lose spiritual content when it is not the vehicle for the worship of spiritual men. Then it declines from religion to magic and from a living worship to a ceremonial routine, in which the exact recitation of the accepted formula, or the correct performance of the ordained act, is held to satisfy the full obligations of religion." The rhythm of the ritual can be mistaken for the spiritual adoration which lifts the soul into communion with God ; the sacrificial rite or the giving of offerings may obscure the true outcome of worship—the offering of the whole personality, heart, mind, and soul, as a living sacrifice ; and endless repetition can come perilously near to the heathen worship, condemned by Jesus because it expects to be heard for its much speaking, of which the Tibetan prayer-wheel is the logical outcome.

The continual revolt of prophet and reformer against the effects of ritual shows only too plainly its dangers, but equally the movement of all forms of religion toward some form of ritual, whether it be the elaborate sacrificial ceremonial of the Jewish temple or the silence and handclasp of the Quaker, shows the need for an "agreed pattern" as a framework for corporate expression of the social side of worship. Priest and prophet, ritualist and rebel, need to exist within the same Church continually reacting to each other, developing a form of worship in which all can partake, and removing any primitive and traditional survivals which have ceased to have significance and no longer aid men in their adoration. Probably we should recognize that nothing in the cultus has an absolute intrinsic value for itself alone ; it is a means to an end, and " its value lies in its power to suggest, to express, and to evoke worship and to unite in one adoring action worshippers at many different stages of development."

Bound up with ritual is the use of symbols. Every approach of the finite mind to the infinite must make use of symbols, if we define a symbol as " a material or mental image which helps the worshipper to apprehend spiritual reality." Dr. Bevan [2] has reminded us that such words as Lofty, Eternal, Great, when applied to God are mental symbols enabling the user to express and apprehend spiritual reality ; many people who would reject the use of material symbols such as incense, lights, crucifixes, or the sign of the Cross, do not realize that they themselves continually use mental images as symbols to express what would otherwise be inexpressible.

Skinner writes :

The symbolism of the second temple with its graduated series of sacred spaces culminating in the inmost shrine or most Holy Place, its different classes of ministers, and its minutely regulated ceremonial was so designed as to form an impressive exhibition to the Israelite of the ruling idea of holiness.

Much of the symbolism of Jewish and Christian worship has in the same way the object of exhibiting by images, words, or actions the attributes of God, his holiness, his continual presence, his sacrificial love. But, as we have seen, symbolic acts, whether of prophet or priest, are often not simply symbolic—they are what has been called functional. As the prophetic action was regarded as influencing the future, and as making the event prophesied actually happen, so the priestly acts made God approachable and secured forgiveness and atonement for sin. In a similar way actions may become sacraments—actions which release the spiritual forces of God. To most Christians the act of baptism which constitutes the form of entrance into the fellowship of the Church and the " breaking of bread " which is the expression of the continual nourishing of the Church's life, constitute such sacraments ; baptism as an act of surrender to the Kingdom of God and later to Jesus, and communion as an act of allegiance—" the new covenant in my blood "—both open the life to the Spirit of God or the indwelling Christ.

As corporate worship included the intellectual approach of the synagogue as well as the sensuous approach to God through eye, ear, and hand in the temple, so, as we have seen, the symbols through which we express spiritual reality may be word images as well as material objects or ceremonial actions. That words, like acts, had a functional force is clear from the story of the blessing by Isaac of his two sons, Jacob and Esau, and from the use made in the New Testament of the name of Jesus ; and most branches of the Christian Church retain both verbal and material symbols as well as symbolic actions. There is the water of baptism, broken bread, and poured-out wine, the cross and crucifix ; there is the sacramental act of baptism and communion, the handclasp of fellowship, corporate prayer through silence or speech, the use of verbal formulæ, and the pronouncing of benedictions.

There is, however, a constant danger of overrating the value of words for the expressing of ideas and emotions ; often actions are not only a more social form of expression but more natural and nearer to life ; also the precision of language is not always an advantage, and words have a danger which acts do not possess. Ritual and ceremonial actions are nearly always older than the current interpretation of them ; people will continue to observe a familiar rite, even though they utterly repudiate the idea in which it originated, and common ritual is never a safe indication of common beliefs. Infant baptism, for example, may have originated in the doctrines of baptismal regeneration and original sin, but the rite continues to be observed by many Christians who would completely reject these doctrines. A creed, too, that is expressed in the form of a symbolic act is always capable of reinterpretation in the light of new thought or fresh discoveries ; it unites people at very different stages of development, and allows

progress from one level to another without the heat of controversy. When words are used as symbols, development is
more difficult ; it is not so easy to reinterpret them. A creed
crystallized into words, a rubric directing a religious act has
become stabilized and static, and has either to be abandoned,
or accepted with a series of mental reservations—a practice of
doubtful morality. Although words like deeds can change
their meaning and convey a vastly different sense to different
people in different times and places, yet precision is, as a rule,
the purpose of verbal formulation, and that precision prevents
the use of the formula with a changed meaning.

§ PRIVATE DEVOTION

The growth of personal religion is not easy to trace ; but
from the account of Enoch walking with God, and Moses
speaking with him face to face as a man speaks with a friend,
to that of Jesus rising up a great while before dawn to be
alone for prayer, there are in the Bible innumerable stories of
men and women whose faith and response to God sprang from
a deep inner fellowship with him. However great the stress
which is rightly placed on the value of corporate devotion
and the social character of worship, the complementary truth
must receive equal emphasis, that the corporate religious life
of any community depends for its quality on the personal
devotional life of each of its members.

Archæological evidence has shown that whatever may
have been the stage of development reached by the Israelite
nomads who entered Palestine, it is not possible to differentiate
either their public or private worship from that of other
peoples. Yahweh was one among many gods and had his
consorts ; the people had images and amulets on their persons
and in their homes, and practised various forms of magic.
To both Israelite and Canaanite, religion was an essential part
of daily life, and no part of life was free from the activities
of God. There are rites and ceremonies incumbent on every
individual all through his life ; and however lofty his idea of

the character of the God he worshipped, this interpenetration of life by rites and rules always remained part of Jewish worship.

Moore suggested that "the ground of the remarkable unity of Judaism is to be found not so much in a general agreement in fundamental ideas as in community of observance throughout the whole Jewish world," and Israel Abrahams said that the Jew has an ingrained belief in the organic union of ritual with religion, and does not appreciate the difference between the abiding principles of religion and the rules and conduct by which it is sought to realize them in daily life. This becomes clear when we read the Psalms, and explains why the rich depth of private devotion within the Psalter can be mingled with the sincerest and warmest love for the temple, its courts, its ritual, and processions, as well as for the Law which later replaced the temple. The performance by the individual of ceremonies in the temple, the synagogue, or the home, the rigid obedience to the demands of oral or written codes, was not merely ritual or submission to a law book : it was an act of worship and adoration.

Some embodiment in external forms is as necessary to private devotion as to public worship. They provide the framework around which we can build those regular habits of devotion which save us from becoming creatures of moods ; they give us the discipline which enables us to lose ourselves in adoration, meditation, or intercession ; and they unite all aspects of our personality, thought, feeling, and will, so that we may the more fully respond in humble, joyous submission to the Objective Reality we call God. When we reject these external aids, our spiritual life is in danger of growing weak through monotony and vagueness, and through the loss of the vision of "The Lord high and lifted up," before whom Seraphim hide their faces—the vision which alone enables us to catch the spirit of him who was "meek and lowly in heart." And yet when we use them it is possible to mistake the means for the end : the ritual act, recital of prayers, reading of scripture, meditation on the mysteries of the life and death of Christ, can satisfy us instead of leading us to the ultimate goal of personal devotion—loving attention to God, listening to his guidance, and actively co-operating with him as we pray, " Thy will be done."

The essential basis of both Jewish and Christian religion is the belief that God is a living reality, lovingly active in the world. This belief colours all private devotion. Philo said that God never ceases working, but as the property of fire is to burn and snow to be cold, so the property of God is to be active, and he is the origin of action in others ; the prophet stressed his activity in history as strongly as the Canaanites had asserted divine activity in nature ; and though Genesis states that God ceased on the seventh day from the work that he had done, Jesus did not accept this as meaning that God rested or became inactive even on that day. When challenged because he had healed a man on the Sabbath, he replied : " My Father worketh up till now, and I work."

The prophets claimed, too, that God had shown the loving nature of his activity by stooping to his people's needs and binding himself in a covenant to them—a relationship that Hosea first describes as grace or loving-kindness. To this covenanted love Israelites appealed when they had sinned, certain that God was " righteous "—the Hebrew word means one who is loyal to his obligations and pays his dues. To Jesus, too, God is lovingly active; he cares for the smallest detail in his world, and has time for each of his children : he clothes the grass, feeds the birds, and can be trusted to know each man's individual needs. In Christianity the advent and death of Jesus have been the proof of God's love ; " he so loved the world that he gave," and he " commended his own love to us in that while we were yet sinners Christ died for us." By his initiative in Jesus Christ God again proved his " righteous-ness," his full and complete loyalty to all the obligations of love. He broke down the barriers of sin and gave men power to enter the family of God, to " become sons of God." Paul uses the picture of the old nomadic community as well as that of the family when he asserts that that righteous act of God restored us to the community of the love of God, and lifted us out of the circle of those who were under his wrath. Hebrew thought places the emphasis on effect rather than on means or purpose, and when Paul translates the Hebrew word for righteousness into Greek he thinks of the resultant relation between God and man and not how the restoration of the relationship is made ; he does not introduce legal terms which were absent from the Old Testament and from the thought of Jesus; he still is thinking in terms of a restored relationship; atonement has been made and we can enter God's community.

This loving activity of God was thought of as admitting the co-operation of individual men. With gratitude awakened by the recognition of all God's mercies, men brought to him their offerings, acknowledged that all their blessings came from him, and " paid their vows unto him in the presence of all his people." But as God became more fully known, vows meant more than an animal or material offering, however costly ; they involved the offering of the whole personality in love and co-operation with the will of God. The basis of the prophetic conscience, of the Jewish belief in reference to the Law, and of the Christian faith in Jesus, is that God can and does make known his will to individuals. The prophets claimed that as individuals they " knew God," had intimate relationship with him, and stood in his councils. This experience of personal fellowship with God passed from prophets to psalmists and was shared by the common people, and from it was born the conviction, emphasised so strongly by one of Streeter's books, that God speaks. Thus the aim of worship, whether public or private, becomes the stimulation of adoration and devotion which can be expressed in a life of sacrifice ; worship is not something apart from life, but a new orientation of daily life Godwards.

§ WORSHIP AS LIFE

The most distinctive contribution made by the Hebrews to religion was that through them morality became essential to worship. It is not possible to say whence this emphasis on morals entered Israel's religion, for even if we say that it was inherent in the nomadic religion we have still to explain why the same development did not take place among other nomadic peoples. We are on safe ground only when we assert that the prophets believed that it was the direct outcome of God's message and the result of the entrance of the Spirit of God into man's consciousness. If the Hebrews had used the word " conscience " for it they would have meant something which comes through knowing God—that is, through intimate fellowship with him—not something which results from intellectual apprehension of his truths; and perhaps their explanation would not have been far wrong.

Where we can trace the growth of this morality it appears to be the application to the larger national community of the principles on which the corporate life of the smaller clan or family was built. Nathan and Elijah would not acquiesce in the king's right to kill a fellow-man in order to obtain his wife or his vineyard, because such conduct would not be tolerated in the tribal life. Amos coming from the wilderness of Judæa and seeing the moral corruption of the northern kingdom, denounced it in the name of God, because such lack of justice and righteousness would inevitably have disintegrated social life in the desert tribe. In the same way all the prophets claimed that worship—the recognition of the worth of God—can be adequately expressed only in life and character. Micah's book stated that God's requirements were that men should do acts of justice, maintain an attitude of loving-kindness, and walk through life in humble reverence with God. Justice, mercy, and humility were attributes of the character of God, and the only complete recognition of their worth is shown by building one's own character around them and incorporating them in one's own daily life. The great confession in Job xxix. contains the same idea of the meaning of worship.

The claim that morality is essential to worship is made as clearly in the New Testament. Jesus said that if you are taking your gift to the altar and on the way remember that your brother has a just cause against you, leave your gift, and first be reconciled to your brother—right human relationships are the doorway into the outer court of God's temple. The character of Jesus is depicted as the embodiment of the loving-kindness which God shows to man, and which he demands from men in their relationships with their fellows ; and one of the few commandments of Jesus challenges his followers to prove the reality of their loyalty by their love: " A new commandment give I unto. you, that ye love one another ; as I have loved you, that ye also love one another. By this shall all men know that ye are my disciples, if ye have love one for another."

It is interesting that humility is claimed as characteristic of Jesus as it had been of Moses. He reveals God to men because he is meek and lowly in heart ; in the great picture drawn of Jesus in the Fourth Gospel we see him—knowing that he came from God and was returning to God—taking a towel and doing the work of the lowest slave, as an example of lowly service (John xiii.). Paul too speaks of the need for a Christian to have the " mind of Christ," who being in the form of God yet took the form of a slave and poured out his life even unto death (Phil. ii. 8).

The New Testament writers agree with the older prophets that morality is the fruit of the Spirit, the difference being that they equated the Spirit of God with the risen Christ dwelling in a human life. James is as emphatic as any pre-exilic prophet that if a man says he loves God and as a matter of fact he hates his brother, he is a liar ; that pure religion is " to visit the fatherless and widows in their affliction and keep oneself unspotted from the world " (James i. 27). In the Fourth Gospel, so deeply influenced by Greek thought, Christianity is still, as to the Hebrews, a way of life, not a system of thought or a pattern of ritual.

It is of considerable interest in view of the modern drift away from institutional religion that many of the prophets appear to have reached the stage where they despaired of institutional forms of religion, and pleaded for a spiritual religion expressed only in daily life. Jeremiah, Second-Isaiah,

and Jesus all envisaged the destruction of the temple and its
cult, and looked forward to the time when men should worship
God in spirit and in truth ; Paul appears even to think of
religion without one day set apart as a special holy day, but in
which all days are alike days on which men serve and worship
God (Rom. xiv. 5). Though this may be an ultimate goal,
what has been said about the necessity for ritual and symbolism
applies to this vision. Dr. E. R. Bevan [2] suggests that a holy
day set apart from the other six may express the conception
of a transcendent God, just as the recognition of the immanence
of God appears in the idea of worship as life. The beauty of
Church buildings, equipment, and ceremonial, can convey
the beauty of holiness, while the simplicity of unadorned
bare walls can encourage men to express their belief in the
beauty of God through a life that reflects his beauty—the
puritan ideal of " plain living and high thinking."

Bishop Frere says that " No one can hope to judge fairly of
matters of ceremonial who does not see that the reason why
they cause such heat of controversy is that they signify so
much." It is that significance which explains the sharp exclusive divisions, and the bitter as well as heated controversies
that have marred the spirit of the Christian Church and of the
Jewish community. The truth seems to be that in the final
analysis worship is more than man's response to the eternal ;
it is a response that opens human personality to the presence
of the Spirit of God, and on that Spirit the very existence of our
spiritual life is dependent. In our thought of world reconstruction we are beginning to realize that forms of national
government may be a purely domestic affair and of secondary
importance, but that world peace demands that the economic
resources of the world on which national existence depends
shall be made available to all nations. Perhaps we should
apply the same principle of reconstruction to religion. Whatever form of government a particular religious community
may possess, the spiritual resources of each community should
be freely available to all. The more highly we value our own
ceremonial, sacraments, and fellowship as a means of spiritual

life, the more eager we should be to make them available to
nourish the spiritual life of others.   Church unity in which
various forms of worship are practised within the one community might only lead to the position in the Church of the
Holy Sepulchre at Jerusalem, or that of the Nativity at Bethlehem ; there the professional Arab guide, with some pardon-
able contempt, tells visitors that " this is the place where all
the various Christian sects worship, and that is the Arab police-
man who keeps order and peace among them."   But if all
—whatever rites or ceremonies they have undergone or
omitted—were encouraged to share each other's spiritual
means of sustenance, we should not only be showing in a
practical way the spirit of true religion, but would grow in
fellowship and understanding, and perhaps attract those who
care more for the growth of spiritual life than for our differences and controversies.

Most people worship God in the way they do, not because
of deeply rooted principles, but because they are perpetuating
traditional forms handed down to them by their fathers and
confirmed by the habits formed in youth ; many so-called
principles are in reality prejudices.   In any reconstruction of
religion nothing must be done which would in any way limit
or interfere with the freedom of the individual to worship
God in his own way ; but it must equally be recognized that
freedom—whether it be national or individual, economic or
religious—does not confer the right to do as we like even with
our own, but the responsibility of so using our resources that
we and our fellows achieve the highest possible good.

CHAPTER 19

SOCIAL CONSCIENCE

A JEWISH Rabbi of the first century B.C. is reported to have said that on three things the world is established : on the Torah, on Prayer, and on the giving of alms.[1] Each of these three appears to be part of a larger whole—God's revelation of himself, man's response to the revelation, and the social expression of that response in help to one's fellows; and just as God's revelation is greater than the Jewish law, and man's response includes prayer as a part of worship, so almsgiving is not the whole of social life. The Hebrew word used by the Rabbi has a wider significance, however, than our word almsgiving; it is the word previously translated "Righteousness," and includes, as we have seen, the recognition of all our obligations and the payment of every due. The stress on it as one of the three bases of the world arose naturally from the Hebrew emphasis on morality as an essential element in worship.

§ CORPORATE PERSONALITY

We have seen that the earliest conception of the relationship between the individual and the group, at least among nomadic people, is one that can be described in Dr. Wheeler Robinson's phrase as " Corporate Personality." The individual as a self-conscious unit had not emerged. Every man was part of a blood group, a family, clan, or tribe bound together by the fact that the same blood flowed through the veins of all the members. For some purposes he appears to have been treated as part of the family of which he was chief, and, for others, as part of the larger group of which he was a son, so that for some offences the sins of the fathers were visited upon the children, and for others the fathers suffered for their children's sins. The group provided each member with food and clothing ; it gave him social security and justice ; it protected him against his foes, and the individual's life was so bound up with his group that he would never question the value of community life. Apart from it, he had no rights, freedom, or property ; within it, all these were guaranteed.

Some writers have assumed that within the nomadic groups there were no individual rights or property, but this is probably an exaggeration. We know of the tribal courts in which disputes between members of the same group were settled by the sheikh, or, if there were no witness or precedent, by ordeal. These disputes concerned blows, breaches of social tabu, and matters that presuppose the possession of at least a minimum of personal rights and property. But there was no private property in things that were necessary to the maintenance of life ; herds and flocks, pastures and wells, and all the means of sustaining life were the common possession of the whole group, and while a man remained within his group he shared its property as well as its victories and defeats, its joys and its sufferings.

In return for his communal rights he had well-defined responsibilities. He took his share of the work in the tents, among the cattle, and upon the battlefield ; justice was administered by the head of the community with the help of elders, but always with the consent and support of every member ; the worship of the tribal god was the duty of all, and each man had his place in the festivals and the ceremonial ; the maintenance of the tribe and its property against any aggression was the responsibility of every member, and each willingly offered his life to avenge wrongs done to the community. Within the group there was a rigid discipline and a strict code of behaviour, and for a breach of that discipline or code a man was liable to the drastic punishment of " being cut off from his people."

The group had clearly defined limits beyond which no man had any responsibilities or obligations. Any attachment, however strong, which he might make outside his own community, might at any time be cut through by the paramount

duty of blood revenge. Between the different " corporate
personalities " there was no moral code apart from that imposed by this desert law. Strong tribes raided the encampments
and pastures of others, carrying off their cattle and stealing their
property ; if by inadvertence blood was shed during one of
these raids, then blood revenge meant that between the two
peoples strife went on for generations. In such a society,
where a man was the member of one group only, there were
no clashes of loyalty, and the problems of the relationship of
the individual to the group were easily solved. It is the conflict of loyalties which in the modern world constitutes one
of the basic problems of social life ; men belong to many
groups which cannot be arranged in concentric circles, and
these groups have different standards of morality, and each
makes its own peculiar demands. It must be recognized that
nomadic society was distinguished from our own, not, as is
usually stated, by the fact that the individual had no rights, but
that he had no conflicting loyalties. There was only one group
within which he had to apply his moral standard, and everyone
within the group lived by the same absolute standard; outside
the group " every man did what was right in his own eyes."

How long and to what extent the group consciousness
survived among the Israelites after they had settled in Palestine
is not easy to decide, but there were many influences that would
tend to break it down. We have seen that excavations in
Palestine, as well as the laws of Leviticus, reveal the fact that
attempts were made to carry this communal society into the
agricultural and industrial life of a settled people. Property
could not be permanently alienated from the family group,
and no man could be enslaved without hope of redemption ;
but it was difficult to apply the same laws to town property as
to country land, and the growing religious communities to
which no property had been originally apportioned were
given the right to acquire land in perpetuity. Social inter-
course with the natives among whom the Israelites settled was
impossible so long as neither observed any moral code in his
dealings with the other, and it became necessary to accept the

code of the stronger party, to treat a Canaanite as a protected member of one's own group, or to live according to the Canaanite laws where the Canaanite was dominant. Laws of blood revenge were modified ; there were cities of refuge where the slayer could be safe from the hand of the avenger until the case had been laid before the elders, and where he could be protected if the crime had been accidental. Stories are told of David suggesting that he claimed, and was given, the right to overrule the desert law among his subjects as well as within his family. Just as, among our own forebears, the breakdown of the feudal system left the land without any central authority sufficiently strong and disinterested to check the selfish use of power and the growth of private property, so in Palestine the same development took place, and by the eighth century B.C. had given rise to many social evils. Men became individuals even though they were not conscious of the fact, and just as groups had oppressed each other without any regard to a moral code, so individuals had no sense of responsibility to one another. The wealthy or powerful man used his riches or influence to achieve his own ends, the poor and unprotected —fatherless and widow—were exploited and oppressed. Private property, both in land, houses, and commerce, replaced communal ownership, and none recognized either the rights or needs of his fellows.

Against this the great prophets protested, regarding the old group morality as a religious obligation demanded by the national God. Though they still treated men as members of a group—the larger national group—all their influence was used to develop an individual conscience to govern relationships between persons within the national group.

§ INDIVIDUALISM

Dr. T. R. Glover, with his usual terseness, remarks : " The savage emphasized the tribe and had a social religion : the Greek discovered the individual and we have to put up with the consequences." The self-conscious individual emerged early in Greek thought, and by the sixth century B.C. in such Greek writers as Theognis the individual had replaced the family as the unit of social interest. In Hebrew thought it was the prophets who laid the foundation for the later Christian doctrine of the rights of the individual. Their attention to morality necessarily involved eventually the discovery of the individual as a separate entity, and brought in its wake revolutionary changes in man's ideas about himself and about his God. But it must be remembered that the prophets began their thinking from the ancient standpoint of corporate personality, not from our modern standpoint of individualism ; and just as it is difficult for the modern mind to put itself back into the circle of ideas of a people who knew nothing of the central nervous system, so it is difficult to think as the prophets thought. In early days it was possible to speak of an evil eye or hand as apart from an evil will of the whole personality ; in the same way it was possible for the eighth-century prophets to use terms to express moral ideas which to us necessarily involve individualism, but it is not right to say that our conceptions of individualism were implicit in the prophetic teaching. The prophets—even as late as Jeremiah and Ezekiel—still addressed themselves to the whole people, and thought not in terms of the individual but of the nation. When they called the nation to repentance and made righteousness the bond between God and man, they thought of a penitent people, not of individual men or individual hearts, hands, or eyes.

It is because of their interest in the future ideal community that Jeremiah and Ezekiel were forced to recognize human beings as separate units whose rewards and punishments could be separated from those of the group. To them the recognition was bound up with ideas of retribution. Both, as we have seen, laid down the principle that the son shall not die for the iniquity of the father, but that father and son shall die each for his own sins ; and this principle received legal sanction in the code of Deuteronomy. Both prophets made a vital and necessary contribution to religious progress by their emphasis on morality and personality, but it cannot be too strongly stated that they did not place their main stress on the individual as such—his value or rights as an individual ; that stress would have been outside the main stream of religious development in the Bible.

The dominant note in these prophets as elsewhere was individual responsibility—man not as a unit but as a limb of a body. To both of them Yahweh's dealings with the individual were directed to the formation of a new community, the fashioning of another body. The new covenant written on the hearts of men was made with the whole house of Israel ; and Ezekiel's individualism was subordinated to the formation of the post-exilic " Church of Israel," comprising Isaiah's righteous remnant.

The growth of belief in the importance of individuals is still more marked in the post-exilic period. Professor G. F. Moore writes :

Judaism thus made religion in every sphere a personal relation between the individual man and God, and in bringing this to clear consciousness and drawing the consequences lies its most significant advance beyond the older religion of Israel.

But even here there is no approach to absolute individualism, or the independence which has marked much Christian thought, and Moore goes on to say :

It was, however, a relation of the individual to God, not in isolation but in the fellowship of the religious community, and ideally of the whole Jewish people. Thus Judaism became in the full sense a personal religion without ceasing to be a national religion.[2]

One important factor in this development of individualism was the exile and the dispersion of the Jews throughout the world as self-conscious individuals separated from their environment. Perhaps the destruction of the northern kingdom was partly responsible for the growth of such thoughts in Jeremiah and Ezekiel, and Dr. Glover suggests that always from storm and stress, confusion of war, tribes and traditions, the individual emerges more sure of his separate existence as every organized form of thought and government collapses. In the Diaspora, the extent to which a man was loyal to the national faith of his fathers was a personal matter, and it was necessary for him to make himself consciously part of the worshipping community of his own people from whom he was separated. " Older ideas of national solidarity were supplemented and to some extent superseded by personal responsibility." [2]

The development can be seen most clearly in the growth of the ideas of individual retribution found in Jeremiah and Ezekiel, and of individual eschatology. That these ideas did not necessarily carry with them a belief in the value of the individual can be seen from Egyptian religion. There, according to Breasted, from an early time conscience can be traced, and there was the belief that each man passed through the portals of the next world as an individual and was judged according to his deeds and character. But the ruins of some of the great buildings show that human life continued to be held cheap. Ezekiel's doctrine was an *ad hoc* one preached to men whose national home had been destroyed, an attempt to convince them that the entail of the past could be broken, and although the belief in individual rewards and punishments remained in Judaism, there is little trace of an interest in individual salvation. This belief arose only as a refuge when national hopes had been baffled. One reason why the belief in personal immortality developed so late in Judaism, and was accepted by part only of the nation, was that the individual was not thought of as a separate unit.

The ease with which Hebrew thought can pass from the plural to the singular, both in syntactical constructions and in the descriptions of nations and ideals, witnesses to a blending of the individual with the community. God, as we have seen, can be translated into Hebrew as a singular or a plural word, and can be construed with singular or plural verbs and adjectives ; Israel can be spoken of as " she " or " he " or " they " ; the Messianic hope can be envisaged as an individual or as part of Israel, personified as the " Servant of Yahweh " or as " the Saints of the Most High."

A marked emphasis on individuality which makes man an end in himself has been regarded as characteristic of Christianity, and it is clear that there is an emphasis in the New Testament on the value of individual man. In the teaching of Jesus we hear parables that teach the untold value of the one lost sheep or coin, and how the bells of heaven ring out their joy when one sinner repents. To every man is offered the power to become the son of God, and whosoever believes on Jesus shall not perish but have everlasting life. The doctrine of the infinite value of each human soul in the sight of God, and the belief that God deals with men as individuals, has been the dominant religious belief in some branches of the Christian Church and in some forms of Christian thought. It has been the mainspring of much social reform; but care is needed before we emphasize the belief too absolutely. The emphasis is perhaps a legacy from oriental mystery religions rather than from the religion of the Old and New Testaments. It was in the mysteries that men were treated as individuals, initiates were offered personal salvation, and no organized communities were built to incorporate the separate individuals. It is possible to stress the rights and sanctity of every human being as though the whole aim of the creation of the universe were to produce strong independent personalities ; too often such an emphasis has resulted in dominating, self-centred persons without a vestige of social sense, who ruin every community of which they form a part. Many Church fellowships have been ruined by such men and women, and the dictator in a modern totalitarian state is the logical and necessary outcome of over emphasis on the individual. It must be recognized that there is little room in either true Jewish or Christian thought for the strong individualism of a dominant personality (although to many it is an ideal for themselves) for greatness must be expressed in losing one's life in humble service to the community. Often, pursuit of strength of character and personal development, whether in home life or in secular and religious education, has resulted only in the vices of self-assertiveness and selfishness.

§ The Individual as a Member of Society

Dr. Wheeler Robinson has written, " It is no small contribution to the Christian doctrine of man that the individualism through which the Gospel makes its appeal was penetrated through and through with the sense of social relationship." [3] We have seen that even the prophets, who are claimed as the great exponents of individualism, put their stress on the value not of separate human beings but of the community. The prophetic stress is continued without abatement in the New Testament record of the teaching of Jesus and Paul. It was because God so loved the world that he sent his son that the world through him might be saved. Although his method was to send an individual and to win individual response, yet individual salvation is not an end in itself, but is part of a larger aim of winning the world—even though with S. W. Green we accept the fact that in the Fourth Gospel the word " world " means " the great mass of mankind hostile to God and his purpose." [4] It was the world, as in the Old Testament it had been Israel, that God loved enough to send his son to save. To change the metaphor, man's value arose from the fact that as a son he became part of the family circle, as a subject he entered the community of the Kingdom of God. Paul too uses a strong community picture when he speaks of the body of Christ in which individual members are limbs compacted together, or when he describes the great divine event toward which all creation moves, and for which all the ages stretch out their neck in eager anticipation, as the revelation of men as sons of God, who cry " Abba " as they become consciously part of the Father's family. The individual thus finds his true worth not in egoistic self-assertion but as he loses himself in membership of a community.

The emphasis in Christian doctrine has tended to be on the relationship between individuals. In both Jewish and Christian thought a fairly comprehensive system or code of individual morality has grown up, and is generally recognized in theory though not always in practice. But not nearly the same attention has been given to the important problem of how to apply biblical teaching to the relation of the individual to the community, and of one community to another. Too often it has been assumed that the elaborate individual code can be applied as a social ethic and govern these larger relationships, and that men must always be treated as individuals and not as members of a group ; but it is doubtful whether there is any more ground for such an idea in biblical religion than there is for the emphasis on individual rights.

In the world as in the Christian Church there are two opposing ideals : on the one side the democratic or protestant conception which regards the individual as of paramount importance ; on the other the totalitarian or catholic ideal which subordinates the individual to the community. Both —like the exponents of ritual and spiritual worship—can find support for their views in the Bible, but the problems of Church reunion no less than those of world reconstruction demand a careful and dispassionate study of the biblical evidence and the recognition that for sane and healthy development both ideals must find their place within the same society and continually check and modify each other.

The most precious experience of religion is personal fellowship of the individual soul with God, and no emphasis on the value of the community must be allowed to obscure that possibility, or deprive men of the privilege. The Spirit of God known through the highest levels of Judaism and through Jesus can and does invade human personality ; not only the chosen priest, prophet, " Servant," and Son, but each individual who is willing to respond to the loving activity of God can enter into the Holy of Holies, and within the veil can in spirit meet God face to face and talk with him as a man talks to his friend ; to each one is open the comfort of eternal love, the guidance of infinite wisdom, the resources of omnipotent strength, the inspiration and joy of co-operating with the creator in his universal purpose. Whether it be mediated through Church, priest, prophet, Bible, or comes direct to the individual conscience, God's message is always primarily to the individual, to him comes the call to repentance, and through his regenerated conscience shines the vision which is the incentive to all progress.

But the individual is always the member of a community. Often he has the power to move from one community to another, but unless he moves to some uninhabited island his movement is into another set of circumstances and another social group. In religious life he can, to use biblical phrases, pass from death unto life, from darkness to light, he can leave the circle of those under the wrath of God and enter the fellowship of those who enjoy his love. But the essential truth behind Pauline doctrines, which often seem so remote to the modern reader, is that God treats men as members of the group to which they belong ; if we join the group of followers of Jesus we are treated as having fulfilled all the obligations incumbent on that group—that is, by " faith " in Christ we are " justified " and have " righteousness."

In modern warfare we have seen how at the beginning of the conflict it is possible to say that " We have no quarrel with the common people of the enemy nation, only their leaders are guilty." Gradually it is realized that the people cannot be separated from their leaders, and the war becomes one of nation against nation. The change is not due to the growth of hatred which always accompanies war, nor to the hardening of hearts through bitterness, but to the recognition that the enemy has to be treated as a community, and each member who remains within it shares responsibility for the actions of the leaders and of the nation as a whole. Fairbairn writes that those who appear to us as single persons—

may appear to the Creator as a unity, co-ordinated as a collective mind, or incorporated in the organism of nature and of race. In other words, man is to God a whole, a colossal individual, whose days are centuries, whose organs are races . . . and this unity has at once an ethical and a physical character.[5]

Jeremiah saw a glimpse of the same truth when he said: "A wonderful and horrible thing is come to pass in the land ;

the prophets prophesy falsely, and the priests bear rule by their power; and my people love to have it so" (v. 30ff.). We are slowly learning a truth dormant in the primitive idea of "corporate personality," that there is corporate responsibility and corporate sin which must be borne by each member of the group.

Does not the age-old problem of the sufferings of the innocent spring partly from a failure to recognize that God treats men as part of their community? Whether there is war, epidemic, social injustice, a national or a religious persecution, the innocent suffer with the guilty. It was inevitable that when Jesus came into the world he should bear the sins of the world of which he became part. The fellowship of an individual with God does not take him out of the world, enable him to contract out of its responsibility and sin, nor entitle him to privileged treatment—the sun and rain pour down on good and bad—but it changes his attitude. While ensuring that he does not add to the burden of corporate sin, he shares its suffering that through suffering he may work with God in bringing redemption to the world.

Modern, unlike primitive, man, belongs to many groups and is often torn by conflicting loyalties. Some of the groups represent circles, such as family, profession or work, state and Church, within each of which there are many smaller concentric circles. Conflict seldom arises within a particular set of concentric circles, for we recognize that although loyalty, like charity, begins at home, it must not end there. Although the warmest loyalty will always be given to the inmost circle, yet each successive circle has its value, its claims upon us, and in numerous ways modifies our primary loyalty. The recognition of our obligation to the wider circles saves us from that self-centredness which is the denial of religion.

Conflict comes between different sets of circles, and the Bible speaks with no definite message to a situation which its writers did not contemplate. Certain passages suggest that where there is conflict the religious individual or group can best witness to truth by isolating itself—" Come ye out from among them and be ye separate "—the ideal being that of a holy people who, by their fidelity to the truth as they see it, spread that truth. On the other side we have ambiguous statements, perhaps due to the Jewish power of holding together opposing ideas, " Render unto Cæsar the things that are Cæsar's, and to God the things that are God's," and " Fear God, honour the King," statements that have been given interpretations as varied as the predilections of their interpreters.

Christians must be influenced by the meaning of the Incarnation ; God did not remain aloof but sent his son into the world to save it, and Jesus prayed not that his disciples might be taken out of the world, but that they might be kept safe within it. The duty of the individual—as of the Church—is to be a regenerative conscience within the world, and in those circles in which the majority do not accept its ideals ; as Dr. Temple has pointed out, the standard of a community must be based on how most of the people within it are willing to act.[6] Often it is easier and pleasanter to " resign," to escape to the Decapolis with the Greeks who have come up to worship at the feast (John xii. 20ff.) than to bring salvation by remaining in the Jerusalem which offers only crucifixion ; but the way to raise the standard is to remain within the community, step by step translating ideals into facts.

At each decisive epoch in the long story of the development of religion there has been advance because the man who was given the vision of the heavenly pattern on the mount descended, and, with self-sacrificing devotion to his people, patiently co-operated with them and with God in first laying foundations, and then, stage by stage, raising a building which was within the capabilities of those who built. " And these all, having obtained a good report through faith, received not the promise : God having provided some better thing for us, that they without us should not be made perfect " (Heb. xi. 39f.).

NOTES AND BIBLIOGRAPHY

FOR the sake of the general reader, reference where possible is made to books containing good bibliographies, and it has not been thought necessary to reprint such lists here.

The following abbreviations are used :

A.J.S.L.	*American Journal of Semitic Languages.*
A.S.O.R.	American School of Oriental Research.
H.B.B.	*Historical Background of the Bible,* 1938.
H.D.B.	Hastings' *Dictionary of the Bible.*
I.L.N.	*Illustrated London News.*
J.T.S.	*Journal of Theological Studies.*
Q.D.A.P.	*Quarterly of Palestine Department of Antiquities.*
Q.S.	*Quarterly Statement, Palestine Exploration Fund.*
R.H.P.R.	*Revue d'Histoire et de Philosophie religieuses.*
Z.A.T.W.	*Zeitschrift für die Alttestamentliche Wissenschaft.*

CHAPTER I

1 For a concise history of the course of Pentateuchal criticism see *Encyclopædia Biblica*, art. " Hexateuch," vol. ii. col. 2045. As examples of some later movements compare Volz, *Theologische Literature Zeitung*, 48, 390 ; Wolfe, *Z.A.T.W.*, 1935, 90ff., " The editing of the book of the Twelve " ; Rudolph, *Z.A.T.W.*, Beihefte 68 ; Chadwick, *Growth of Literature*, 1936, vol. ii. 629ff.

2 *Progress of Religion*, 1922, 3.

3 *Cf.* periodicals and books referred to in the writer's *Historical Background of the Bible*, 1938 ; and also add W. F. Albright, *From the Stone Age to Christianity*, 1940; A. G. Barrois, *Manuel d'Archéologie biblique*, 1939 ; and the periodicals, *Syria, Palästinajahrbuch, Revue biblique.*

4 T. R. Glover, *op. cit.*, page 6f.

5 S. A. Cook, " The Development of the Religion of Israel," Mélanges Franz Cumont, 1936, 539ff.

6 Q.D.A.P., vi., 3-4, 218ff.

7 *Cambridge Biblical Essays*, 1909, 1ff.

CHAPTER 2

1 *Authority and Archæology*, ed. D. G. Hogarth, 1899, 6f.

2 *Syria and the Holy Land*, 1918. For other works on geography compare the same author's *Historical Geography of the Holy Land*, and Abel, *Géographie de la Palestine*, 1933.

3 *Campaigns in Palestine from Alexander the Great*, 1927.

4 Compare literature cited by Olmstead, *History of Palestine and Syria*, 1931 ; Moret, *The Nile and Egyptian Civilization*, 1927.

5 Woolley, *The Sumerians*, 1929 ; *The Development of Sumerian Art*, 1935 ; Olmstead, *History of Assyria*, 1923.

6 Albright, *op. cit.*, 319, note 16, accepts the approximate dating of 1792–50 B.C.

7 S. A. Cook, *Laws of Moses and the Code of Hammurabi*, 1903.

8 Forrer, *Geschichtliche Texte aus Boghaz-Köi*, 1926.

9 *Illustrated London News*, October 9, 1937.

10 Hogarth and Woolley, *Carchemish*, 1914–21.

11 C. F. Burney, *The Book of Judges*, 1930, lxv.ff.

12 Erman, *Handbook of Egyptian Religion*, 1907.

13 Breasted, *Development of Religion and Thought in Ancient Egypt*, 1912.

14 Albright, *op. cit.*, 165, traces the beginning of this reform to Amenhotep III (1413–1377).

15 Discoveries at Tell Halaf, *Z.A.T.W.*, 1929.

16 Delaporte, *Mesopotamia*, 1925 ; Jastrow, *Religion of Babylonia and Assyria*, 1911.

17 Various vols. of Ur Excavations, published jointly by British Museum and the University of Pennsylvania, 1934ff.

18 Henri Berr, Foreword to Lods, *Israel*, 1932.

19 *I.L.N.*, February 20, 1937, but compare Albright, *op. cit.*, 197 and note.

CHAPTER 3

1 S. H. Hooke, *Origins of Early Semitic Ritual*, 1938 ; *Myth and Ritual*, 1933.

2 G. A. Barton, *Semitic and Hamitic Origins*, 1934.

3 G. A. Barton, *Royal Inscriptions of Sumer and Akkad*, 1929, 251 ; and Graham and May, *Culture and Conscience*, 1936, 96.

CHAPTER 4

1 *Ancient Religion of Palestine in the Light of Archæology*, 1925.
2 Present writer's articles in *In His Steps*, Amal. Press, 1939.
3 *Cf. Cambridge Ancient History*, vol. ii.

CHAPTER 5

1 For literature *cf.* Graham and May, *Culture and Conscience*, 1936; and the books of Albright and S. A. Cook already mentioned.
2 S. A. Cook, *op. cit.*, 11ff.
3 *Cf.* Reports in Liverpool University Annuals.
4 Report of excavations at Athlit in Q.D.A.P., vi. 3.
5 A. Mallon, *Teleilat Ghassul*, ii. (Bea and Koeppel), 1940; and description by Albright, *op. cit.*, 102.
6 G. E. Wright, *The Pottery of Palestine from the Earliest Times to the end of the Early Bronze Age*, 1937, 137.
7 *Cf.* Trumbull, *The Threshold Covenant*, 1896, for suggestions as to origin.
8 *I.L.N.*, February 20, 1937, Ras Shamra had houses with spacious funerary crypts.
9 *Die Ursprünge des israelitischen Rechts*, 1934.
10 Rowe, *Topography and History of Bethshan*, 1930.
11 Tufnell, and others, *Lachish II, The Fosse Temple*, 1940.
12 *Cf.* S. A. Cook, *op. cit.*; Ginsburg, *The Ugarit Texts* (in Hebrew), 1936.

CHAPTER 6

1 W. R. Smith, *Religion of the Semites*, third ed. with notes by S. A. Cook, 1927.
2 Hastings' *Dictionary of the Bible*, extra volume.
3 A. Causse, *Du Groupe ethnique à la Communauté religieuse*, 1937.
4 *Cf.* A. R. Johnson, *The One and the Many in the Israelite conception of God*, 1942.
5 Lods, *op. cit.*, 292.
6 Lods, *Israel*, 437ff.
7 G. A. Barton, *op. cit.*, for discussion of Passover.

8 *Cf.* references in Lods, *op. cit.*, 268.

9 *L'Évolution religieuse d'Israël*, 1937.

10 For general discussion of problems of sacrifice, *cf.* G. B. Gray, *Sacrifice in the Old Testament*, 1925 ; E. O. James, *Origins of Sacrifice*, 1933 ; Dussaud, *Les Origines cananéennes du Sacrifice israélite*, 1921.

CHAPTER 7

1 Petrie, *Gerar*, 1928.

2 Alt, *Der Gott der Väter*, 1929.

3 Burney, *op. cit.*, 243ff. G. R. Driver, *Z.A.T.W.*, 1928, 7ff.

4 *Studies in Hebrew Proper Names*, 1896 ; *cf.* Noth, *Die israelitischen Personennamen*, 1928.

5 G. Duncan, *New Light on Hebrew Origins*, 1936 ; H.D.B. vol. ii. 58ff., 113.

6 *Q.S.*, 1937, 220.

CHAPTER 8

1 *Q.S.*, 1927.

2 *H.B.B.*, 126.

3 *Culture and Conscience*, and literature there cited; H. G. May, *A.J.S.L.*, July 1936.

4 Annual, *American School of Oriental Research (A.S.O.R.)*, No. 4.

5 Badé, *Excavations at Tell en Nasbeh*, 1928 ; and later reports in *American Journal of Archæology*.

6 May and Engberg, *Material Remains of Megiddo Cult*, 1935.

7 *Cf.* also the name *Tobshalem*, " Good is Shalem," on Lachish letters.

8 Illustrated in *H.B.B.*, 182.

9 Hollis, *The Archæology of Herod's Temple*, 1934.

10 Loehr, *A History of Religion in the Old Testament*, 1936.

CHAPTER 9

1 *Re* nature of prophecy *cf.* Lods, *The Prophets and the Rise of Judaism*, 1937, 51f. ; Von Rad, *Z.A.T.W.*, 1933, 109ff.

2 Streeter, *The God Who Speaks*, 1936.

3 *Culture and Conscience*, Chap. VII.f.

4 Essay, " The Function of Criticism."

5 *J.T.S.*, April 1939.

6 S. A. Cook, *The Truth of the Bible*, 1938.

CHAPTER 10

1 Skinner, *Prophecy and Religion*, 1922.

2 The standpoint of the writer in reference to the date and origin of Deuteronomy can be seen in *H.B.B.* and in his essay on " The Significance of the Prophets for the dating of Deuteronomy," *Studies in History and Religion*, edit. Payne, 1942, where some of the evidence and literature is cited.

3 *Religion of the Semites*, third ed., 625.

CHAPTER 11

1 *Bulletin A.S.O.R.*, February 1928.

2 *Cf.* Lam. ii. to show that Jeremiah's interpretation of Jerusalem's fall was accepted.

3 For discussion as to whether the purpose of Deuteronomy was " Einheit " or " Reinheit " compare Welch, *The Code of Deuteronomy*.

4 *Cf.* Causse, *R.H.P.R.*, 1933, 1ff., 289ff. ; E. Meyer, *Israeliten u. ihre Nachbarstämme*, 1906, *s.v.* " Rationalische."

5 Vincent, *La Religion des Judéo-Araméens d'Éléphantine*, 1937 ; Cowley, *Aramaic Papyri of the Fifth Century*, 1923 ; S. A. Cook, *American Journal of Theology*, 1915.

CHAPTER 12

1 For a review of recent criticism compare G. A. Cooke, *Ezekiel*, 1936 ; Leslie, *Old Testament Religion*, 1936, stresses the fertility motif in Ezekiel ; Oesterley and Robinson, *Hebrew Religion*, 1930, the prophet's familiarity with Babylonian myth and ritual.

2 Contrast Lev. x. 17, where sin is in the flesh and priests bear the iniquity by eating.

3 *Cf.* Eissfeldt, *Einleitung* ; Skinner, *Cambridge Bible* ; Torrey, *Second Isaiah*, 1928.

4 H. W. Robinson, *The Cross of the Servant*, 1936 ; C. R. North, *Expository Times*, February 1941.

5 For a vivid account of Zechariah's cartoons *cf.* H. R. Kennett, Peake's *Commentary*, *ad loc.*

CHAPTER 13

1 Oesterley and Robinson, *History of Israel*, 1934, vol. ii.
2 *Post-Exilic Judaism*, 1935.
3 A. C. Welch, *The Work of the Chronicler*, 1939 ; Von Rad, " Das Geschichtbild des chronistischen Werkes," 1930.
4 Lods, *The Prophets and the Rise of Judaism*, 290ff.
5 *H.D.B.*, Macalister, *s.v.*
6 Benzinger, *Hebräische Archäologie*, 1927.
7 *Religious Ideas of the Old Testament*, 1913.
8 *Q.S.*, 1937, 94.
9 *Persae*, 407ff.
10 *Q.S.*, 1937, 171ff.
11 Jeremias, *Das alte Test. im Lichte des alten Orients*, 29f.
12 *Cf.* R. Otto, *Reich Gottes und Menschensohn*, 1934.

CHAPTER 14

1 Bousset, *Religion des Judentums*, 1903 ; for magic in the Psalter, *cf.* *Ency. Brit.*, 14th edition, vol. xviii., 663f.
2 S. A. Cook, *Ancient Religion of Palestine*.
3 For an account of monotheistic movements in Hellenism *cf.* Dodd, *The Bible and the Greeks*, 1935.
4 *Jews and Judaism during the Greek Period*, 1941, 96f.
5 *Cf.* English translation by Danby, *Mishna*, 1933.
6 *Les dispersés d'Israël*, 1929.
7 *Book of Proverbs*, 1929
8 Ranston, *The Old Testament Wisdom Books and their Teaching*, 1930 ; *Ecclesiastes and the Early Greek Wisdom Literature*, 1925 ; Cheyne, *Jewish Religious Life after the Exile*, 1898.
9 Cheyne, *op. cit.*, 156.
10 *La Religion d'Israël*, 1939.
11 *Judaism and Christianity*, three vols., ed. Oesterley, Loewe, Rosenthal, 1937–38 ; Moore, *Judaism*, three vols., 1927–30 ; works by I. Abrahams, C. G. Montefiore, and T. Herford.
12 *Ancient Synagogues in Palestine and Greece*, 1934.
13 Bab. Talmud, Sukka 53*a*.

14 Strack, *Einleitung in Talmud und Midras*, 1921.

15 *Op. cit.*, 68.

16 *Christian Beginnings*, 1924.

17 H. R. Kennett, *Old Testament Essays*, 1928, 219ff.

18 *Cf.* McNeile, *Cambridge Biblical Essays*, 1909 ; and Charles, *Eschatology, Hebrew, Jewish and Christian*, 1913.

CHAPTER 15

1 Rowley, "Jewish Proselyte Baptism," *Hebrew Union College Annual*, xv., 1940.

2 Dodd, *The Parables of the Kingdom*, 1936 ; *Apostolic Preaching*, 1937.

3 Manson, *The Teaching of Jesus*, 1935.

4 *Messianic Prophecy*, 1891.

5 Kennett, *op. cit.*

6 *Op. cit.*, I, 116.

7 *Cf.* H. W. Robinson, *The Cross of the Servant*.

8 Herford, *Judaism in the N.T. Period*, 1928, 213f.

9 Fairbairn, *Christ in Modern Theology*, 1894, 339.

CHAPTER 16

1 *Judaism*, 1913.

2 *Le VIᵉ siècle, moment décisif dans l'histoire du Judaïsme*, R.H.P.R., 1938, 4.

3 *Cf.* Abrahams, *Pharisaism and the Gospels*, 1924.

4 Klausner, *Jesus of Nazareth*, 1929 ; Herford, *Judaism in the New Testament Period*, 1928.

5 *The Age of Transition*, 186.

6 *Cambridge Ancient History*, vol. ix.

7 Levine, *op. cit.*

CHAPTER 17

1 *Cf.* Kennedy, *Century Bible*, ad. loc.

2 W. R. Smith, *Religion of the Semites* ; *cf.* Albright, *op. cit.*, 18 and 314.

3 Cheyne, *op. cit.*

4 *Ency. Biblica*, 3883ff.

CHAPTER 18

1 *Worship*, 1937.
2 *Symbolism and Belief*, 1938.

CHAPTER 19

1 *Sayings of the Jewish Fathers.*
2 *Judaism*, I.
3 *Christian Doctrine of Man*, 1934.
4 Hastings, *Dictionary of the Bible, sub verb.*
5 Fairbairn, *The Philosophy of the Christian Religion*, 1902.
6 Temple, *Christianity and Social Order*, 1942.

INDEX